Adobe® Premiere Pro® CS6

CLASSROOM IN A BOOK®

The official training workbook from Adobe Systems

Adobe

WHAT'S ON THE DISC

Here is an overview of the contents of the Classroom in a Book disc

The *Adobe Premiere Pro CS6 Classroom in a Book* disc includes the lesson files that you'll need to complete the exercises in this book, as well as other content to help you learn more about Adobe Premiere Pro CS6 and use it with greater efficiency and ease. The diagram below represents the contents of the disc, which should help you locate the files you need.

● **Note:** The disc also includes a bonus lesson, "Authoring DVDs with Adobe Encore," along with associated lesson files.

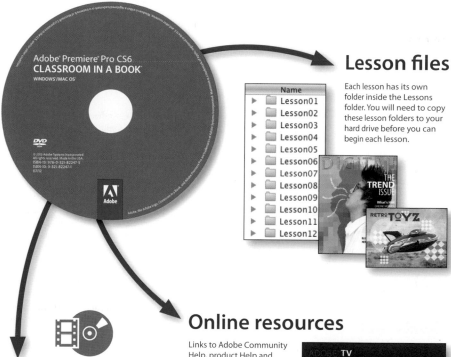

Lesson files

Each lesson has its own folder inside the Lessons folder. You will need to copy these lesson folders to your hard drive before you can begin each lesson.

Online resources

Links to Adobe Community Help, product Help and Support pages, Adobe certification programs, Adobe TV, and other useful online resources can be found inside a handy HTML file. Just open it in your Web browser and click on the links, including a special link to this book's product page where you can access updates and bonus material.

Learn by Video bonus tutorials

A bonus 2-hour set of "Adobe Premiere Pro CS6: Learn by Video" tutorials is included on this disc, from video2brain and Adobe Press. "Learn by Video" is one of the most critically acclaimed training products on Adobe software and is the only Adobe-approved video courseware for the Adobe Certified Associate Level certification.

CONTENTS

GETTING STARTED

Adobe® Premiere® Pro CS6, the essential editing tool for video enthusiasts and professionals, enhances your creative power and freedom. Adobe Premiere Pro is the most scalable, efficient, and precise video-editing tool available. It supports a broad range of video formats including AVCHD, HDV, XDCAM, P2 DVCPRO HD, XDCAM, AVC-Intra, Canon XF, RED, ARRIRAW, QuickTime, and many more. The superior performance of Adobe Premiere Pro lets you work faster and more creatively. The complete set of powerful and exclusive tools lets you overcome any editorial, production, and workflow challenges to deliver the high-quality work you demand.

About Classroom in a Book

Adobe Premiere Pro CS6 Classroom in a Book® is part of the official training series for Adobe graphics and publishing software. The lessons are designed so that you can learn at your own pace. If you're new to Adobe Premiere Pro, you'll learn the fundamental concepts and features you'll need to use the program. This book also teaches many advanced features, including tips and techniques for using the latest version of this software.

The lessons in this edition include opportunities to use features such as multicamera editing, keying, dynamic trimming, color correction, tapeless media, and audio and video effects. You'll also learn how to create files for the Internet and mobile devices with Adobe Media Encoder or send a sequence to Adobe Encore CS6 without rendering or intermediate exporting to output to DVD, Blu-ray Disc, or Adobe Flash. Performance has been significantly enhanced with the new Mercury Playback Engine, which provides both software- and hardware-assisted performance breakthroughs. Adobe Premiere Pro CS6 is available for both Windows and Mac OS.

Prerequisites

Before beginning to use *Adobe Premiere Pro CS6 Classroom in a Book*, make sure your system is set up correctly and that you've installed the required software and hardware. You can view updated system requirements by visiting *www.adobe.com/products/premiere/tech-specs.html*.

You should have a working knowledge of your computer and operating system. You should know how to use the mouse and standard menus and commands and also how to open, save, and close files. If you need to review these techniques, see the printed or online documentation included with your Windows or Mac OS system.

Installing Adobe Premiere Pro CS6

You must purchase the Adobe Premiere Pro CS6 software separately from this book. It can be purchased as a stand-alone product or included in the Creative Suite or Creative Cloud families. Install Adobe Premiere Pro from the software DVD onto your hard disk; you cannot run the program from the DVD. If you purchased a downloadable version, follow the instructions included with the download for launching the installation process.

Adobe Premiere Pro CS6 trial

Adobe offers a 30-day trial of Adobe Premiere Pro CS6. You can download this trial from the Adobe product website. After 30 days, the software will stop functioning. If you decide to purchase Adobe Premiere Pro, you can enter your purchased serial number into the trial version you have installed to convert it to a full version of Adobe Premiere Pro CS6.

Optimizing performance

Editing video is memory- and processor-intensive work for a computer. A fast processor and a lot of memory will make your editing experience much faster and more efficient; 4 GB of memory is the minimum, and 8 GB or more is better for high-definition (HD) media. Adobe Premiere Pro CS6 takes advantage of multicore processors on Windows and Macintosh systems.

A dedicated 7200 RPM or faster hard drive is recommended for high-definition video (HD) media. A RAID 0 striped disk array or SCSI disk subsystem is strongly recommended for HD. Performance will be significantly affected if you attempt to store media files and program files on the same hard drive. Be sure to keep your media files on a second disk if at all possible.

The Mercury Playback Engine in Adobe Premiere Pro can operate in software-only mode or GPU acceleration mode. The GPU acceleration mode provides significant performance improvement. The GPU acceleration is possible with select video cards. You can find a list of these video cards on the Adobe website at *www.adobe.com/products/premiere/tech-specs.html.*

Copying the lesson files

The lessons in *Adobe Premiere Pro CS6 Classroom in a Book* use specific source files, such as video clips, audio files, and image files created in Adobe Photoshop CS6 and Adobe Illustrator CS6. To complete the lessons in this book, you must copy all the files from the *Adobe Premiere Pro CS6 Classroom in a Book* DVD (inside the back cover of this book) to your hard drive. You will need about 4 GB of storage space in addition to the 4 GB you need to install Adobe Premiere Pro CS6.

Although each lesson stands alone, some lessons use files from other lessons, so you'll need to keep the entire collection of lesson assets on your hard drive as you work through the book. Here's how to copy those assets from the DVD to your hard drive:

1   Open the *Adobe Premiere Pro CS6 Classroom in a Book* DVD in My Computer or Windows Explorer (Windows) or in Finder (Mac OS).

2   Right-click (Windows) or Control+click (Mac OS; if you're using a super mouse or pen, you can right-click) the folder called Lessons, and choose Copy.

3   Navigate to the location you set to store your Adobe Premiere Pro CS6 projects.

The default location is My Documents\Adobe\Premiere Pro\6.0 (Windows) or Documents/Adobe/Premiere Pro/6.0 (Mac OS).

4   Right-click (Windows) or Control+click (Mac OS) inside the 6.0 folder, and choose Paste.

Following these steps will copy all the lesson assets to your local folder. This process may take a few minutes to complete, depending on the speed of your hardware.

Relinking the lesson files

It is possible that the file path to the lesson files may need to be updated. If you open an Adobe Premiere Pro project and it cannot find a media file, a dialog may open and ask you "Where is the File MEDIA.mov'?" If this happens, you will need to navigate to one of the offline files in order to reconnect. Once you've reconnected one file in the project, the rest should reconnect.

- You can navigate to the same location where you copied the files you copied from the DVD. The path will be Premiere Pro CS6 CIB > Lessons > Assets. You may need to look in some of the included folders to find the media file (especially if it involves tapeless media).

- You can use the search field in the OS dialog box to search for the file by name.

When you locate a file, just select it and click the Open button.

How to use these lessons

Each lesson in this book provides step-by-step instructions for creating one or more specific elements of a real-world project. The lessons stand alone, but most of them build on previous lessons in terms of concepts and skills. So, the best way to learn from this book is to proceed through the lessons in sequential order.

The organization of the lessons is workflow-oriented rather than feature-oriented, and the book uses a real-world approach. The lessons follow the typical sequential steps video editors use to complete a project, starting with acquiring video, laying down a cuts-only sequence, adding effects, sweetening the audio track, and ultimately exporting the project to the Web, a portable device, a DVD, a Blu-ray Disc, or Flash.

Additional resources

Adobe Premiere Pro CS6 Classroom in a Book is not meant to replace documentation that comes with the program or to be a comprehensive reference for every feature. Only the commands and options used in the lessons are explained in this book. For comprehensive information about program features and tutorials, please refer to these resources:

Adobe Community Help: Community Help brings together active Adobe product users, Adobe product team members, authors, and experts to give you the most useful, relevant, and up-to-date information about Adobe products.

To Access Community Help: To invoke Help, press F1 or choose Help > Premiere Pro Help.

Adobe content is updated based on community feedback and contributions. You can add comments to content and forums (including links to web content), publish your own content using Community Publishing, or contribute Cookbook recipes. Find out how to contribute at www.adobe.com/community/publishing/download.html.

See community.adobe.com/help/profile/faq.html for answers to frequently asked questions about Community Help.

Adobe Premiere Pro CS6 Help and Support: www.adobe.com/support/premiere is where you can find and browse Help and Support content on adobe.com.

Adobe Forums: forums.adobe.com lets you tap into peer-to-peer discussions, questions, and answers on Adobe products.

Adobe TV: tv.adobe.com is an online video resource for expert instruction and inspiration about Adobe products, including a How To channel to get you started with your product.

Adobe Design Center: www.adobe.com/designcenter offers thoughtful articles on design and design issues, a gallery showcasing the work of top-notch designers, tutorials, and more.

Adobe Developer Connection: www.adobe.com/devnet is your source for technical articles, code samples, and how-to videos that cover Adobe developer products and technologies.

Resources for educators: www.adobe.com/education offers a treasure trove of information for instructors who teach classes on Adobe software. Find solutions for education at all levels, including free curricula that use an integrated approach to teaching Adobe software and can be used to prepare for the Adobe Certified Associate exams.

Also check out these useful links:

Adobe Marketplace & Exchange: www.adobe.com/cfusion/exchange is a central resource for finding tools, services, extensions, code samples, and more to supplement and extend your Adobe products.

Adobe Premiere Pro CS6 product home page: www.adobe.com/products/premiere

Adobe Labs: labs.adobe.com gives you access to early builds of cutting-edge technology, as well as forums where you can interact both with the Adobe development teams building that technology and with other like-minded members of the community.

Adobe certification

The Adobe training and certification programs are designed to help Adobe customers improve and promote their product-proficiency skills. There are four levels of certification:

- Adobe Certified Associate (ACA)
- Adobe Certified Expert (ACE)
- Adobe Certified Instructor (ACI)
- Adobe Authorized Training Center (AATC)

The Adobe Certified Associate (ACA) credential certifies that individuals have the entry-level skills to plan, design, build, and maintain effective communications using different forms of digital media.

The Adobe Certified Expert program is a way for expert users to upgrade their credentials. You can use Adobe certification as a catalyst for getting a raise, finding a job, or promoting your expertise.

If you are an ACE-level instructor, the Adobe Certified Instructor program takes your skills to the next level and gives you access to a wide range of Adobe resources.

Adobe Authorized Training Centers offer instructor-led courses and training on Adobe products, employing only Adobe Certified Instructors. A directory of AATCs is available at partners.adobe.com.

For information on the Adobe Certified programs, visit www.adobe.com/support/certification/index.html.

Checking for updates

Adobe periodically provides updates to software. You can easily obtain these updates through Adobe Updater, as long as you have an active Internet connection.

1 In Premiere Pro, choose Help > Updates. Adobe Updater automatically checks for updates available for your Adobe software.

2 In the Adobe Updater dialog box, select the updates you want to install, and then click Download and Install Updates to install them.

For book updates and bonus material, visit the book's page on the Web at www.peachpit.com/prcs6cib.

1 TOURING ADOBE PREMIERE PRO CS6

Lesson overview

In this lesson, you'll learn about the following:

- What's new in Adobe Premiere Pro CS6

- Nonlinear editing in Adobe Premiere Pro

- Exploring the standard digital video workflow

- Enhancing the workflow with high-level features

- Incorporating Adobe Creative Suite 6 Production Premium into your workflow

- Exploring the Adobe CS6 Production Premium workflow

- Touring the Adobe Premiere Pro CS6 workspace

- Exploring the workspace layout

- Customizing your workspace

 This lesson will take approximately 45 minutes.

Before you begin, you'll walk through a brief overview of video editing and an explanation of how Adobe Premiere Pro functions as the hub of the video production workflow. Even experienced editors will find this tour a useful guide to Adobe Premiere Pro CS6.

Adobe Premiere Pro CS6 is a video-editing system that supports the latest technology and cameras with powerful tools that are easy to use and that integrate perfectly with almost every video acquisition source.

Getting started

Today we're seeing an increasing demand for high-quality video content as well as an ever-changing landscape of old and new technologies. Despite all of this rapid change, however, the goal of video editing is the same: You want to take your footage and shape it using your original vision so that you can effectively communicate with your audience (or even the world).

In Adobe Premiere Pro, you'll find a video-editing system that supports the latest technology and cameras with powerful tools that are easy to use and that integrate perfectly with almost every video acquisition source, as well as a wide range of plug-ins and other post-production tools.

You'll begin by reviewing the essential workflow that most editors follow. Next you'll see how Premiere Pro fits into Adobe CS6 Production Premium. Finally, you'll learn about the main components in the Adobe Premiere Pro interface and how to create your own custom workspaces.

Nonlinear editing in Adobe Premiere Pro

Premiere Pro is a *nonlinear editor* (NLE). Like a word processor, Premiere Pro lets you place, replace, and move footage anywhere you want in your final edited video. You can also adjust any parts of the video clips you use at any time. You don't need to perform edits in a particular order, and you can make changes to any part of your video project at any time.

You'll combine multiple clips to create a sequence that you can edit simply by clicking and dragging with your mouse. You can edit any part of your sequence, in any order, and then change the contents, move clips so that they play earlier or later in the video, blend layers of video together, add special effects, and more.

You can work on any part of your sequence, in any order, and even combine multiple sequences. You can jump to any moment in a video clip without needing to fast-forward or rewind. It's as easy to organize clips as it is to organize files on your computer.

Adobe Premiere Pro supports both tape and tapeless media formats, including XDCAM EX, XDCAMHD 422, AVCCAM, DPX, Panasonic P2, AVCHD, AVC-Intra, and DSLR video. It also supports the latest in raw video formats with enhanced RED camera support and the addition of ARRI Alexa. Bringing footage into your project is fast and easy, and it is usually unnecessary to convert your video files before using them.

Presenting the standard digital video workflow

As you gain editing experience, you'll develop your own preference for the order in which to work on the different aspects of your project. Each stage requires a particular kind of attention and different tools. Also, some projects call for more time spent on one stage than another.

Whether you skip through some stages with a quick mental check or spend hours (even days!) dedicated to perfecting an aspect of your project, you'll work through the following steps:

1 Acquire the video. This can mean recording original footage or gathering assets for a project.

2 Capture (transfer or ingest) the video to your hard drive. With tape-based formats, Adobe Premiere Pro (with the appropriate hardware) can convert the video into digital files. With tapeless media, Adobe Premiere Pro can read the media directly—there's no need for conversion. If working with tapeless media, be sure to back up your files to a second location.

3 Organize your clips. These days, there can be quite a lot of video shots to choose from in your project. Spend the time to organize clips together into special folders (called *bins*) in your project. You can also add color labels and other metadata (additional information about the clips) to help keep things organized.

4 Build your edited sequence by selecting the parts of the video and audio clips you want and adding them to the Timeline.

5 Place special transition effects between clips, add video effects, and create combined visual effects by placing clips on multiple layers (*tracks*).

6 Create titles or graphics, and add them to your sequence in the same way you would add video clips.

7 Mix your audio tracks to get the combined level just right, and use transitions and special effects on your audio clips to improve the sound.

8 Export your finished project to videotape, to a file for a computer or for Internet playback, to a mobile device, or to a DVD or Blu-ray Disc.

Adobe Premiere Pro supports each of these steps with industry-leading tools.

Enhancing the workflow with Adobe Premiere Pro

Adobe Premiere Pro has easy-to-use tools for standard video editing. It also provides advanced tools for manipulating, adjusting, and fine-tuning your projects.

You may not incorporate all of the following features in your first few video projects. However, as your experience and understanding of nonlinear editing grows, you'll want to expand your capabilities.

The following topics will be covered in this book:

- **Advanced audio editing:** Adobe Premiere Pro provides audio effects and editing unequaled by any other nonlinear editor. Create and place 5.1 surround-sound audio channels, make sample-level edits, apply multiple audio effects to audio clips or tracks, and use the included state-of-the-art plug-ins as well as third-party Virtual Studio Technology (VST) plug-ins.

- **Color correction:** Correct and enhance the look of your footage with advanced color-correction filters. You can also make secondary color-correction selections that allow you to adjust isolated colors and adjust parts of an image to improve the composition.

- **Keyframe controls:** Premiere Pro gives you the precise control you need to fine-tune visual and motion effects without exporting to a compositing or motion graphics application. Keyframes use a standard interface design, so learn how to use them once, and you'll know how to use them in all Adobe Creative Suite products.

- **Broad hardware support:** Choose from a wide range of dedicated capture cards and other hardware to assemble a system that best fits your needs and budget. Adobe Premiere Pro system specifications extend from low-cost computers for digital video (DV) and compressed HDV editing up to high-performance workstations capturing full HD and 3D stereoscopic video.

- **Mercury Playback Engine graphics card acceleration:** The Mercury Playback Engine operates in two modes: software-only and GPU acceleration. The GPU acceleration mode requires a compatible graphics card in your workstation. See *www.adobe.com/products/premiere/tech-specs.html* for a list of compatible graphics cards.

- **Multicam editing:** You can easily and quickly edit productions shot with multiple cameras. Adobe Premiere Pro displays multiple camera sources in a split-view monitor, and you can choose a camera view by clicking the appropriate screen or using shortcut keys.

- **Project Manager:** Manage your media through a single dialog box. View, delete, move, search for, and reorganize clips and bins. Consolidate your projects by moving just the media actually used in a project and copying that media to a single location. Then reclaim drive space by deleting unused media.

- **Metadata: Adobe** Premiere Pro supports Adobe XMP, which stores additional information about media as metadata that can be accessed by multiple applications. This information can be used to locate clips or communicate valuable information such as preferred takes.

- **Creative titles:** Create titles and graphics using the Premiere Pro Title Designer. You can also use graphics created in almost any suitable software, plus Adobe Photoshop documents can be used as automatically flattened images or as separate layers you can incorporate, combine, and animate selectively.

- **Advanced trimming:** Use special trimming tools to adjust each clip and cut point in a sequence. Adobe Premiere Pro CS6 includes significant improvements to its trimming tools, allowing you to make complex trimming adjustments to multiple clips.

- **Media encoding:** Export your sequence to create a video and audio file that is perfect for your needs. Use the advanced features of Adobe Media Encoder to create multiple copies of your finished sequence in several different formats.

Expanding the workflow

While it is possible to work with Premiere Pro as a stand-alone application, it is really meant to be a team player. Chances are high that you're using Adobe Premiere Pro as part of Creative Suite 6, which means you have access to other specialized tools. Even if you are using the stand-alone version, it comes bundled with Adobe Encore (for authoring DVD and Blu-ray Discs) and Adobe Media Encoder (for creating digital video files). Knowing how the software components work together will improve your efficiency and expand your capabilities.

Incorporating other CS6 components into the editing workflow

Adobe Premiere Pro is a versatile video and audio post-production tool, but it is just one component of Adobe CS6, Adobe's complete post-production environment that includes software for the following:

- High-end 3D motion effects creation

- Complex text animation generation

- Layered graphics production

- Vector artwork creation

- Audio production

To incorporate one or more of these features into a production, you can use other components of Adobe Creative Suite 6 Production Premium. The software set has everything you need to produce advanced, professionally finished videos.

Here's a brief description of the other components:

- **Adobe After Effects CS6:** The tool of choice for motion graphics and visual effects artists.

- **Adobe Photoshop CS6 Extended:** The industry-standard image-editing and graphic-creation product. You can work with photos, video, and 3D objects to prepare them for your project.

- **Adobe Audition CS6:** A powerful tool for audio editing, audio cleanup, audio sweetening, music creation, and automatic speech alignment.

- **Adobe Encore CS6:** A high-quality DVD-authoring software designed to work closely with Adobe Premiere Pro, After Effects, and Photoshop CS6. Encore produces DVDs, Blu-ray Discs, and interactive SWF files. Encore CS6 is included with Premiere Pro.

- **Adobe Illustrator CS6:** Professional vector graphics creation software for print, video production, and the Web.

- **Adobe Dynamic Link:** A cross-product connection that allows you to work in real time with media, compositions, and sequences shared natively between After Effects, Premiere Pro, and Encore CS6, without rendering, exporting, or importing.

- **Adobe Bridge CS6:** A visual file browser that provides centralized access to your Creative Suite project files, applications, and settings. Bridge CS6 is included with Adobe Premiere Pro CS6.

- **Adobe Flash Professional CS6:** The industry standard for creating rich, interactive web content.

- **Adobe SpeedGrade CS6:** Professional, sophisticated color grading/finishing with support for high-end and 3D (visual stereo) video formats.

- **Adobe Prelude CS6:** Ingest and add metadata, markers, and tags to file-based footage to speed up your post-production workflow.

- **Adobe Media Encoder CS6:** Batch-process files to produce content for any screen from Premiere Pro and Adobe After Effects CS6. Adobe Media Encoder CS6 is included with Adobe Premiere Pro CS6.

Adobe Creative Suite 6 Production Premium workflow

Your Premiere Pro/Creative Suite 6 Production Premium workflow will vary depending on your production needs. Here are a few scenarios:

- Use Photoshop CS6 to touch up and apply effects to still images from a digital camera, a scanner, or a video clip. Then use them in Premiere Pro.

- Create a layered graphic in Photoshop CS6, and then open it in Premiere Pro. You can opt to work with each layer independently, allowing you to apply effects and animation to selected layers.

- Import large numbers of media files with Adobe Prelude CS6, adding valuable metadata, temporal comments, and tags. Create sequences from subclips in Adobe Prelude and send them to Premiere Pro to continue editing them.

- Send a clip straight from the Premiere Pro timeline to Adobe Audition for professional audio cleanup and sweetening.

- Send your Premiere Pro sequence to Adobe Audition to complete a professional audio mix. Premiere Pro can create an Adobe Audition session based on your sequence, with mixed-down video so you can compose based on the action.

- Using Dynamic Link, open Premiere Pro video clips in After Effects CS6. Apply special effects and animation, and then view the results in Premiere Pro. You can play After Effects compositions in Premiere Pro without waiting to render them and also benefit from After Effects CS6 Global Cache, which saves RAM previews for later use.

- Use After Effects CS6 to create and animate text in ways far beyond the capabilities of Premiere Pro. Use those compositions in Premiere Pro with Dynamic Link. Adjustments made in After Effects appear inside Premiere Pro immediately.

- Send video projects created in Premiere Pro into Encore CS6 using Dynamic Link, without rendering or saving an intermediate file. Use Encore to create a DVD, Blu-ray Disc, or interactive Flash application.

Most of this book will focus on a standard workflow involving only Premiere Pro. However, several lessons and sidebars will demonstrate how you can use Adobe Creative Suite 6 Production Premium components as part of your workflow for powerful effects work and fine finishing.

Touring the Adobe Premiere Pro interface

It's helpful to begin by getting a little familiarity with the editing interface so you can recognize the tools as you work with them in the following lessons. To make it easier to configure the user interface, Premiere Pro offers *workspaces*. Workspaces quickly configure the various panels and tools on-screen in ways that are helpful for particular activities, such as editing, special effects work, or audio mixing.

To begin with, you'll take a brief tour of the Editing workspace. In this exercise, you'll use an Adobe Premiere Pro project from this book's companion DVD. Be sure to copy the lesson files from the DVD to your computer's hard drive for best performance.

Note: It's best to copy all the lesson assets from the DVD to your hard drive and leave them there until you complete this book; some lessons refer to assets from previous lessons.

1   Make sure you've copied all the lesson folders and contents from the DVD to your hard drive. The suggested directory is My Documents/Adobe/Premiere Pro/6.0/Lessons (Windows) or Documents/Adobe/Premiere Pro/6.0/Lessons (Mac OS).

2   Launch Premiere Pro.

On the welcome screen of Premiere Pro, you can start a new project or open a saved one.

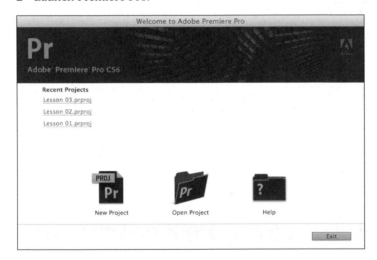

Note: You may be prompted with a dialog box asking where a particular file is. This will happen when the original files are saved on a hard drive (or hard drive letter) different from the one you're using. You'll need to tell Premiere Pro where the file is. In this case, navigate to the Lessons/Assets folder, and select the file that the dialog box is prompting you to open. Premiere Pro will remember this location for the rest of the files.

3   Click Open Project.

4   In the Open Project window, navigate to the Lesson 01 folder in the Lessons folder, and then double-click the Lesson 01.prproj project file to open the first lesson in the Premiere Pro workspace.

Note: All Adobe Premiere Pro project files have a .prproj extension.

The workspace layout

Before you begin, make sure you are looking at the default workspace. Choose Window > Workspace > Editing. Then, to reset the Editing workspace, choose Window > Workspace > Reset Current Workspace. Click Yes in the confirmation dialog.

If you're new to nonlinear editing, the default workspace might look like an awful lot of buttons. Don't worry. Things become much simpler when you know what the buttons are for. The interface is designed to make video editing easy. The principal elements are shown here.

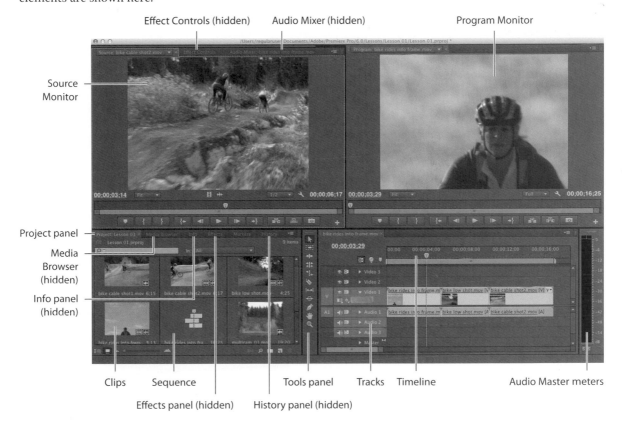

Each workspace item appears in its own panel, and multiple panels can be combined into a single frame. Some items with common industry terms stand alone, such as Timeline, Audio Mixer, and Program Monitor. The main user interface elements are as follows:

- **Timeline panel:** This is where you'll do most of your actual editing. You view and work on *sequences* (the term for edited video segments or entire projects) in the Timeline panel. One strength of sequences is that you can *nest* them (place sequences inside other sequences). In this way, you can break up a production into manageable chunks or create unique special effects.

- **Tracks:** You can layer—or *composite*—video clips, images, graphics, and titles on an unlimited number of tracks. Video clips on upper video tracks cover whatever is directly below them on the Timeline. Therefore, you need to give clips on higher tracks some kind of transparency or reduce their size if you want clips on lower tracks to show through.

- **Monitor panels:** You use the Source Monitor (on the left) to view and trim raw clips (your original footage). To view a clip in the Source Monitor, double-click it in the Project panel. The Program Monitor (on the right) is for viewing your sequence. Some editors prefer working with only one monitor screen. The lessons throughout this book reflect a two-monitor configuration. You can change to a single-monitor view if you choose. Click the Close button on the Source tab to close that monitor. In the main menu, choose Window > Source Monitor to open it again.

- **Project panel:** This is where you place links to your project's media files: video clips, audio files, graphics, still images, and sequences. You can use bins—similar to folders—to organize your assets.

- **Media Browser:** This panel helps you browse your hard drive to find footage. It's especially useful for file-based camera media.

- **Effects panel:** This panel contains all the clip effects you will use in your sequences, including video filters, audio effects, and transitions (docked, by default, with the Project panel). Effects are grouped by type to make them easier to find.

- **Audio Mixer:** This panel (docked, by default, with the Source and Effect Controls panels) is based on audio production studio hardware, with volume sliders and panning knobs. There is one set of controls for each audio track on the Timeline, plus a master track.

Effects panel

Audio Mixer

- **Effect Controls panel:**
  This panel (docked, by
  default, with the Source
  and Audio Mixer
  panels, or accessible via
  the Window menu)
  displays the controls for
  any effects applied to a
  clip you select in a
  sequence. Motion,
  Opacity, and Time
  Remapping controls are
  always available for
  visual clips. Most effect
  parameters are adjustable over time.

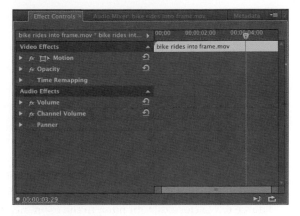

Effect Controls panel

- **Tools panel:** Each icon in this panel represents a tool that performs a specific function, typically a type of edit in a sequence. The Selection tool is context-sensitive, which means it changes appearance to indicate the function that matches the circumstances. If you find your cursor doesn't work as you expect it, it might be because you have the wrong tool.

- **Info panel:** The Info panel (docked, by default, with the Project panel and Media Browser, or accessible via the Window menu) presents information about any asset you select in the Project panel or any clip or transition selected in a sequence.

- **History panel:** This panel (docked, by default, with the Effects and Info panels) tracks the steps you take and lets you back up easily. It's a kind of visual Undo list. When you select a previous step, all steps that came after it are also undone.

Tools panel

Customizing your workspace

In addition to customizing the default workspaces (based on tasks), you can adjust the position and location of panels to create a workspace that works best for you. You can then store a workspace or even create multiple workspaces for different tasks.

- As you change the size of a frame, other frames change size to compensate.

- All panels within frames are accessible via tabs.

- All panels are dockable—you can drag a panel from one frame to another.

- You can drag a panel out of a frame to become a separate floating panel.

In this exercise, you'll try all these functions and save a customized workspace.

1 Click the Source Monitor panel (selecting its tab if necessary), and then position your pointer on the vertical divider between the Source panel and the Program panel. Then, click and drag left and right to change the sizes of those frames. You can choose to have different sizes for your video displays.

Note: All panels are adjustable in the same way, even the Tools and Audio meters.

2 Place the pointer on the horizontal divider between the Source panel and the Timeline. Drag up and down to change the sizes of these frames.

Note: As you move a panel, Premiere Pro displays a drop zone. If the panel is a rectangle, it will go into the selected frame as an additional tab. If it's a trapezoid, it will go into its own frame.

3 Click the gripper area in the upper-left corner of the tab for the Effects panel (to the left of the name), and drag it to the middle of the Source panel to dock the Effects panel in that frame.

The drop zone is displayed as a center highlight.

When many panels are combined in a single frame, you may not be able to see all the tabs. A navigation slider appears above the tabs to navigate between them. Slide it left or right to reveal hidden tabs. You can also display a panel by choosing it in the Window menu.

4 Click and drag the Effects drag handle to a point near the right of the Project panel to place it in its own frame.

The drop zone is displayed as a trapezoid.

You may need to resize your panels to see the controls you want.

The drop zone is a trapezoid that covers the right portion of the Project panel. Release the mouse button, and your workspace should look something like the example on the right.

You can also pull panels out into their own floating panel.

5 Click the Source Monitor's drag handle, and hold down the Control (Windows) or Command (Mac OS) key while dragging it out of its frame. Its drop zone image is much more distinct, indicating that you are about to create a floating panel.

6 Drop the Source Monitor anywhere, creating a floating panel. Resize it by dragging from a corner or a side like any other panel.

7 As you gain experience, you might want to create and save the layout of your panels as a customized workspace. To do so, choose Window > Workspace > New Workspace. Type a name, and click OK.

8 If you want to return a workspace to its default layout, choose Window > Workspace > Reset Current Workspace. To return to a recognizable starting point, choose the preset Editing workspace and reset it.

Introducing preferences

The more you edit video, the more you'll want to customize Premiere Pro to match your specific needs. There are several types of preferences, all grouped into one panel for easy access. Preferences will be covered in depth as they relate to the individual lessons in this book. Let's look at a simple one:

1 Choose Edit > Preferences > Appearance (Windows) or Premiere Pro > Preferences > Appearance (Mac OS).

▶ **Tip:** Notice as you approach the darkest setting, the text switches to white on gray. This is to accommodate those editors who work in editing bays in darkened rooms.

2 Drag the Brightness slider to the left or right to suit your needs. When done, click OK, or click cancel to return to the default setting.

The default brightness is a neutral gray to help you see colors correctly.

Review questions

1 Why is Premiere Pro considered a nonlinear editor?

2 Describe the basic video-editing workflow.

3 What is the Media Browser used for?

4 Can you save a customized workspace?

5 What is the purpose of the Source Monitor? What is the purpose of the Program Monitor?

6 How can you drag a panel to its own floating panel?

Review answers

1 Premiere Pro lets you place video clips, audio clips, and graphics anywhere in a sequence; rearrange items already in a sequence; add transitions; apply effects; and do any number of other video-editing steps in any order that suits you.

2 Shoot your video; transfer it to your computer; create a sequence of video, audio, and still-image clips on the Timeline; add effects and transitions; add text and graphics; mix your audio; and export the finished product.

3 The Media Browser allows you to browse and import media files without having to open an external file browser. It is particularly useful when you're working with file-based camera footage.

4 Yes. You can save any customized workspace by choosing Window > Workspace > New Workspace.

5 You use the monitor panels to view your original clips and your sequence. You can view and trim your original footage in the Source Monitor and use the Program Monitor to view the Timeline sequence as you build it.

6 Drag the panel with your mouse while holding down Control (Windows) or Command (Mac OS).

2 SETTING UP A PROJECT

Lesson overview

In this lesson, you'll learn about the following:

- Choosing project settings
- Choosing video rendering and playback settings
- Choosing video and audio display settings
- Choosing capture format settings
- Creating scratch disks
- Using sequence presets
- Customizing sequence settings

 This lesson will take approximately 45 minutes.

Before you begin editing, you need to create a new project and choose some settings for your first sequence. If you're not familiar with video and audio technology, all the options might be a little overwhelming. Luckily, Adobe Premiere Pro CS6 gives you easy shortcuts. Plus, the principles of video and sound reproduction are the same no matter what you're creating.

It's just a question of knowing what you want to do. To help you plan and manage your projects, this chapter contains quite a lot of information about formats and video technology. You may decide to revisit this chapter later, as your familiarity with Adobe Premiere Pro grows.

In practice, you are likely to make very few changes to the default settings, but it's good to know what all the options mean.

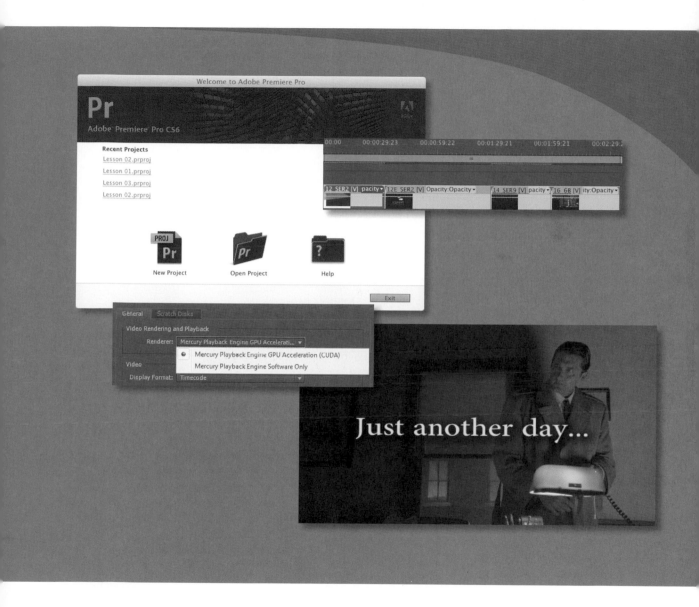

In this lesson, you'll learn how to create a new project and choose sequence settings that tell Adobe Premiere Pro how to play your clips.

Getting started

An Adobe Premiere Pro project file stores links to all the video and sound files—aka *clips*—used in your Adobe Premiere Pro project. A project file also has at least one *sequence*—that is, a series of clips that play, one after another, with special effects, titles, and sound, to form your completed creative work. You'll choose which parts of your clips to use and in which order they'll play. The beauty of editing with Adobe Premiere Pro is that you can change your mind about almost anything.

Remember that Adobe Premiere Pro project files have the file extension .prproj.

● **Note:** Many of the terms used in Adobe Premiere Pro come from film editing, including the term *clip*. In traditional film editing, film editors cut a piece of celluloid with a clipper and then put the piece aside for use in the edit.

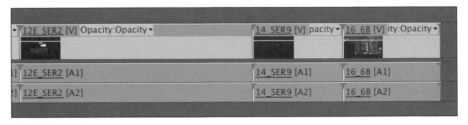

Video and audio clips in a sequence play in order as a completed edit.

Most often, starting a new Adobe Premiere Pro project is simple. You create a new project, choose a sequence preset, and get on with editing.

New Project

When you create a new project, Adobe Premiere Pro invites you to create a sequence. It's important to understand how sequence settings change the way Adobe Premiere Pro plays your video and audio clips. You can change the settings selected by a preset if it is almost, but not exactly, what you want.

● **Note:** Presets preselect several settings, saving you time. You can use an existing sequence preset or create a new one for use next time.

You need to know the kind of video and audio your camera records because your sequence settings will usually be based on your original source clips. To make it easier for you to choose the right settings, Adobe Premiere Pro sequence presets are named after different camera recording formats, so if you know the video format that your camera records, you'll know what to choose.

In this lesson, you'll learn how to create a new project and choose sequence settings that tell Adobe Premiere Pro how to play your clips. You'll also learn about different kinds of audio tracks, what preview files are, and how to open projects created in Apple Final Cut Pro 7 and Avid Media Composer.

Setting up a project

Let's begin by creating a new project.

1 Launch Adobe Premiere Pro. The Welcome screen appears.

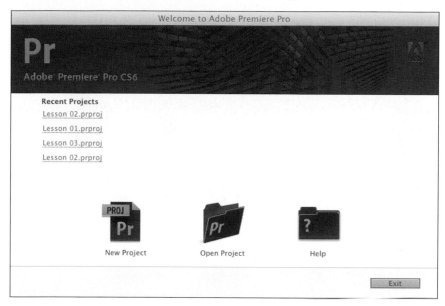

Recent Projects is a list of previously opened projects. If this is your first time launching Adobe Premiere Pro, it will be blank.

There are four buttons in this window:

- **New Project:** Opens the New Project dialog.

- **Open Project:** Lets you browse to an existing project file and open it to continue working on it.

- **Help:** Opens the online Help system. You'll need to be connected to the Internet to access online Adobe Premiere Pro Help.

- **Exit:** Exits Adobe Premiere Pro.

2 Click New Project to open the New Project dialog.

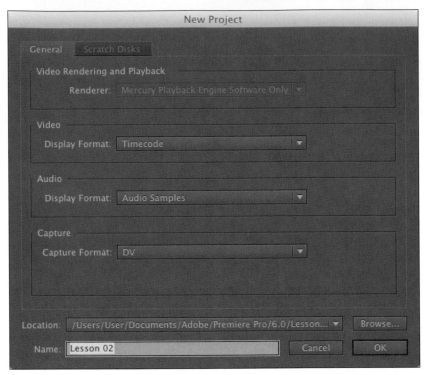

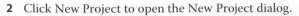

 Note: You'll notice that tabbed panels and dialogs appear a lot in Adobe Premiere Pro. They are a useful way of packing extra options into a smaller space.

This dialog has two tabs: General and Scratch Disks. All of the settings in this dialog can be changed later. In most cases, you'll want to leave them as they are. Let's take a look at what they mean.

Video rendering and playback settings

While working creatively with video clips in your sequences, it's likely you'll apply some visual effects. Some special effects can be played immediately, combining your original video with the effect and displaying the results as soon as you click Play. When this happens, it's called *real-time playback*.

Real-time playback is desirable because it means you can watch the results of your creative choices right away. Many special effects in Adobe Premiere Pro are designed to be in real time.

If you use lots of effects or if you use effects that are not designed to be played in real time, your computer may not be able to display the results at the full frame rate. That is, Adobe Premiere Pro will attempt to display your video clips, combined with the special effects, but it will not show every single frame each second. When this happens, it is described as *dropping* frames.

What do *rendering* and *real time* actually mean?

Think of rendering as an artist's rendering, where something is visualized, taking up paper and taking time. Imagine you have a piece of video that is too dark. You add a special effect to make it brighter, but your video-editing system is unable to both play the original video *and* make it brighter. In this situation, you'd have your system render the effect. When this happens, a new video file is created that looks like your original video combined with the special effect to make it brighter.

When the part of your sequence is played that contains the clip with the rendered effect, your system invisibly, and seamlessly, switches to playing the newly rendered video file instead. That file plays back like any other regular file. Although it looks like your original video with an effect on it, it's actually just a simple video clip that plays back normally.

When the part of your sequence with the brightened clip is finished, your system invisibly, and seamlessly, switches back to playing your other original video files.

The downside with rendering is that it takes up extra space on your hard drive, and it takes time. It also means you are viewing a new video file, based on your original media, and that might introduce some loss of quality. The upside with rendering is that you can be confident your system will be able to play the results of your effect at full quality, with all the frames per second.

Real-time is...instant! When using a real-time special effect, your system plays the original video clip combined with the special effect right away, without waiting for it to render. The only downside with real-time performance is that the amount you can do without rendering depends on how powerful your system is. In the case of Adobe Premiere Pro, you can dramatically improve real-time performance by using the right graphics card (see "The Mercury Playback Engine GPU Acceleration [CUDA]" on the next page). Plus, you'll need to use effects that are designed for real-time playback—and not all effects are.

Adobe Premiere Pro displays colored lines along the top of the Timeline panel to tell you when extra work is required to play back your video.

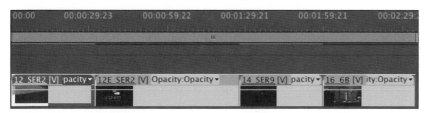

Not seeing every frame when you play your sequence is OK! It won't affect the final results. When you're done editing and you output your finished sequence (more on that in Chapter 18, "Exporting Frames, Clips, and Sequences"), it'll be full quality, with all the frames. However, it can make a difference to your editing experience and your ability to preview the effects you apply with confidence. There is a simple solution: rendering.

When you choose to render, Adobe Premiere Pro produces a new video file that looks exactly like the part of your sequence you have selected—known as the *work area*—with all the special effects applied. Every time that part of your sequence is played, Adobe Premiere Pro automatically, and invisibly, switches to the new video file and plays that instead. When that part of your sequence finishes, Adobe Premiere Pro invisibly switches back to playing the next clips in your sequence.

This means Adobe Premiere Pro can play back the results of your special effects at full quality, and at full frame rate, without your computer having to do any more work than playing a regular video file.

In practice, telling Adobe Premiere Pro to render is as simple as pressing a single key on your keyboard (the Enter key) or choosing an option in a menu.

| Render Effects in Work Area | ↵ |
| Render Entire Work Area | |

If the Renderer menu is available, it means you have the right graphics hardware for GPU Acceleration in your computer and it is installed correctly.

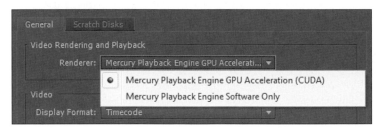

You'll see two options:

- **Mercury Playback Engine GPU Acceleration (CUDA):** If you choose this option, Adobe Premiere Pro will send many playback tasks to the graphics hardware on your computer, giving you lots of real-time effects and easy playback of mixed formats in your sequences.

- **Mercury Playback Engine Software Only:** This is still a major advancement on non-real-time playback, giving you excellent performance that uses all of the available power in your computer. If you don't have the right graphics hardware on your computer, only this option is available, and you won't be able to click this menu.

You can achieve much better performance by choosing GPU Acceleration, if you have a compatible graphics card. It allows Adobe Premiere Pro to give some of the work of playing back video and applying visual effects to the GPU.

You will almost certainly want to choose the GPU option and benefit from the additional performance if you can.

Do so now, if the option is available.

The Mercury Playback Engine

With Adobe Premiere Pro CS5, Adobe introduced a playback engine called Mercury. The Mercury Playback Engine dramatically improved playback performance, making it faster and easier than ever to work with multiple video formats, multiple special effects, and multiple layers of video (for effects such as picture-in-picture).

The Mercury Playback Engine was enhanced with version CS5.5 and again with version CS6. It has three main features:

- **Playback performance**: The way Adobe Premiere Pro plays back video files was improved, especially for some of the types of video that are really difficult to play back. If you're filming with a DSLR camera, for example, chances are your media is recorded using the H.264 codec, which is particularly hard to play back. With the new Mercury Playback Engine, you'll find these files play back with ease.

- **64-bit and multithreading**: Adobe Premiere Pro is a 64-bit application, which simply means it can use all of the random access memory (RAM) on your computer. This is particularly useful when you're working with very high-resolution video. The Mercury Playback Engine is also multithreaded, which means it uses all of the CPU cores in your computer. The more powerful your computer is, the more performance you get in Adobe Premiere Pro.

- **CUDA and Open CL support**: If you have the right graphics card or an Apple MacBook Pro laptop with the right graphics hardware, Adobe Premiere Pro can delegate some of the work for playing back video to the graphics card, rather than putting the entire processing burden on the CPU in your computer. The result is even better performance and responsiveness when working with your sequences and lots of special effects that will play in real time.

For a list of supported graphics cards, see *www.adobe.com/products/premiere/tech-specs.html*.

Video/audio Display Format settings

The next two options tell Adobe Premiere Pro how to measure time for your video and audio clips.

In most cases, you'll choose the default options: Timecode for video and Samples for Audio. These settings don't change the way Adobe Premiere Pro plays video or audio clips, only the way time is measured.

About seconds and frames

When a camera records video, it captures a series of still images of the action. If there are enough images captured each second, it looks like moving video when played back. Each picture is called a *frame*, and the number of frames each second is usually called *frames per second* (fps).

The fps will vary depending on your camera format and settings. It could be 23.976, 24, 25, 29.97, 50, or 59.94fps. Some cameras allow you to choose between more than one frame rate, with different options for accompanying frame sizes.

Adobe Premiere Pro will play back video at all common frame rates.

Video Display Format

There are four options for Video Display Format. The correct choice for a given project largely depends on whether you are working with video or film as your source material.

The choices are as follows:

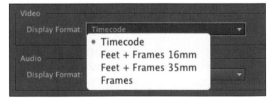

- **Timecode:** This is the default option. Timecode is a universal standard for counting hours, minutes, seconds, and individual frames for video files or tape. The same system is used by cameras, professional video recorders, and nonlinear editing systems all around the world.

- **Feet + Frames 16mm or Feet + Frames 35mm:** If your source files are captured from film and you intend to give your editing decisions to a lab so they can cut the original negative to produce a finished film, you may want to use this standard method of measuring time. Rather than measuring time, it's the number of feet plus the number of frames since the last foot. It's a bit like feet and inches but with frames rather than inches. Because 16mm film and 35mm film have different-sized frames (and so different numbers of frames per foot), there is an option for each.

- **Frames:** This option simply counts the number of frames of video, starting at 0. This is sometimes used for animation projects and is another way that labs like to receive information about edits for a film-based project.

For this exercise, leave Video Display Format set to Timecode.

Audio display format

When playing audio files, time can be displayed as samples or milliseconds.

- **Audio Samples:** When digital audio is recorded, a sound sample is taken, as captured by the microphone, thousands

of times a second. In the case of most professional video cameras, this happens 48,000 times per second. In Audio Samples mode, Adobe Premiere Pro will display time in your sequences as hours, minutes, seconds, and samples. The number of samples per second will depend on your sequence settings.

- **Milliseconds:** With this mode selected, Adobe Premiere Pro will display time in your sequences as hours, minutes, seconds, and thousandths of a second.

By default, Premiere Pro lets you zoom in to your sequences to view individual frames. However, you can easily switch to displaying your audio display format. This powerful feature lets you make the tiniest adjustments to your sound.

For this project, leave the Audio Display Format option set to Audio Samples.

Capture Format settings

The Capture Format settings menu tells Adobe Premiere Pro what format to use when recording video to your hard drive from videotape.

DV and HDV capture

Without additional third-party hardware, Adobe Premiere Pro can record from DV and HDV cameras using the FireWire connection on your computer, if it has one. FireWire is also known as IEEE 1394 and i.Link.

FireWire is a convenient connection for tape-based media because it uses just one cable to transmit video and sound information, device control (so your computer can tell the video deck to play, fast-forward, pause, and so on), and timecode.

Third-party hardware capture

Not all video decks use a FireWire connection, so you may need additional third-party hardware installed to be able to connect your video deck for capture.

If you have additional hardware, you should follow the directions provided by the manufacturer to install it. Most likely you'll install software supplied with your hardware, and this will discover Adobe Premiere Pro is installed on your computer, automatically adding extra options to this menu (and others).

Follow the directions provided with your third-party equipment to configure new Adobe Premiere Pro projects.

For more information about video capture hardware and video formats supported by Adobe Premiere Pro, visit *www.adobe.com/products/premiere/extend.html*.

Ignore this setting for now because we will not be capturing from a tape deck in this exercise, and the setting can be changed at any time.

● **Note:** The Mercury Playback Engine can share performance with video capture cards for monitoring, thanks to Adobe Mercury Transmit—a new feature in CS6.

Scratch Disks settings

Whenever Adobe Premiere Pro *captures* (records) from tapes or renders your special effects, new media files are created on your hard drive.

Scratch disks are the places these new files are stored. They can be separate disks, as the name suggests, or any file storage locations. Scratch disks can be created all in the same place or in separate locations, depending on your hardware and workflow requirements. If you're working with really large media files, you may get a performance boost by putting all of your scratch disks on different hard drives.

There are generally two approaches to storage for video editing:

- **Project-based setup:** All associated media files are stored with the project file in the same folder.

- **System-based setup:** Media files associated with multiple projects are saved to one central location, and the project file is saved to another.

Using a project-based setup

By default, Adobe Premiere Pro keeps any newly created media together with the project file (this is the Same as Project option). Keeping everything together this way makes finding associated files simple. You can stay even more organized by moving any media files you intend to import into your project into the same folder before you import them. When you're finished with your project, you can remove everything from your system by deleting the folder your project file is stored in.

Using a system-based setup

Some editors prefer to have all of their media stored in a single location. Others choose to store their capture folders and preview folders in a different location from their project. This is a common choice in editing facilities where multiple editors share multiple editing systems, all connected to the same storage drives. It's also common among editors who have one very fast hard drive for video media and a slower hard drive for everything else.

Typical drive setup and network-based storage

Although all file types can coexist on a single hard drive, a typical editing system will have two hard drives: drive 1, dedicated to the operating system and programs, and drive 2 (often a faster drive), dedicated to footage items, including captured video and audio, video and audio previews, still images, and exported media.

Some storage systems use local computer networks to share storage between multiple systems. If this is the case for your Adobe Premiere Pro setup, check with your system administrators to make sure you have the right settings.

For this project, we recommend you leave your scratch disks all set to the default option: Same as Project.

1 Click in the Name: box and give your new project the name *Lesson 02-01*.

2 Click the Browse button; then choose a preferred location on your computer hard drive for these lessons.

3 If your project is set up correctly, the General and Scratch Disks tabs in your New Project window should look identical to the screen shown here. If the settings match, click OK to create the project file.

● **Note:** When choosing a location for your project file, you might be able to choose a recently used location from the drop-down menu.

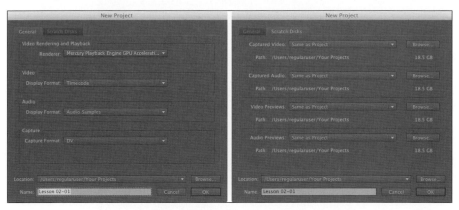

Setting up a sequence

Immediately after you create your project, you'll see another dialog box prompting you to set parameters for your first sequence. Adobe Premiere Pro always assumes you want at least one sequence, so you are prompted to create one when starting a new project. Adobe Premiere Pro adapts video and audio clips that you put into a sequence so they match the settings for that sequence. Each sequence in your project can have different settings, and you'll want to choose settings that match your original media as precisely as possible. Doing so reduces the work your system must do to play back your clips, improves real-time performance, and maximizes quality.

The New Sequence dialog has three tabs: Sequence Presets, Settings, and Tracks. We'll start with Sequence Presets.

Sequence Presets tab

The Sequence Presets tab makes setting up a new sequence much easier. When you choose a preset, Adobe Premiere Pro chooses settings for your sequence that closely match a particular video and audio format. After choosing a preset, you can tweak these settings on the Settings tab.

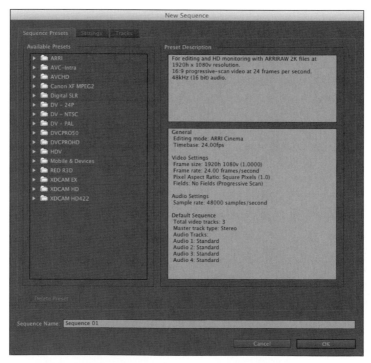

You'll find a wide range of preset configuration options for the most commonly used and supported media types. These settings are organized based on camera formats (with specific settings inside a folder named after the recording format).

Click the disclosure triangle to see specific settings in a group. These settings are typically designed around frame rates and frame sizes. Let's look at an example.

Note: The Preset Description area of the Sequence Presets tab often describes the kind of camera used to capture media in this format.

1   Click the disclosure triangle next to the group DVCPROHD.

You can now see three subfolders, based on frame sizes and interlacing methods. Remember, video cameras can often shoot video using different-sized flavors of HD, as well as frame rates and recording methods. The media used for the next exercise will be DVCPRO HD at 720p and a frame rate of 24fps.

2   Click the disclosure triangle next to the 720p subgroup.

3   To best match the footage we'll be using, choose the DVCPROHD 720p24 preset by clicking its name.

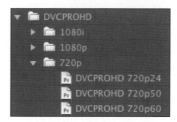

▶ **Tip:** If your system has additional third-party hardware for capture and playback, you may find you have additional sequence presets available.

Choosing the correct preset

When starting out in video editing, you may find the number of formats available a little overwhelming. Adobe Premiere Pro can play back and work with a very wide range of video and audio formats and will often play back mismatched formats smoothly.

However, when Adobe Premiere Pro has to adjust video for playback because of mismatched sequence settings, your editing system must expend extra effort to play the video, and this will impact real-time performance. It's worthwhile to take the time before you start editing to make sure you have sequence settings that closely match your original media files. You'll notice that all of the presets are based on types of camera to make it easier to select the right one.

The essential factors are always the same: the number of frames per second, the frame size (the number of pixels in the picture), and the codec. If you were to turn your sequence into a file, then the frame rate, audio format, frame size, and so on, would all match the settings you choose here.

When you output to a file, you can choose any export format you like (for more on exporting, see Chapter 18, "Exporting Frames, Clips, and Sequences").

Settings tab

Once you've selected the sequence preset that most closely matches your source video, you may want to adjust the settings to suit the specifics of your sequence.

To begin making adjustments, you would click the Settings tab and choose any options that better suit the way you would like Adobe Premiere Pro to conform your video and audio files for playback. Remember, Adobe Premiere Pro will automatically adapt footage you add to your Timeline so that it matches your sequence settings, giving you a standard frame rate and frame size, regardless of the original format.

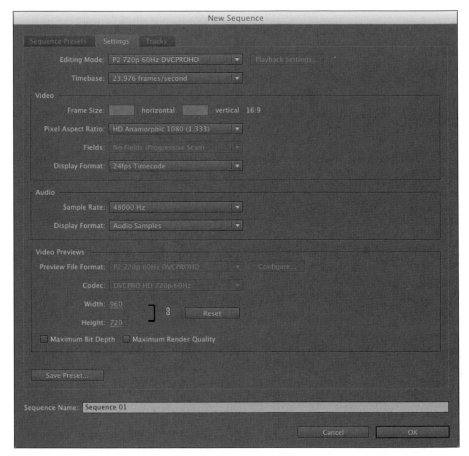

You will notice some settings cannot be changed when you use a preset. This is because they are optimized for the media type you selected on the Preset tab. To have complete flexibility, change the Editing Mode menu to Custom, and you will be able to change all of the available options.

The Settings tab allows you to customize the individual settings of a preset. If your media matches one of the presets, it's not necessary to make changes on the Settings tab. In fact, it's recommended that you do not.

For now, leave the settings alone, but examine how the preset is going to configure the new sequence. Look at each setting from top to bottom on the tab to get familiar with all of the choices required to properly configure a video-editing sequence.

Maximum bit depth and maximum render quality

If you enable Maximum Bit Depth, Adobe Premiere Pro can render special effects at the maximum quality possible. For many effects, this means 32-bit floating-point color, which allows for trillions of color combinations. This is the best possible quality for your effects but requires more work for your computer, so expect less real-time performance if you enable it.

If you enable Maximum Render Quality or if you have GPU acceleration, Adobe Premiere Pro uses a more advanced system for scaling images smaller. Without this option, you might see artifacts or noise in the picture when making images smaller. Without GPU acceleration, this option will impact performance.

Both of these options can be turned off or on at any time, so you can edit without them and then turn them on when you output your finished work. Even with both options on, you can use real-time effects and get good performance from Adobe Premiere Pro.

Custom presets

While the standard presets usually fit, you may need to create a custom setting. To do so, first choose a sequence preset that matches your media closely and then make custom selections in the Settings tab. You can save your custom preset by clicking the Save Preset button near the bottom of the Settings tab. Give your customized project settings preset a name in the Save Settings dialog, add notes if you want, and click OK. The preset will appear in the Custom folder under Available Presets.

If you use an Apple Macintosh and have the Apple ProRes codec installed, you can use this as your preview file codec. Choose a custom editing mode, and then choose QuickTime as your preview file format and Apple ProRes as your codec.

Formats and codecs

Video file types like Apple QuickTime and Microsoft AVI are containers that can carry many different video and audio codecs. The file is referred to as the *wrapper*, and the codec is referred to as the *essence*.

Codec is a shortening of compressor/decompressor. It is the way video and audio information is stored.

If you output your finished sequence to a file, you'll choose both a file type and a codec.

Tracks tab

When you add a video or audio clip to a sequence, you'll put it on a *track*. Tracks are horizontal areas in the sequence that hold clips in a specific position in time. If you have more than one video track, any video placed on an upper track will be in front of clips on a lower track (if they occupy the same moment in time). So, if you have text or a graphic on your second video track and video on your first video track, you'll see a composite of both.

All your audio tracks are played at the same time. This makes it easy to create an audio mix. You simply position your audio clips on different tracks, lined up in time. Narration, sound bites, sound effects, and music can be organized by putting them on dedicated tracks, making it easier to find your way around your sequence.

Adobe Premiere Pro lets you specify how many video and audio tracks will be added when the sequence is created. You can add and remove audio or video tracks later, but you can't change your Audio Master setting.

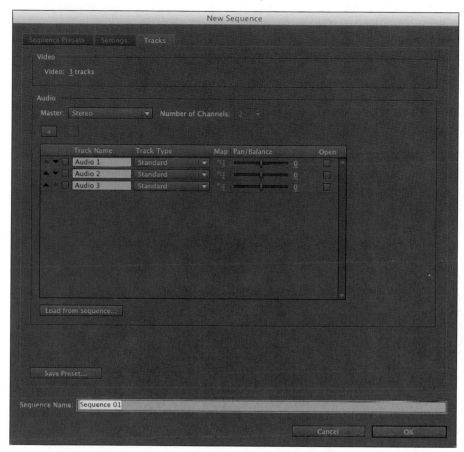

Note: After a sequence is created, you can't change the Audio Master setting. This setting is for choosing mono, stereo, 5.1-, or multi-channel output. For the purposes of these lessons, we'll choose Stereo. If you are new to video editing, it's likely you'll want to choose Stereo for the majority of your projects. The other options are used for advanced professional workflows such as surround-sound mixing for feature films.

You can choose from several audio track types. Each track type is designed for you to add specific types of audio file. When you choose a particular track type, Adobe Premiere Pro gives you the right controls to make adjustments to the sound.

When you add a clip to a sequence that has both video and audio, Adobe Premiere Pro makes sure the audio part goes to the right kind of track. You can't accidentally put an audio clip on the wrong track; Adobe Premiere Pro will automatically create the right kind of track if one doesn't exist.

Let's take a quick overview of each type (we'll explore audio more in Chapter 11, "Editing and Mixing Audio").

Audio tracks

Audio tracks are the horizontal areas where you'll put your audio clips. The types of audio tracks available in Adobe Premiere Pro are as follows:

- **Standard:** These tracks can take both mono and stereo audio clips.

- **5.1:** These tracks can take only audio clips with 5.1 audio (the kind used for surround sound).

- **Adaptive:** This track type is new in Adobe Premiere Pro CS6. Adaptive tracks will take both mono and stereo audio.

- **Mono:** This track type will take only mono audio clips.

Submixes

Submixes are a special feature of the audio finishing tools in Adobe Premiere Pro CS6. You can send the output from a track in your sequence to a submix, rather than directly to the master output. If you do this, you can then use the submix to apply special audio effects and make changes to the volume. This may not seem so useful for a single track, but you can send as many regular audio tracks as you like to a single submix. That means you could have, for example, ten audio tracks controlled by a single submix. Put simply, this means far less clicking and much more action.

Your submix options are as follows:

- **Stereo Submix:** For submixing stereo tracks

- **5.1 Submix:** For submixing 5.1 tracks

- **Adaptive Submix:** For submixing mono or stereo tracks

- **Mono Submix:** For submixing mono tracks

For this first sequence, we'll use the default settings. Be sure to take a moment, though, to click the available options to familiarize yourself with the available choices.

1 For now, click into the Sequence Name box and call your sequence *First Sequence*.

2 Click OK to create the sequence.

3 Choose File > Save. Congratulations! You have made a new project and sequence with Adobe Premiere Pro.

   If you have not already copied the media and project files to your computer, please do so now (you'll find instructions in the introduction to this book).

Importing Final Cut Pro projects

Adobe Premiere Pro CS6 can import and export sequences and links to media files using Final Cut Pro 7 XML. XML files store information about editing decisions in a way that can be understood by both Final Cut Pro and Adobe Premiere Pro.

This makes it ideal for sharing creative work between both applications.

Exporting an XML file from Final Cut Pro 7

You'll need to open the Final Cut Pro project file in Final Cut Pro to create an XML file. When you import the XML file to Adobe Premiere Pro, you'll need the media files used by Final Cut Pro. Adobe Premiere Pro can share the same files.

1   Open the existing project in Final Cut Pro.

2   Either choose nothing in the project, in which case you'll export the whole project, or select some specific items, in which case only those will be included.

3   Choose File > Export > XML.

    In the XML dialog you'll see a report of how many bins, clips, and sequences are selected.

4   Choose the Apple XML Interchange Format, version 4 option for maximum compatibility with Adobe Premiere Pro.

5   Save the XML file in an easy-to-find location (such as with your project).

Importing a Final Cut Pro 7 XML file

You import a Final Cut Pro 7 XML file into Adobe Premiere Pro just like any other kind of file (for more detail, see Chapter 3, "Importing Media"). When you import an XML file, Adobe Premiere Pro guides you through connecting the sequence and clip information to the original media files used by Final Cut Pro. There is a limit to the amount of information Final Cut Pro will include in an XML file, so you will find proprietary effects (such as color correction) will not make it to Adobe Premiere Pro. Test this workflow before you depend upon it.

Media best practice

If you intend to work with both Final Cut Pro and Adobe Premiere Pro, you'll want to use a media format that both editing systems can work with easily. Adobe Premiere Pro has wide-ranging support for media formats and can easily work with Final Cut Pro ProRes media files.

For this reason, it's best to use Final Cut Pro to import your media and capture video from tapes. You can set up your project using ProRes media in Final Cut Pro and then easily exchange projects with Adobe Premiere Pro.

See *www.adobe.com/products/premiere/extend.html* for more information about sharing projects with Final Cut Pro.

Importing Avid Media Composer projects

Adobe Premiere Pro CS6 can import and export sequences and links to media files using AAF files exported from Avid Media Composer. AAF files store information about editing decisions in a way that can be understood by both Avid and Adobe Premiere Pro.

This makes it ideal for sharing creative work between both applications.

Exporting an AAF file from Avid Media Composer

You'll need to open the Avid project file in Avid Media Composer to create an AAF file. When you import the AAF file to Adobe Premiere Pro, you'll need the media files used by Avid Media Composer—Adobe Premiere Pro can share the same files.

1   Open an existing project in Media Composer.

2   Choose the sequence you'd like to transfer.

3   Choose File > Export. Click the Options button.

In the standard Avid Export dialog, there's a menu at the bottom that contains templates. The Options button at the bottom allows customization.

4   From the Export Settings dialog, choose the following:

   • Select AAF Edit Protocol.

   • Include all video tracks in the sequence.

   • Include all audio tracks in the sequence.

   • On the Video Details tab for Export Method, choose Link to (Don't Export) Media.

   • On the Audio Details tab for Export Method, choose Link to (Don't Export) Media.

   • On the Audio Details tab, select Include Rendered Audio Effects.

   • (Optional.) Include marks—export only between In/Out points.

   • (Optional.) Use enabled tracks.

5   Save the AAF file in an easy-to-find location.

Importing an Avid AAF file

You import an Avid AAF file like any other kind of file (see Chapter 3). When you import an AAF file, Adobe Premiere Pro guides you through connecting the sequence and clip information to the original media files used by Avid. There is a limit to the amount of information Avid will include in an AAF file, so you will find that proprietary effects (such as color correction) will not make it to Adobe Premiere Pro. Test this workflow before you rely upon it.

Importing Avid Media Composer projects (continued)

Media best practice

Avid Media Composer uses a media management system that's completely different from the Adobe Premiere Pro system. However, since version 3.5 of Media Composer, a new system called AMA has permitted linking to media outside of Avid's own media organizational system. Media files imported to Avid Media Composer using AMA tend to relink better when an AAF file is imported into Adobe Premiere Pro. Media in an Avid Media Composer AMA folder can be anything that Apple QuickTime can play, including P2, XDCAM, and even RED. You'll need to have the appropriate codec available on your Adobe Premiere Pro editing system.

You will usually achieve the best results if you use Avid Media Composer's AMA system to link to original media with P2 or XDCAM media.

See *www.adobe.com/products/premiere/extend.html* for more information about sharing projects with Avid Media Composer.

Creating a sequence that automatically matches your source

If you're not sure what sequence preset you should choose, don't worry. Adobe Premiere Pro has a special shortcut to create a sequence based on your original media.

At the bottom of the Project panel, there is a New Item menu button 🔳. You can use this menu to create new items such as sequences and titles.

To automatically create a sequence that matches your media, drag and drop any clip in the Project panel onto this New Item menu button.

▶ **Tip:** If the first clip you add to a sequence does not match the playback settings of your sequence, Adobe Premiere Pro asks if you would like to change the sequence settings automatically to fit.

Adobe Premiere Pro creates a new sequence with the same name as the clip and a matching frame size and frame rate. Now you're ready to start editing, and you can be confident your sequence settings will work.

Review questions

1. What is the purpose of the Settings tab in the New Sequence dialog?

2. How should you choose a sequence preset?

3. What is timecode?

4. How do you create a custom sequence preset?

5. What capture settings are available inside Adobe Premiere Pro with no additional hardware?

Review answers

1. The Settings tab is used to customize an existing preset or to create a new custom preset. If you're using a standard media type, a sequence preset is all you should need to select.

2. It's generally best to choose a preset that matches your original footage. Adobe Premiere Pro makes this easy by describing the presets in terms of camera systems.

3. Timecode is a universal professional system for measuring time in hours, minutes, seconds, and frames. The number of frames per second varies depending on the recording format.

4. When you've selected the settings you want for your custom preset, click the Save Preset button, give a name and a description, and click OK.

5. Adobe Premiere Pro records DV and HDV files if you have a FireWire connection on your computer. If you have additional connections via installed hardware, consult the documentation for that hardware for the best settings.

3 IMPORTING MEDIA

Lesson Overview

In this lesson, you'll learn about the following:

- Using the Media Browser to load video files
- Using the Import command to load graphic files
- Choosing where to place cache files
- Capturing from tape

 This lesson will take approximately 75 minutes.

To edit your video assets, you need to first get the sources into your project. Because Adobe Premiere Pro can work with so many types of assets, there are multiple methods for browsing and importing media.

Getting started

In this lesson, you'll learn to import media assets into Adobe Premiere Pro CS6. For most files, you will use the Adobe Media Browser—a robust asset browser that works with all the media types you may need to import into Adobe Premiere Pro. You'll also learn about special cases such as importing graphics or capturing from videotape.

For this lesson, you'll use the project file you set up in Lesson 2.

1 Continue to work with the project file from the previous lesson, or open it from your hard drive.

2 Choose File > Save As.

3 Rename the file to *Lesson 03.prproj.*

4 Choose a preferred location on your hard drive, and click Save to save the project.

   If you do not have the previous lesson file, you can open the file Lesson 03.prproj from the Lesson 03 folder.

Importing assets

When you import items into an Adobe Premiere Pro project, you are creating a link from the original media to a pointer that lives inside your project. This means you are not actually modifying the original files; you're just manipulating them in a nondestructive manner. For example, if you choose to edit only part of a clip into your sequence, you're not throwing away the unused media.

You'll import media into Adobe Premiere Pro in two principal ways:

• Standard importing by choosing File > Import

• By using the Media Browser panel

Let's explore the benefits of each.

When to use the Import command

Using the Import command is straightforward (and may match what you're used to from other applications). To import any file, just choose File > Import. You can also use the keyboard shortcuts, Control+I (Windows) or Command+I (Mac OS), to open the standard Import dialog.

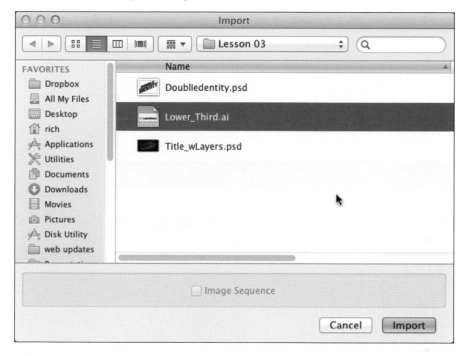

This method works best for self-contained assets such as graphics and audio, especially if you know exactly where those assets are on your drive and you want to quickly navigate to them. This importing method is not ideal for camera format files, which often use complex folder structures with separate files for audio and video. For camera-originated media, you'll instead rely on the Media Browser.

▶ **Tip:** Another way to open the Import dialog box is to simply double-click an empty area of the Project panel.

When to use the Media Browser

The Media Browser is a robust tool for reviewing your media assets and then importing them into Adobe Premiere Pro. The Media Browser is designed to properly show you media formats acquired by modern digital video cameras and can convert the complex camera folder structures into easy-to-browse icons and metadata. Being able to see this metadata (which contains important information such as duration, date, and file type) makes it far easier to select the correct clip from long lists of files or shots.

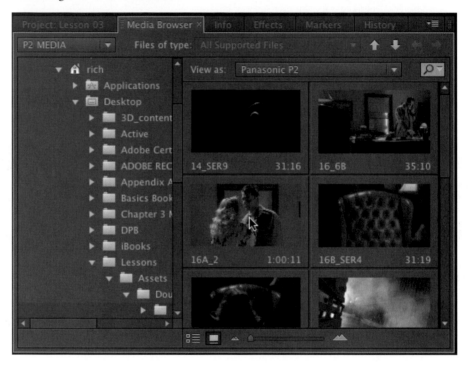

By default, you'll find the Media Browser in the lower-left corner of your Adobe Premiere Pro workspace (if your workspace is set to Editing). It's docked in the same frame as the Project panel. You can also quickly access the Media Browser by pressing Shift+8.

You can position the Media Browser elsewhere on-screen by dragging it, or you can undock it and make it a floating panel by clicking the submenu in the corner of the panel and choosing Undock Panel.

You'll find that working in the Media Browser is not significantly different from browsing using your computer's operating system. There are a series of navigation folders on the left side and standard up, down, left, and right arrows in the upper-right corner to change levels of browsing. You can use the up and down arrows to select items within a list and the left- and right-arrow keys to move further along a file directory path (such as stepping into a folder to examine its contents).

Importing from Adobe Prelude

A component of Adobe Creative Suite CS6 is Adobe Prelude, which you can use to organize footage in a simple, streamlined interface. The use of Adobe Prelude is beyond the scope of this book, but you will find extensive coverage in the component's documentation on how to use it and best practices for organizing clips. Adobe Prelude is designed so producers or assistants can quickly ingest, log, and even transcode media for tapeless workflows.

If you have an Adobe Prelude project, here's how to send it to Adobe Premiere Pro:

1 Launch Adobe Prelude.

2 Open the project you want to transfer.

3 Switch to Adobe Premiere Pro and make sure the project you want to receive the media is open.

4 Switch back to Adobe Prelude and click the Project panel.

5 Select the individual clips you want to send by Control+clicking (Windows) or Command+clicking (Mac OS), or select all clips.

6 Choose File > Send to Adobe Premiere Pro.

7 Switch to Adobe Premiere Pro. The files should appear in the Project panel.

You can now quit Adobe Prelude and close the project.

The major benefits of the Media Browser include the following:

- Narrowing the display to a specific file type, such as JPEG, Photoshop, XML, AAF, and more.

- Autosensing camera data—AVCHD, Canon XF, P2, RED, ARRIRAW, Sony HDV, and XDCAM (EX and HD).

- Viewing and customizing the display of metadata associated with your clips.

- Correctly displaying media that has spanned clips across multiple camera media cards. This is common in professional cameras, and Adobe Premiere Pro will import the files as a single clip, even if two cards were used to record the longer file.

▶ **Tip:** If you need to use assets from another Adobe Premiere Pro project, you can import that project into your current one. Just use the Media Browser to locate it; then drag it into your current project.

Working with the Media Browser

The Media Browser in Adobe Premiere Pro allows you to easily browse for files on your computer. It can also stay open all the time, giving you immediate access to the media files on your hard drive. It's fast and convenient and highly optimized for locating and importing footage.

● **Note:** To complete this lesson, you will be importing files from your computer. Be sure you have copied the entire DVD included with this book to your computer. For more details, see the "Getting Started" section in the front of the book.

Using a tapeless workflow

A *tapeless workflow* (also known as a *file-based workflow*) is simply the process of importing video from a tapeless camera, editing it, and exporting it. Adobe Premiere Pro makes this especially easy because, unlike many competing nonlinear editing systems, Adobe Premiere Pro CS6 does not require the media from these tapeless formats to be converted before editing. Adobe Premiere Pro can edit tapeless formats (such as P2, XDCAM, AVCHD, and even DSLRs that shoot video) natively with no conversions.

For best results when working with your own camera media, follow these guidelines:

1 Create a new folder for each project.

2 Copy the camera media to your editing hard drive (being sure to keep the existing folder structure intact). Be sure to transfer the complete data folder directly from the root directory of the card. You can also use a transfer

application that is often included by the camera manufacturer to move your video clips for best results. Be sure to visually inspect it to ensure that all media files have been copied and that the card and new folder sizes match.

3   Clearly label the folder of the media with the camera information including card number and date of shoot.

4   Create a second copy of the cards on a second drive.

5   Ideally, create a long-term archive using another backup method such as Blu-ray Disc, LTO tape, and so on.

Supported video file types

It's not unusual to work on a project and end up with video clips from different cameras using different file formats. This is no problem for Adobe Premiere Pro because you can mix clips of different frame sizes on the same Timeline. The Media Browser can see just about any file format. It is particularly well suited for native support for tapeless formats.

The major tapeless formats supported by Adobe Premiere Pro include the following:

*   Any DSLR camera that shoots H.264 directly as a .mov or .mp4 file

*   Panasonic P2 (DV, DVCPRO, DVCPRO 50, DVCPRO HD, AVC-Intra)

*   RED ONE, RED EPIC, and the RED Mysterium X

*   ARRIRAW

*   XDCAM SD, XDCAM EX, XDCAM HD, and HD422

*   Sony HDV (when shot on removable tapeless media)

*   AVCHD cameras

*   Canon XF

Finding assets with the Media Browser

▶ **Tip:** Filter the assets you're looking for by using the Files of Type menu in the Media Browser.

The good news is that the Media Browser is pretty self-explanatory. In many ways, it's like a web browser (it has forward and back buttons to go through your recent navigation). It also has a list of shortcuts on the side. Finding materials is pretty easy.

1 Work with the Lesson 03.prproj file from earlier. This project should have no assets imported yet.

2 Let's reset the workspace to the default; choose Window > Workspace > Editing. Then choose Window > Workspace > Reset Current Workspace and click Yes.

3 Click the Media Browser (it should be docked with the Project panel by default). Make it larger by dragging its right edge to the right.

4 Using the Media Browser, navigate to the Lessons/Assets/Double Identity/ P2 MEDIA folder. You can open each folder by double-clicking.

● **Note:** The Media Browser filters out nonmedia files, making it easier to browse for video or audio assets.

5 Let's make the Media Browser easier to see. Place your mouse pointer over the panel; then press the ` (grave) key. It is often in the upper-left corner of your keyboard.

The Media Browser panel should now fill the screen.

6 Drag the resize slider in the lower-left corner of the Media Browser to enlarge the thumbnails of the clips. You can use any size you like.

7 Single-click the first clip in the bin to select it.

You can now preview the clip using keyboard shortcuts.

8 Press the L key to preview a clip forward.

9 To stop playback, press the K key.

10 Rewind the clip by pressing the J key.

11 Experiment with playing back other clips. If the volume of your computer is turned up, you should be able to hear the audio playback clearly.

You can also press the J or L key multiple times to increase the playback rate for fast previews. Use the K key or the spacebar to pause.

12 Let's import all of these clips into our project. Press Control+A (Windows) or Command+A (Mac OS) to select all of the clips.

13 Right-click one of the selected clips and choose Import.

Alternately, you can drag all of the selected clips onto the Project panel's tab and then down into the empty area to import the clips.

14 Switch back to the Project panel.

Importing images

Graphics have become an integral part of the modern video edit. People expect graphics to both convey information and add to the visual style of a final edit. Fortunately, Adobe Premiere Pro can import just about any image and graphic file type. Support is especially excellent when you use the native file formats created by Adobe's leading graphic tools, Adobe Photoshop and Adobe Illustrator.

Importing flattened Adobe Photoshop files

Anyone who works with print graphics or does photo retouching has probably used Adobe Photoshop. It is the workhorse of the graphic design industry. Adobe Photoshop is a powerful tool with great depth and versatility, and it is becoming an increasingly important part of the video production world. Let's explore how to properly import two files from Adobe Photoshop.

To start, let's import a basic Adobe Photoshop graphic:

1 Click the Project panel to select it.

2 Choose File > Import or press Control+I (Windows) or Command+I (Mac OS).

3 Navigate to Lessons/Lesson 03.

4 Select the file DoubleIdentity.psd, and click Import.

The graphic is a simple logo file and imports into the Adobe Premiere Pro project.

Importing layered Adobe Photoshop files

Adobe Photoshop can also create graphics using multiple layers. Layers are similar to tracks in your Timeline and allow for separation between elements. These layers can be imported into Adobe Premiere Pro to allow for isolation or animation.

1 Double-click an empty area of the Project panel to open the Import dialog box.

2 Navigate to Lessons/Lesson 03.

3 Select the file Title_wLayers.psd, and click Import.

4 A new dialog opens, giving you a choice of how to interpret the layered file. There are four ways to import the file, controlled by a pop-up menu in the Import Layered File dialog box:

- **Merge All Layers:** Merges all layers, importing the file into Adobe Premiere Pro as a single, flattened clip.

- **Merged Layers:** Merges only the layers you select into Adobe Premiere Pro as a single, flattened clip.

- **Individual Layers:** Imports only the layers you select from the list into a bin, making one clip for each source layer.

- **Sequence:** Imports only the layers you select, each as a single clip. Adobe Premiere Pro also then creates a new sequence (with its frame size based on the imported document) containing each layer on a separate track (that matches the original stacking order).

Choosing Sequence or Individual Layers allows you to select one of the following options from the Footage Dimensions menu:

- **Document Size:** Brings the selected layer in at the size of the original Photoshop document.

- **Layer Size:** Matches the frame size of the clips to the frame size of their content in the original Photoshop file. Layers that do not fill the entire canvas may be cropped smaller as transparent areas are removed.

5 For this exercise, choose Sequence and use the Document Size option. Click OK.

6 Looking in the Project panel, locate the new bin Title_wLayers. Double-click to open it and to reveal its contents.

7 Double-click the sequence Title_wLayers to load it.

8 Examine the sequence in the Timeline panel. Try turning the visibility icons off and on for each track to see how the layers are isolated.

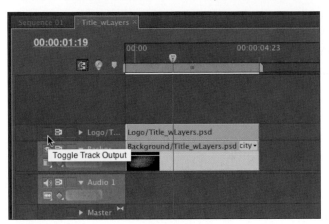

Image tips for Adobe Photoshop files

Here are a few tips for importing images from Adobe Photoshop:

- You can import images up to 16 megapixels in size (4096 x 4096). Remember that when you import a layered Photoshop document as a sequence, the frame size will be the pixel dimensions of the document.

- If you don't plan to zoom or pan, try to create files with a frame size at least as large as the frame size of the project. Otherwise, you have to scale up the image, and it will lose some of its sharpness.

- Importing overly large files uses more memory and can slow down your project.

- If you plan to zoom or pan, create images such that the zoomed or panned area has a frame size at least as large as the frame size of the project. For example, if you were working in 1080p and you wanted to do a 2X zoom, you'd need 3840 x 2160 pixels.

Importing Adobe Illustrator files

Another graphics component in Adobe Creative Suite is Adobe Illustrator. Unlike Adobe Photoshop, which is primarily designed to work with pixel-based (or *raster*) graphics, Adobe Illustrator is a vector application. This means it is typically used for things such as technical illustrations, line art, and complex graphics that can be scaled infinitely inside Adobe Illustrator.

Let's import a vector graphic.

1 Double-click an empty area of the Project panel to open the Import dialog box.

2 Navigate to Lessons/Lesson 03.

3 Select the file Lower_Third.ai, and click Import.

   This file type is Adobe Illustrator Artwork. Here's how Adobe Premiere Pro deals with Adobe Illustrator files:

   • Like the Photoshop CS6 file you imported in the previous exercise, this is a layered graphic file. However, Adobe Premiere Pro doesn't give you the option to import Adobe Illustrator files in separate layers. It merges them.

   • It also uses a process called *rasterization* to convert the vector (path-based) Adobe Illustrator art into the pixel-based (raster) image format used by Adobe Premiere Pro. This conversion happens during the import stage, so be sure your graphics are large enough in Illustrator before importing into Adobe Premiere Pro.

   • Adobe Premiere Pro automatically *anti-aliases*, or smoothes the edges of, the Adobe Illustrator art.

   • Adobe Premiere Pro converts all empty areas into a transparent alpha channel so that clips below those areas on the Timeline can show through.

● **Note:** If you right-click Lower_Third.ai in the Project panel, you'll note that one option is Edit Original. If you have Illustrator installed on your computer, selecting Edit Original will open this graphic in Illustrator, ready to be edited. So, even though the layers are merged in Adobe Premiere Pro, you can return to Adobe Illustrator, edit the original layered file, and save it, and the changes will immediately show up in Adobe Premiere Pro.

Recording a scratch narration track

Many times, you may be working with a video project that has a narration track. While most choose to eventually get these recorded by professionals (or at least in a location quieter than their desks), you can still record a temporary track right into Adobe Premiere Pro. This can be helpful if you need something to edit your video to.

Here's how to go about recording a scratch audio track:

1   If you're not using a built-in microphone, make sure your external microphone is properly connected to your computer. You may need to see the documentation for your computer or sound card.

2   Choose Edit > Preferences > Audio Hardware (Windows) or Premiere Pro > Preferences > Audio Hardware (Mac OS) to properly configure your microphone so Adobe Premiere Pro can use it. Use one of the choices from the Default Device pop-up menu, such as System Default Input/Output or Built-in Microphone/Built-in Output, and click OK.

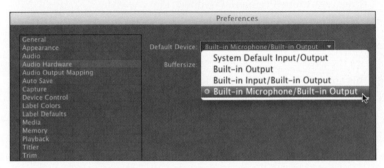

3   Turn down the speakers on your computer to prevent feedback or echo.

4   Open a sequence, and select an empty track in the Timeline.

5   Choose the Audio Mixer (which is likely to be docked in the same frame as your Source Monitor).

6   In the Audio Mixer, click the Enable Track For Recording icon (R) for the track you want to use for your audio device.

Recording a scratch narration track (continued)

7 Choose the recording input channel from the Track Input Channel menu.

8 Click the Record button at the bottom of the Audio Mixer to enter Record mode.

9 Click the Play button to start recording.

10 If the levels are too loud or quiet, you can adjust the track volume slider up (louder) or down (quieter) as you record. If you see red indicators at the top of the VU meters light up, you likely have distortion. A good target to aim for is loud audio registering near 0 dB and quiet audio registering around –18 dB.

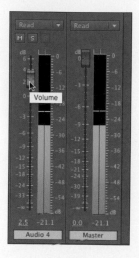

11 Click the Stop icon to stop recording.

12 Locate both instances of the recorded audio. The newly recorded audio appears both on the audio track in the Timeline and as a clip in the Project panel. You can select the clip in the Project panel and rename or delete it from your project.

The media cache

When you import certain video and audio formats, Adobe Premiere Pro may need to process and cache a version. This is particularly true for highly compressed formats. Imported audio files are conformed to a new .cfa file. Most MPEG files are indexed to a new .mpgindex file. You'll know that the cache is being built if you see a small progress indicator in the lower-right corner of the screen when importing media.

The benefit of the media cache is that it greatly improves performance for previews. It does this by lessening the load on a computer's CPU. You can fully customize the cache to further improve responsiveness. This media cache database is shared with Adobe Media Encoder, Adobe After Effects, Adobe Premiere Pro, Adobe Encore, and Adobe Audition, so each of these applications can each read from and write to the same set of cached media files.

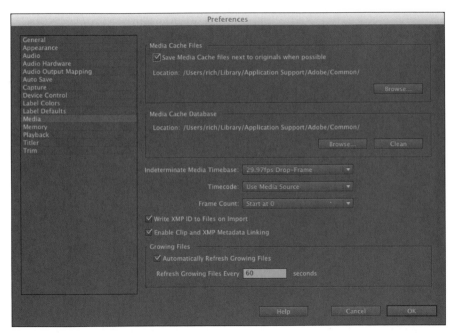

To access controls for the cache, choose Edit > Preferences > Media (Windows) or Premiere Pro > Preferences > Media (Mac OS). Here are the relevant options to consider:

- To move the media cache or the media cache database to a new disk, click the respective Browse button, select the desired location, and click OK. In most cases, you should not move the media cache database after you start to edit. However, on a regular basis, it should be cleaned.

- To clean the cache to remove conformed and indexed files, click the Clean button. Any connected drives will have their cache files removed. It's a good idea to do this after you wrap up projects because it removes unneeded previews.

- Choose "Save Media Cache files next to originals when possible" in order to keep cache files stored on the same drive as the media. This will distribute the media cache files to the same drive as the media, which is generally desirable. If you want to keep everything in one central folder, leave this box unchecked.

An introduction to Dynamic Link

One way to work with Adobe Premiere Pro is with a suite of tools. You may be using a version of Adobe Creative Suite that includes other components for the related tasks for video editing. To make things easier, you'll find several options for speeding up post-production workflow.

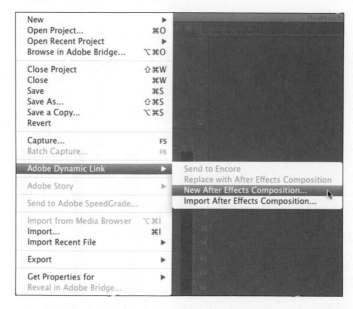

The options for Dynamic Link exist between several applications but behave a little differently depending upon the pair being used. The principal goal with Dynamic Link is to minimize time lost from rendering or exporting. Dynamic Link is supported by Adobe Premiere Pro, Adobe After Effects, and Adobe Encore.

We'll explore the Dynamic Link workflow throughout this book, but this is a good time to point out an example that will help you understand how Adobe software components can work together. Using Dynamic Link, you can import Adobe After Effects compositions to an Adobe Premiere Pro project. Once added, the Adobe After Effects compositions will look and behave like any other clip in your project. If you make changes in Adobe After Effects, they'll automatically update in the Adobe Premiere Pro project. This sort of time savings is useful as you begin to set up your projects.

Capturing from videotape

While tapeless media has become the most common video format, there are still plenty of video cameras around that record to tape. Fortunately, tape is still a relevant source and fully supported by Adobe Premiere Pro. To bring footage into an Adobe Premiere Pro project, you can capture it.

You capture digital video from a tape to the hard disk before using it in a project. Adobe Premiere Pro captures video through a digital port, such as a FireWire or Serial Digital Interface (SDI) port installed on your computer. Adobe Premiere Pro saves captured footage to disk as files and imports the files into projects as clips.

Adobe Premiere Pro features tools that take some of the manual labor out of the capturing process. There are three basic approaches:

- You can capture your entire videotape as one long clip.

- You can log each clip's In and Out points for automated batch capturing.

- You can use the scene detection feature in Adobe Premiere Pro to automatically create separate clips based on every time you pressed the Pause/Record button on your camcorder.

● **Note:** To do these exercises, you will need a DV or HDV camera or deck. You may also need a FireWire port and appropriate cable. If you don't have the hardware available, you can still read the exercises to explore the process. If you don't plan on using tape, you can skip to Chapter 4, "Organizing media."

Capturing other formats with third-party hardware

By default, you can use DV and HDV sources with Adobe Premiere Pro if your computer has a FireWire port. If you'd like to capture other higher-end professional formats, you'll need to add a third-party capture device. They come in several form factors including internal cards as well as breakout boxes that connect via FireWire, USB 3.0, and Thunderbolt ports. Adobe Premiere Pro CS6 helps unify support for third-party hardware, which can now often take advantage of Mercury Engine Playback features for previewing effects and video to a connected professional monitor. You can find a detailed list of supported hardware by visiting *www.adobe.com/products/premiere/extend.html*.

Capturing an entire tape

Because hard drive space is relatively cheap, many choose to capture entire tapes at once. After editing your project, you can choose to manually remove the unused portions using media management options in Adobe Premiere Pro.

Here's how to capture an entire tape:

1 Make sure to quit Adobe Premiere Pro before connecting any hardware. This is necessary so the hardware can be detected when the application launches.

2 Connect the camera or tape deck to your computer with the appropriate cable.

3 Turn on your camera or tape deck, and set it to playback mode: VTR or VCR. Do not set it to camera mode.

4 Depending on your operating system, additional dialog boxes may open:

- In Windows, an AutoPlay dialog may pop up. Click "View more AutoPlay options in Control Panel." Set the option to "Take no action." (The next time you fire up your camcorder, you should not see this connection query.)

- In Mac OS X, if iMovie or another application starts up, simply quit it. You can then use Adobe Premiere Pro to capture.

5 Start Adobe Premiere Pro, click Open Project, and navigate to the Lesson 03 file you've been working with. Create a new bin called *Captured Footage*.

6 Choose File > Capture to open the Capture panel.

● **Note:** If you get a No Device Control or Capture Device Offline message, you'll need to do some troubleshooting. The most obvious fix is to make sure the camcorder is turned on and the cables are connected. For more troubleshooting tips, refer to the Adobe Community Help website.

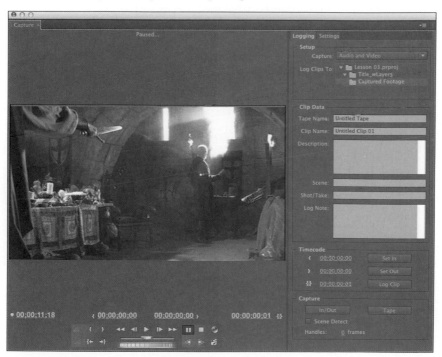

7 Look above the Capture panel preview pane to make sure your camcorder is connected properly.

8 Insert a tape into your camera or deck. Adobe Premiere Pro prompts you to give the tape a name.

▶ **Tip:** To help you identify these buttons, move the pointer over them to see tool tips.

9 Type a name for your tape in the textbox. Be sure not to give two tapes the same name; Adobe Premiere Pro remembers clip in/out data based on tape names.

10 Use the VCR-style device controls in the Capture panel to play, fast-forward, rewind, pause, and stop your tape. If you've never used a computer to control a camcorder, this may seem pretty cool.

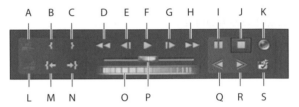

A. Next Scene	**F.** Play	**K.** Record	**P.** Shuttle
B. Set In Point	**G.** Step Forward	**L.** Previous Scene	**Q.** Slow Reverse
C. Set Out Point	**H.** Fast Forward	**M.** Go To In Point	**R.** Slow Play
D. Rewind	**I.** Pause	**N.** Go To Out Point	**S.** Scene Detect
E. Step Back	**J.** Stop	**O.** Jog	

11 Try some of the other VCR-style buttons:

- Shuttle (the slider toward the bottom) enables you to move slowly or zip quickly—depending on how far you move the slider off-center—forward or backward through your tape.

- Single-frame Jog control (below the Shuttle slider).

- Step Forward and Step Back, one frame at a time.

- Slow Reverse and Slow Play.

12 Rewind the tape to its beginning or to wherever you want to start recording.

13 In the Setup area of the Logging tab, note that Audio and Video is the default setting. If you want to capture only audio or only video, change that setting.

14 Click the Tape button in the Capture area of the Logging tab or the Record button in the Capture panel to start recording.

You'll see (and hear) the video in the Capture panel and on your camcorder. Since there is a slight delay during capture, you'll hear what sounds like an echo. Feel free to turn down the speaker on either your camcorder or your computer.

15 Press the Escape key when you want to stop recording.

The Save Captured Clip dialog appears.

16 Give your clip a name (add descriptive information if you want), and click OK.

Adobe Premiere Pro stores all the clips in the same folder as your project file. You can change the default location by choosing Project > Project Settings > Scratch Disks.

> **Note:** You may not see the preview window update when capturing HDV footage on your computer. Be sure to directly attach a monitor to your tape deck or camera so you can monitor the video signal.

Using batch capture

Adobe Premiere Pro offers a feature called *batch capture*. This allows you to log a tape and set In and Out points to describe a number of clips. Use the logging process to critically view your raw footage. You want to look for useful video, the best interview sound bites, and any natural sound that will enhance your production. Adobe Premiere Pro can then automatically transfer the logged clips to your computer. This method is beneficial because it lets you log in faster than real time and then walk away and let the clips capture.

When you log each clip, you must assign it a unique name. Think through how you're going to name your clips. You might end up with dozens of clips from each tape, and if you don't give them descriptive names, it'll slow down editing.

Here are the steps to follow:

1 In the Capture panel, click the Logging tab.

2 Change the Handles setting (at the bottom of the Logging tab) to 30 frames.

This adds one second to the start and finish of each captured clip for NTSC 29.97, which will give you enough head and tail frames to add transitions without covering up important elements of the clip. If you're working in PAL, set this to 25 frames.

> **Note:** Handles are extra frames at the beginning and end of a clip. For example, adding 30 frames as handles would add one second of video to the start and end of your clips if you're working in NTSC 29.97. This can be useful for transitions.

3 In the Clip Data area of the Logging tab, give your tape a unique name.

4 Log your tape by rewinding and then playing it.

5 When you see the start of a segment you want to transfer to your computer, stop the tape, rewind to that spot, and click the Set In button in the Timecode area of the Logging tab.

6 When you get to the end of that segment (you can use Fast Forward or simply Play to get there), click Set Out. The in/out times and the clip length will appear.

7 Click Log Clip to open the Log Clip dialog.

8 Change the clip name, if needed, and add appropriate notes if you want; then click OK.

That adds this clip's name with its in/out times and tape name information to the Project panel (with "Offline" next to it). You'll go there later to do the actual capture.

9 Log clips for the rest of your tape using the same method.

Each time you click Log Clip, Adobe Premiere Pro automatically adds a number to the end of your previous clip's name. You can accept or override this automated naming feature.

10 When you've finished logging your clips, close the Capture panel.

All your logged clips will be in the Project panel, with the offline icon next to each.

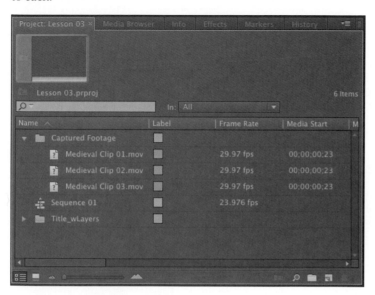

11 In the Project panel, select all the clips you want to capture.

12 Choose File > Batch Capture.

A Batch Capture dialog opens, allowing you to override the camcorder settings or add more handle frames.

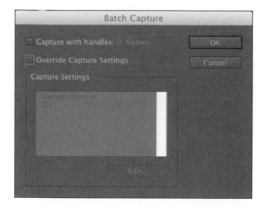

13 Leave the Batch Capture options unselected, and click OK.

The Capture panel opens, as does another little dialog telling you to insert the proper tape (in this case, it's probably still in the camcorder).

14 Insert the tape, and click OK.

Adobe Premiere Pro now takes control of your camcorder, cues up the tape to the first clip, and transfers that clip and all other clips to your hard drive.

15 When the process is complete, take a look at your Project panel to see the results. The offline icon is now a movie icon, and your footage is ready to be edited.

Using scene detection

Instead of manually logging In and Out points, you might want to use the scene detection feature. Scene detection analyzes your tape's time/date stamp, looking for breaks such as those caused when you press the camcorder's Pause/Record button while recording.

When scene detection is on and you perform a capture, Adobe Premiere Pro automatically captures a separate file at each scene break it detects. Scene detection works whether you are capturing an entire tape or just a section between specific In and Out points.

To turn on scene detection, do either of the following:

• Click the Scene Detect button (below the Record button in the Capture panel).

• Select the Scene Detect option in the Capture area of the Logging tab.

Then you can either set In and Out points and click Record or cue your tape to wherever you want to start capturing and click Record. In the latter case, click Stop when done.

Your clips will show up in the Project panel. You don't need to batch capture them—Adobe Premiere Pro captures each clip on the fly. Adobe Premiere Pro then names the first captured clip by putting a "01" after the name you put in the Clip Name box and increments the number in each new clip name by one.

Review questions

1 Does Adobe Premiere Pro CS6 need to convert P2, XDCAM, or AVCHD footage when it is imported?

2 What is one advantage of using the Media Browser to import tapeless media over the File > Import method?

3 What should you check if you see "Capture Device Offline" at the top of the Capture panel?

4 What does scene detection do when selected?

5 During the capture process, how do you add extra frames to ensure you have enough footage for transitions?

6 Is the actual media captured to your hard disk during the logging stage of a batch capture?

Review answers

1 No. Adobe Premiere Pro CS6 can edit P2, XDCAM, and AVCHD natively.

2 The Media Browser understands the P2 and XDCAM folder structures and shows you the clips in a visually friendly way.

3 Check that your camcorder or deck is connected to the computer and that it is turned on and in VCR mode.

4 Enabling scene detection causes clips to be automatically logged at each point where the camcorder was stopped or paused.

5 Type a number of frames in the Handles option in the Capture area of the Logging tab.

6 Only information about the clip, such as the tape name and In and Out points, is captured when creating the batch list. The clip will be displayed as "Offline" in the Project panel. The media is captured when you go to the Project panel and perform the batch capture of offline files.

4 ORGANIZING MEDIA

Lesson Overview

In this lesson, you'll learn about the following:

- Using the Project panel

- Staying organized with bins

- Adding metadata to your clips

- Using essential playback controls

- Interpreting footage

- Making changes to your clips

 This lesson will take approximately 50 minutes.

Once you have some video and sound assets in your project, you'll want to get on with looking through your footage and adding clips to a sequence. Before you do, it's well worth spending a little time organizing the assets you have. Doing so can save you hours of hunting for things later.

Getting started

When you have lots of clips in your project, imported from several different media types, it can be a challenge to stay on top of everything and always find that magic shot when you need it.

In this lesson, you'll learn how to organize your clips using the Project panel, which is the heart of your project. You'll create special folders, called *bins*, to divide your clips into categories. You'll also learn about adding important metadata and labels to your clips.

You'll begin by getting to know the Project panel and organizing your clips.

Before you begin, make sure you are using the default Editing workspace.

1 Click Window > Workspace > Editing.

2 Click Window > Workspace > Reset Current Workspace.

3 Click Yes in the Reset Workspace dialog.

 For this lesson, you'll use the project file you used in Lesson 3.

4 Continue to work with the project file from the previous lesson, or open it from your hard drive.

5 Choose File > Save As.

6 Rename the file to *Lesson 04.prproj*.

7 Choose a preferred location on your hard drive, and click Save to save the project.

 If you do not have the previous lesson file, you can open the file Lesson 04.prproj from the Lesson 04 folder.

The Project panel

Anything you import into your Adobe Premiere Pro CS6 project will appear in the Project panel. As well as giving you excellent tools for browsing your clips and working with their metadata, the Project panel has special folders, called *bins*, you can use to organize everything.

No matter how you import your clips, everything that appears in a sequence must appear in the Project panel. If you delete a clip in the Project panel that is already used in a sequence, the clip will automatically be removed from the sequence. Don't worry, though, because Adobe Premiere Pro will warn you if you do this.

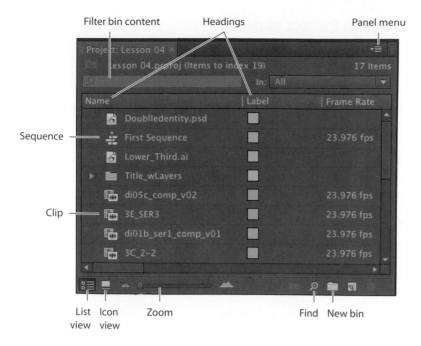

Filter bin content   Headings   Panel menu

Sequence

Clip

List view   Icon view   Zoom   Find   New bin

As well as acting as the repository for all of your clips, the Project panel gives you important options for interpreting media. All of your footage will have a frame rate and pixel aspect ratio, for example, and you may want to change these settings for creative reasons. You could, for example, interpret 30fps video as 24fps to achieve a subtle slow-motion effect. You might also receive a video file that has the wrong pixel aspect ratio setting.

Adobe Premiere Pro uses metadata associated with footage to know how to play it back. If you want to change the metadata, you can use the Project panel to do so.

It's all too easy to leave things with names like "untitled" or "new." Although this might work out fine with only two or three clips, how would you find anything with two or three hundred?

Even if your clips have individual names, as in the case of our current project, they may not be super clear or easy to identify.

Let's look at some ways to get organized.

Customizing the Project panel

▶ **Tip:** There's a very quick way to toggle between seeing the Project panel in a frame and seeing it full-screen. Just press the ` (grave) key. You can do this with any panel in Adobe Premiere Pro.

It's quite likely that you will want to resize the Project panel from time to time. You'll be alternating between looking at your clips as a list or as thumbnails, and sometimes it's quicker to resize the panel than scroll over to see more information.

The default Editing workspace is designed to keep the interface as clean as possible so you can focus on your creative work rather than the buttons. Part of the Project panel that's hidden from view, called the Preview Area, gives additional information about your clips.

Let's take a look at it:

1 Click the panel menu for the Project panel.

2 Choose Preview Area.

● **Note:** Be sure to follow the instructions in the "Getting Started" section that begins this lesson.

The Preview Area shows you several kinds of useful information about a clip when you select it in the Project panel, including the frame size, pixel aspect ratio, and duration.

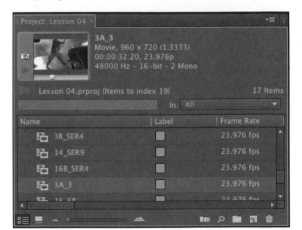

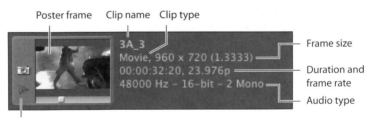

Poster frame   Clip name   Clip type
                                        — Frame size
                                        — Duration and frame rate
                                        — Audio type

Play/Stop

If it is not already selected, click the List View button ≣ at the bottom-left corner of the Project panel. In this view, a lot of information is available about each clip in the Project panel, but you need to scroll horizontally to see it.

The Preview Area gives you a mix of information about clips when you need it.

3 Click the panel menu for the Project panel.

4 Choose Preview Area to hide it.

Finding assets in the Project panel

Working with clips is a little like working with pieces of paper at your desk. If you have just one or two clips, it's easy. Once you have one or two hundred, you need a system!

One way you can help make things smoother during the edit is to take a little time to organize your clips at the very beginning. If you can name your clips during capture or after importing them, it can help enormously. Even if you don't give each individual clip its own name during capture from tape, you can give a name to each type of shot and let Adobe Premiere Pro add 01, 02, 03, and so on (see Chapter 3, "Importing Metadata").

▶ **Tip:** You can scroll the Project panel view up and down using the mouse wheel.

1   Click the name heading at the top of the Project panel. The items in the Project panel are displayed in alphabetical order or reverse alphabetical order when you click the name heading.

2   Scroll to the right until you can see the Media Duration heading in the Project panel. This shows the total duration of each clip's media file.

3   Click the Media Duration heading. Adobe Premiere Pro displays the clips in order of media duration. Notice the direction arrow on the Media Duration heading. When you click the heading, the direction arrow toggles between showing clips in duration order or reverse duration order.

| Media Duration ∧ | | Media Duration ∨ |

● **Note:** You may need to click and drag to expand the width of a column to see its arrow.

If you're looking for lots of clips with particular features—such as a duration or a frame size—it can be helpful to change the order in which the headings are displayed.

4   Click and drag the Media Duration heading to the left, until you see a blue divider between the Label heading and the Name heading. When you release the mouse button, the Media Duration heading will be repositioned right next to the Name heading.

| Name | | Media Duration ∨ | Label |

The blue divider shows where you will drop the heading.

● **Note:** When you scroll to the right in the Project panel, Adobe Premiere Pro always maintains the clip names on the left so you know which clips you're seeing information about.

● **Note:** Graphic and photo files like Photoshop PSD, JPEG, or Illustrator AI files import with the duration you set in Preferences > General > Still Image Default Duration.

Filter bin content

Adobe Premiere Pro has built-in search tools to help you find your media. Even if you are using the rather nondescriptive original clip names taken from a file-based camera, you can search for things like a frame size or a file type.

At the top of the Project panel, you can type in the Filter Bin Content box to display only clips that match the text you enter. This is a very

quick and easy way of locating a clip if you remember what it is called. Clips that don't match the text you enter are hidden and clips that do are revealed, even if they are inside a bin.

1 Click into the Filter Bin Content box, and type the letters *ser*.

Adobe Premiere Pro displays only the clips with the letters *ser* in the name. Notice the name of the project is displayed above the text entry box, along with "(filtered)."

2 Click the X on the right of the Filter Bin Content box to clear your filter.

3 Type the letters *psd* in the box.

Adobe Premiere Pro displays only clips that have the letters *psd* in their name, along with all the project bins. In this case, it's just one clip that was imported earlier. Using the Filter Bin Content box in this way, you can look for particular types of files.

To the left of the text entry box you should see a button menu that displays a list of recent entries, along with the number of clips that match the search criteria.

● **Note:** The folders you create inside the Project panel are called *bins*. This is a term taken from film editing. The Project panel itself is effectively a bin, since you can contain clips inside it. It functions exactly like any other bin and is referred to as one.

To the right of the Filter Bin Content box, there's an In menu where you can specify whether Adobe Premiere Pro should search for clips based on all of the available metadata, just the metadata displayed currently (see "Working with bins" later in this chapter), or words taken from scripts (see "Organizing media with content analysis" later in this chapter).

Usually, it isn't necessary to choose anything in this menu because the filtering works when using the All option if you type selections carefully. Be sure to click the X on the right of the Filter Bin Content box to clear your filter.

Find

Adobe Premiere Pro also has an advanced Find option. To learn about it, let's import a couple of extra clips.

1   Using any of the methods described in Lesson 3, import Seattle_Skyline.mov and Vegas_Night.mov from the Assets folder, included with these lessons.

2   At the bottom of the Project panel, click the Find button . Adobe Premiere Pro displays the Find panel, which has more advanced options for locating your clips.

There are two sets of searches you can perform at the same time with the Adobe Premiere Pro Find panel. You can choose to display clips that match both search criteria or either search criteria. For example, you could do *either of the following:*

• Search for a clip with the words **dog** AND **boat** in its name.

• Search for a clip with the word **dog** OR **boat** in its name.

Then choose from the following options:

• **Column:** Selects from the available headings in the Project panel. When you click Find, Adobe Premiere Pro will search using only the heading you select.

• **Operator:** Gives you a set of standard search options. Use this menu to choose whether you want to find a clip that contains, matches exactly, begins with, or ends with whatever you search for.

• **Match:** Choose All to find a clip with both your first and second search text. Choose Any to find a clip with either your first or your second search text.

• **Case Sensitive:** Tells Adobe Premiere Pro whether you want your search to exactly match the upper- and lowercase letters you enter.

• **Find What:** Type your search text here. You can add up to two sets of search text.

When you click Find, Adobe Premiere Pro highlights a clip that matches your search criteria. Click Find again, and Adobe Premiere Pro highlights the next clip that matches your search criteria. Click Done to exit the Find dialog box.

Working with bins

Bins have the same icon as a folder on your hard drive and work in almost exactly the same way. They allow you to store your clips in a more organized way, by dividing them into different groups.

Just like folders on your hard drive, you can have multiple bins inside other bins, creating a folder structure as comprehensive as your project requires.

There's one very important difference between bins and folders on your hard drive: Bins exist only inside your Adobe Premiere Pro project file. You won't see individual project bins anywhere on your hard drive.

Creating bins

Let's create a bin.

1   Click the New Bin button at the bottom of the Project panel.

    Adobe Premiere Pro creates a new bin and automatically highlights the name, ready for you to rename it. It's a good idea to get into the habit of naming bins when you create them.

2   We have some clips from a film, so let's give them a bin. Name the bin *Double Identity.*

3   You can also create a bin using the File menu. Choose File > New > Bin.

4   Name this bin *PSD files.*

● **Note:** It can be quite difficult to find a blank part of the Project panel to click when it is full of clips. Try clicking just to the left of the icons, inside the panel.

5   You can also make a new bin by right-clicking a blank area in the Project panel and choosing New Bin. Try this now.

6   Name the new bin *Illustrator files.*

    One of the quickest and easiest ways to create a new bin for clips you already have in your project is to drag and drop the clips onto the New Bin button at the bottom of the Project panel.

7   Drag and drop the clip Vegas_Night.mov onto the New Bin button.

8   Name the bin *City Views.*

9 Press the keyboard shortcut Control+/ (Windows) or Command+/ (Mac) to make a new bin.

10 Name the bin *Sequences*.

If your Project panel is set to List View, bins are displayed in name order among the clips.

● **Note:** When you import an Adobe Photoshop file with multiple layers and choose to import as a sequence, Adobe Premiere Pro automatically creates a bin for the individual layers and their sequence.

Managing media in bins

Now that we have some bins, let's put them to use. As you move clips into bins, use the disclosure triangles to hide their contents and tidy up the view.

1 Drag the clip Lower_Third.ai into the Illustrator files bin.

2 Drag DoubleIdentity.psd into the PSD files bin.

3 Drag the Title_wLayers bin (created automatically when you imported the layered PSD file) into the PSD files bin. Bins inside bins work just like folders inside folders.

4 Drag the clip Seattlc_Skyline.mov into the City Views bin. You might need to resize the panel or switch it to full-screen to see both the clip and the bin.

5 Drag the sequence First Sequence into the Sequences bin.

6 Put all of the remaining clips inside the Double Identity bin.

You should now have a nicely organized Project panel, with each kind of clip in its own bin.

Notice that you can also copy and paste clips to make extra copies if this suits your organizational system. You have a Photoshop document that might be useful for the Double Identity content. Let's make an extra copy.

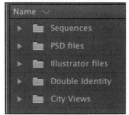

▶ **Tip:** You can make Shift+click and Control+click (Windows) or Command+click (Mac) selections in the Project panel, just as you can with files in your hard drive.

7 Click the disclosure triangle for the PSD files bin to display the contents.

8 Right-click the DoubleIdentity.psd clip, and choose Copy.

9 Click the disclosure triangle for the Double Identity bin to display the contents.

10 Right-click the Double Identity bin, and choose Paste.

Adobe Premiere Pro places a copy of the clip in the Double Identity bin.

Finding your media

If you're not sure where your media is on your hard drive, right-click the clip in the Project panel and choose Reveal in Explorer (Windows) or Reveal in Finder (Mac).

Adobe Premiere Pro will open the folder on your hard drive that contains the media file and highlight it. This can be very useful if you are working with media files stored on multiple hard drives or if you have renamed your clips in Adobe Premiere Pro.

Changing bin views

Though there is a distinction between the Project panel and bins, they have the same controls and viewing options. For all intents and purposes, you can treat the Project panel as a bin.

Bins have two views. You choose between them by clicking the List View or Icon View button at the bottom left of the Project panel.

- **List View:** Displays your clips and bins as a list, with a significant amount of metadata you can scroll through.

- **Icon View:** Displays your clips and bins as thumbnails you can rearrange and play back.

The Project panel has a Zoom control, which changes the size of the clip icons or thumbnails.

1 Double-click the Double Identity bin to open it in its own panel.

2 Click the Icon View button on the Double Identity bin to display thumbnails for your clips.

3 Try adjusting the Zoom control.

Adobe Premiere Pro can display very large thumbnails to make browsing and selecting your clips easy.

4 Switch the view to List View.

5 Try adjusting the Zoom control for the bin.

When in List View, it doesn't make that much sense to zoom, unless you turn on the display of thumbnails in this view.

6 Click the Panel menu, and choose Thumbnails.

Adobe Premiere Pro now displays thumbnails in List View, as well as in Icon View.

7 Try adjusting the Zoom control.

The clip thumbnails show the first frame of the media. In some cases, this is not particularly useful. Look at the clip 16B_SER4, for example. The thumbnail shows an empty armchair, but it would be useful to see who will be sitting in it.

8 Click the Panel menu, and choose Preview Area.

9 Select the clip 16B_SER4 so that information about it is displayed in the Preview Area.

10 The Thumbnail Viewer in the Preview Area allows you to play your clip, drag through it, and set a new poster frame. Drag through the clip using the Thumbnail Viewer until you see the actress sitting in the chair.

11 Click the Poster Frame button on the Thumbnail Viewer.

Adobe Premiere Pro shows your newly selected frame as the thumbnail for this clip.

12 Use the panel menu to turn off thumbnails in List View and to hide the Preview Area.

Assigning labels

Every item in the Project panel has a label color. In List View, the Label heading shows the label color for every clip. When you add your clips to a sequence, they will appear in the Timeline panel with this color.

Let's change the color for the title so that it matches the other clips in this bin.

Note: You can change the label color for multiple clips by choosing them first.

1 Right-click DoubleIdentity.psd and choose Label > Iris.

2 Make sure the DoubleIdentity bin is active by clicking once somewhere inside the panel.

3 Press Control+A (Windows) or Command+A (Mac) to select every clip in the bin.

4 Right-click any of the clips in the bin, and choose Label > Forest.

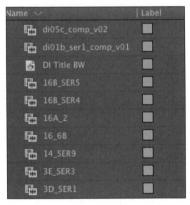

Changing the available label colors

Eight available colors can be assigned as labels to items in your project. There are also eight types of item that label colors can be assigned to, and this means there aren't any spare label colors.

If you choose Edit > Preferences > Label Colors (Windows) or Premiere Pro > Preferences > Label Colors (Mac), you can see the list of colors, each with a color swatch you can click to change the color to something else.

If you select Label Defaults in the preferences, you can choose different default labels for each kind of item in your project.

Changing names

Because clips in your project are separate from the media files they link to, you can rename items inside Adobe Premiere Pro, and the names of your original media files on the hard drive are left untouched. This makes renaming clips safe to do!

1   Right-click the clip DoubleIdentity.psd, and choose Rename.

2   Change the name to *DI Title BW*.

3   Right-click the newly renamed clip, DI Title BW, and choose Reveal in Explorer (Windows) or Reveal in Finder (Mac).

Notice the original filename has not changed. It's helpful to be clear about the difference between your original media files and the clips inside Adobe Premiere Pro because it explains much of the way Adobe Premiere Pro works.

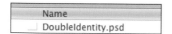

● **Note:** When you change the name of a clip in Adobe Premiere Pro, the new name is stored in the project file. Two project files could easily have different names for the same clip.

Customizing bins

Adobe Premiere Pro displays certain types of information in the Project panel by default. You can easily add or remove headings. Depending on the clips you have and the types of metadata you are working with, you might want to display or hide different kinds of information.

1   If it's not open already, open the Double Identity bin.

2   Click the Panel menu, and choose Metadata Display.

The Metadata Display panel allows you to choose any kind of metadata to use as a heading in the List View of the Project panel (and any bins). All you have to do is select the checkbox for the kind of information you would like to be included.

3   Click the disclosure triangle for Adobe Premiere Pro Project Metadata to show those options.

4   Select the Media Type checkbox.

5   Click OK.

You'll notice that Media Type is now added as a heading for the Double Identity bin but not for any other bins. To make this kind of change to every bin in one step, use the Panel menu on the Project panel, rather than on an individual bin.

Some of the headings are for information only, while others can be edited directly. The Scene heading, for example, allows you to add a scene number for each clip.

Notice that if you enter a number for a scene and then press the Enter key, Adobe Premiere Pro activates the next scene box. This way, you can use the keyboard to quickly enter information about each clip, jumping from one box to the next.

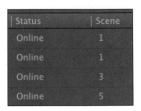

The Scene heading is a special one. It gives you information about what the scene clips are intended for; it also gives Adobe Premiere Pro information about which scene from an original script should be used for automatic analysis of the audio (see "Organizing media with content analysis" later in this chapter).

Adobe Story

Adobe Story is a script-writing application that automates the process of correctly formatting scripts and integrates into your editing workflow with Adobe Premiere Pro.

As well as giving you tools for script writing, Story supports collaboration with other writers, automatic versioning, and tagging scripts with metadata for preproduction planning, and it can generate script reports and schedules to help you prepare for production.

Having multiple bins open at once

When you double-click a bin, by default, Adobe Premiere Pro opens the bin in a floating panel. Every bin panel behaves in the same way, with the same options, buttons, and settings.

If you have room on your computer monitor, you can have as many bins open as you like.

Bins are like any other kind of panel in that you can drag them to any part of the interface, resize them, combine them with other panels, and toggle them between full-screen and frame display using the ` (grave) key.

Bins open in their own panel when you double-click them because of the default preferences, which you can change to suit your editing style.

Choose Edit > Preferences > General (Windows) or Premiere Pro > Preferences > General (Mac) to change the options.

Each of the options lets you choose what will happen when you double-click, double-click with the Control (Windows) or Command (Mac) key, or double-click with the Alt (Windows) or Option (Mac) key.

Organizing media with content analysis

Increasingly, metadata is used to help you stay organized and share information about your clips. The challenge with metadata is in finding efficient ways to create it and add it to your clips.

To make this process much easier, Adobe Premiere Pro can analyze your media and automatically create metadata based on the content. The words that are spoken can be added as time-based text, and clips with faces can be marked as such to make it easier to identify useful shots.

Attaching a script or transcript

Adobe Premiere Pro has a Speech to Text function that listens to the words spoken in your footage and creates text associated with your clips. The text is linked in time to when the words are spoken, so you can easily locate the part of a clip you want.

The accuracy of the analysis depends on several factors. You can help Adobe Premiere Pro correctly identify the words that are spoken by associating a script or transcript with your clips.

Speech analysis

To initiate the Speech to Text function, do the following:

● **Note:** There's a zip file in that folder with an original copy of the video clip, so you can try this again if you'd like. Once you use the Adobe Premiere Pro Speech to Text feature, the original file has the additional metadata added, which will be available whenever you import it.

1 Import the video file CU MAGE STT.mp4 from the Assets/Speech to text folder.

2 Scroll along in the Project panel until you can see the Scene heading. Add the scene number 1 for the CU MAGE STT.mp4 clip.

3 Double-click the CU MAGE STT.mp4 clip. If the Double Identity bin obscures the Source Monitor, you can close the bin by clicking on the X on the bin's panel tab.

Adobe Premiere Pro displays it in the Source Monitor.

4 Click the tab for the Metadata panel to display it. In the default Editing workspace, you'll find the Metadata panel sharing a frame with the Program Monitor. If it isn't there, click the Window menu, and choose Metadata.

The Metadata panel shows you many different kinds of metadata about clips in your project.

5 Click the Analyze button at the bottom right of the Metadata panel.

The Analyze Content panel gives you options for how the automatic analysis will take place. You simply need to decide whether you want Adobe Premiere Pro to detect faces and/or identify speech and then choose the language and the quality settings.

To help the speech detection improve accuracy, we're going to attach a script file.

6 Click the Reference Script menu, and choose Add.

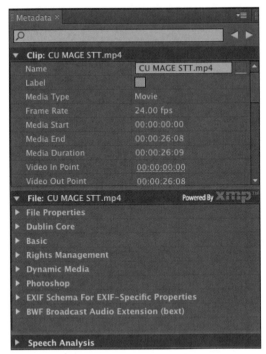

7 Browse to the Assets/Speech to text folder, and open Paladin_Script_Final.astx. Adobe Premiere Pro displays the Import Script dialog so you can confirm you have chosen the right script. Notice there's a checkbox to confirm the script text exactly matches the recorded dialogue. This forces Adobe Premiere Pro to use only the words in the original script (useful for interview transcriptions). Click OK, without selecting the check box.

8 Select the Identify Speakers checkbox in the Analyze Content panel.

This tells Adobe Premiere Pro to separate dialogue from different voices.

9 Leave all of the other settings at their defaults, and click OK.

Adobe Premiere Pro starts the Adobe Media Encoder, which conducts the analysis in the background. This allows you to carry on working in your project while the analysis happens. When the analysis is complete, a text description of the words spoken is displayed for the clip in the Metadata panel.

Adobe Media Encoder starts the analysis automatically and plays a completion sound when it has finished. You can set off multiple clips for analysis, and Adobe Media Encoder will automatically add them to a queue. You can quit Adobe Media Encoder when it has completed its tasks.

▶ **Tip:** Adding a scene number for your clips helps Adobe Premiere Pro identify the part of the script the dialogue relates to.

Face detection

With so many clips in larger projects, anything that makes finding the right shot easier helps. Turning on face detection when analyzing your clips adds an extra way of searching for content.

Now that you have analyzed the CU MAGE STT.mp4 clip, try clicking the Recent Searches button for the Filter Bin Content box in the Project panel and choosing Find Faces. The CU MAGE STT.mp4 shot will be displayed, even if you put it into a bin. Be sure to click the X on the right of the Filter Bin Content box to clear your filter.

Monitoring footage

The greater part of video editing is invested in watching clips and making creative choices about them. It's important to feel really comfortable browsing media.

Adobe Premiere Pro has multiple ways of performing common tasks such as playing video clips. You can use the keyboard, click buttons with your mouse, or use an external device like a jog/shuttle control.

Adobe Premiere Pro CS6 has a new browsing feature called *hover scrub* that allows you to view the contents of your clips quickly and easily right in the bin.

1 Double-click the Double Identity bin to open it.

2 Click the Icon View button at the bottom-left corner of the bin.

3 Drag your mouse, without clicking, across any of the images in the bin.

Adobe Premiere Pro displays the contents of the clip as you drag. The left edge of the thumbnail represents the beginning of the clip, and the right edge represents the end. In this way, the width of the thumbnail represents the whole clip.

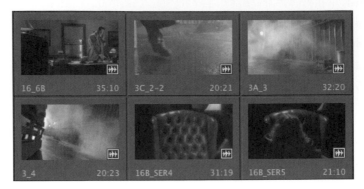

4 Select a clip by clicking it once. Hover scrubbing is now turned off, and a mini scrollbar appears at the bottom of the thumbnail. Try dragging through the clip using the scrollbar.

Adobe Premiere Pro uses the J, K, and L keys on your keyboard to perform playback too, just like the Media Browser.

- **J**: Play backward
- **K**: Pause
- **L**: Play forward

▶ **Tip:** If you press the J or L key multiple times, Adobe Premiere Pro will play the video clips at multiple speeds.

5 Select a clip, and use the JKL keys to play the thumbnail. Be sure to click the clip only once. If you double-click, it will open in the Source Monitor.

When you double-click a clip, not only is it displayed in the Source Monitor, it's also added to a list of recent clips.

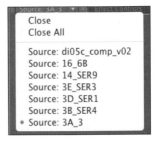

6 Double-click to open four or five clips from the Double Identity bin.

7 Click the Recent Items menu, on the tab at the top of the Source Monitor, to browse between your recent clips.

▶ **Tip:** Notice that you have the option to close a single clip or close all clips, clearing the menu and the monitor. Some editors like to clear the menu and then open several clips that are part of a scene by selecting them all in the bin and dragging them into the Source Monitor together. They can then use the recent items menu to browse only the clips from this short list.

8 Click the Zoom menu at the bottom of the Source Monitor. By default, this is set to Fit, which means Adobe Premiere Pro will display the whole frame, regardless of the original size. Change the setting to 100%.

These Double Identity clips are high-resolution, and they are probably much bigger than your Source Monitor. You are likely to have scrollbars at the bottom and on the right of your Source Monitor now, so you can view different parts of the image.

The benefit of viewing with Zoom set to 100% is that you see every pixel of the original video, which is useful for checking the quality.

9 Set the Zoom back to Fit.

Playback resolution

If you have an older or slower processor, your computer may struggle to play back very high-quality video clips. To work with a wide variety of computer hardware configurations, from powerful desktop workstations to lightweight portable laptops, Adobe Premiere Pro can lower the playback resolution to make playback smoother. You can switch the playback resolution as often as you like, using the Select Playback Resolution menu on the Source (and Program) Monitor.

Timecode information

At the bottom left of the Source Monitor, a timecode display shows the current position of the playhead in hours, minutes, seconds, and frames (00:00:00;00).

At the bottom right of the Source Monitor, a timecode display shows the total selected duration for your clip. Later, you'll be adding special marks to make a partial selection. For now, it shows the complete duration.

Safe margins

Old-style CRT monitors crop the edges of the picture to achieve a clean edge. If you are producing video for a CRT monitor, click the Settings (spanner icon) button at the bottom of the Source Monitor and choose Safe Margins. Adobe Premiere Pro displays white outlines over the image.

The outer box is the Safe Action zone. Aim to keep important action inside this box so that when the picture is displayed, cropping does not hide what is going on.

The inner box is the Title Safe zone. Keep titles and graphics inside this box so that even on a badly calibrated display, your audience will be able to read the words.

Click back into the Settings button at the bottom of the Source Monitor and choose Safe Margins to turn them off.

Essential playback controls

Let's look at the playback controls.

1 Double-click the shot 16_6B in the Double Identity bin to open it in the Source Monitor.

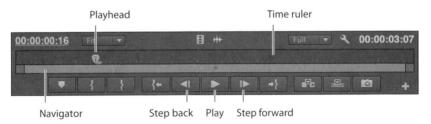

2 At the bottom of the Source Monitor, there's a yellow playhead marker. Drag it along the bottom of the panel to view different parts of the clip. You can also click wherever you want the playhead to go, and it will jump to wherever you click.

3 Below the clip navigation bar and the playhead, there is a scrollbar that doubles as a Zoom control. Drag one end of the scrollbar to zoom in on the clip navigator.

Drag here   Drag here

4 Click the Play button to play the clip. Click it again to stop playback. You can also use the spacebar to play and stop playback.

5 Click the Step back and Step forward buttons to move through the clip one frame at a time. You can also use the left- and right-arrow keys on your keyboard.

6 Use the J, K, and L keys to play your clip.

Customizing the monitors

To customize your monitors, click the Settings button 🔧 on the Source Monitor.

This menu gives you several different display options for your Source Monitor (the Program Monitor has a similar menu). You can choose to view waveforms and vector scopes to analyze your video.

For now, we just want to know how to get regular video on-screen. Make sure Composite Video is selected in this menu.

You can add or remove buttons at the bottom of the Source Monitor.

1 Click the Button Editor button at the bottom right of the Source Monitor.

A special set of buttons appears.

2 Drag the Loop button 🔁 from the floating panel to the right of the Play button on the Source Monitor, and click OK.

3 Double-click the di05c_compv_02 clip in the Double Identity bin to open it in the Source Monitor.

4 Click the Loop button to enable it, and then play the video using the spacebar or the Play button on the Source Monitor. Stop the playback when you have seen enough.

With Loop turned on, Adobe Premiere Pro continuously repeats playback.

Modifying clips

Adobe Premiere Pro uses metadata associated with clips to know how to play them back. Occasionally, this metadata will be wrong, and you'll need to tell Adobe Premiere Pro how to interpret a clip.

You can change the interpretation of clips for one file or multiple files in a single step. To do so, just select the clips you want to change.

Adjusting audio channels

Adobe Premiere Pro has advanced audio management features. You can create complex sound mixes and selectively target output audio channels with original clip audio. You can produce Mono, Stereo, 5.1, and even 16-channel sequences with precise control over which audio goes where.

If you're just starting out, you'll probably want to produce stereo sequences and might well be working with stereo source material. In this case, the default settings are most likely exactly what you need.

When recording audio with a professional camera, it's common to have one microphone record onto one audio channel and a different microphone record onto another audio channel. Though these are the same audio channels that would be used for regular stereo audio, they now contain completely separate sound.

Your camera adds metadata to the video that is recorded to tell Adobe Premiere Pro whether the sound is meant to be mono (separate audio channels) or stereo (channel 1 audio and channel 2 audio combine to produce the complete stereo sound).

You can tell Adobe Premiere Pro how to interpret audio channels when new media files are imported by going to Edit > Preferences > Audio > Channels (Windows) or Premiere Pro > Preferences > Audio > Channels (Mac).

If the setting was wrong when you imported your clips, it's easy to tell Adobe Premiere Pro how to correctly interpret the audio channels.

1 Right-click the CU MAGE STT.mp4 clip in the Project panel, and choose Modify > Audio Channels.

2 Right now, this clip is set to use the file's metadata to identify the channel format for the audio. Click the Preset menu, and change it to Mono.

Adobe Premiere Pro switches the Channel Format menu to mono. You'll see the Left and Right Source Channels are now linked to track Audio 1 and Audio 2. This means that when you add the clip to a sequence, each audio channel will go on a separate track, allowing you to work on them independently.

3 Click OK.

Interpreting footage

For Adobe Premiere Pro to interpret a clip correctly, it needs to know the frame rate for the video, the pixel aspect ratio (the shape of the pixels), and the order to display the fields, if your clip has them. Adobe Premiere Pro can find out this information from the file's metadata, but you can change the interpretation easily.

1 Import RED Video.R3D from the Lesson 04 folder. Double-click it to open it in the Source Monitor. It's full anamorphic widescreen, which is a little too wide for our project.

2 Right-click the clip in the bin, and choose Modify > Interpret Footage.

3 Right now, the clip is set to use the Pixel Aspect Ratio setting from the file: Anamorphic 2:1. This means the pixels are twice as wide as they are tall.

4 Change the Pixel Aspect Ratio setting to Conform to:, and select DVCPRO HD (1.5). Then click OK.

From now on, Adobe Premiere Pro will interpret the clip as having pixels that are 1.5 times wider than they are tall. This reshapes the picture to make it standard 16:9 widescreen. This won't always work—in fact, it usually introduces unwanted distortion—but it can provide a quick fix for mismatched media (a common problem for news editors).

Working with RED files

Adobe Premiere Pro has special settings for R3D files created by RED cameras. R3D files are very similar to the camera raw format used by professional DSLR still cameras. Raw files always have a layer of interpretation applied to them in order to view them. You can change the interpretation at any time without impacting playback performance in Adobe Premiere Pro. This means you can make changes, for example, to the colors in a shot without requiring any extra processing power. You could achieve a similar result using a special effect, but your computer would have to do more work to play the clip.

The added benefit is that the changes made using RED source settings apply to the original media files, so you can update the way colors are interpreted at a later stage in your edit and see the results in clips that are already in a sequence.

1   Right-click the RED Video.R3D clip in the Project panel, and choose Source Settings.

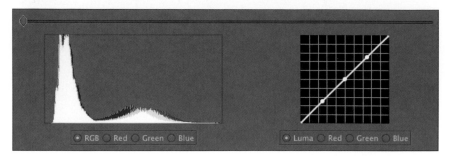

The RED R3D Source Settings dialog appears, giving you access to all of the original interpretation controls for the clip you select. In many ways, this is a powerful color correction tool, with automatic white balance and individual adjustment of the red, green, and blue values.

2   On the right, there is a series of individual controls for adjusting the picture. Scroll down to the very end of the list, where you'll find Gain Settings. Since this is a RED clip, let's increase the Red gain to about 1.5. You can drag the slider control, click and drag the orange number, or click and type over the number.

3   Click OK, and take another look at the clip in the Source Monitor.

The picture has updated. If you had already edited this clip into a sequence, it would update inside the sequence, too.

For more information about working with RED media, go to http://www.adobe.com/go/red/.

Review questions

1 How do you change the List View headings in the Project panel?

2 How can you quickly filter the display of clips in the Project panel to make finding a clip easier?

3 How do you create a new bin?

4 If you change the name of a clip in the Project panel, does it change the name of the media file it links to on your hard drive?

5 What keys can you use to play back video and sound clips?

6 How can you change the type of audio channels on a clip if they are not set up in the way you'd like to work?

Review answers

1 Click the Panel menu for the Project panel, and choose Metadata Display. Select the checkbox for any heading you would like to appear.

2 Click into the Filter Bin Content box, and start typing the name of the clip you are looking for. Adobe Premiere Pro hides any clips that don't match and displays those that do.

3 Click the New Bin button at the bottom of the Project panel. Or, go to the File menu and choose New > Bin. Or, right-click a blank area in the Project panel and choose New Bin. Or, press Ctrl+/ (Windows) or Command+/ (Mac). You can also drag and drop clips onto the New Bin button on the Project panel.

4 No, you can duplicate, rename, or delete clips in your Project panel, and nothing will happen to your original media files. Adobe Premiere Pro is a nondestructive editor and will not modify your original files.

5 The Spacebar plays and stops. J, K, and L can be used like a shuttle controller to play backward and forward, and the arrow keys can be used to move one frame backward or one frame forward.

6 Right-click the clip you want to change, and choose Modify > Audio Channels. Choose the correct option (usually by selecting a preset), and click OK.

5 ESSENTIALS OF VIDEO EDITING

Lesson Overview

In this lesson, you'll learn about the following:

- Working with clips in the Source monitor

- Creating sequences

- Using essential editing commands

- Understanding tracks

 This lesson will take approximately 45 minutes.

This lesson will teach you the core editing skills you will use again and again when creating sequences with Adobe Premiere Pro CS6.

Editing is much more than choosing shots. You time your cuts precisely, placing clips in sequences at exactly the right point in time and on the track you want (to create layered effects), adding new clips to existing sequences, and removing old ones.

Getting started

No matter how you like to approach video editing, there are some very simple techniques you will employ time and again. Essentially, you'll be making partial selections of your clips and selectively placing them in your sequence. There are several ways of doing this in Adobe Premiere Pro.

Before you begin, make sure you are using the default Editing workspace.

1 Choose Window > Workspace > Editing.

2 Choose Window > Workspace > Reset Current Workspace.

3 Click Yes in the Reset Workspace dialog.

   For this lesson, you'll use the project file you used in Lesson 4.

4 Continue to work with the project file from the previous lesson, or open it from your hard drive.

5 Choose File > Save As.

6 Rename the file to *Lesson 05.prproj*.

7 Choose a preferred location on your hard drive, and click Save to save the project.

   If you do not have the previous lesson file, you can open the Lesson 04.prproj file from the Lesson 04 folder.

You'll begin by learning more about the Source monitor and how to premark your clips to get them ready to be added to a sequence. Then you'll learn about the Timeline panel, where you'll work on your sequences, and you'll learn how to put everything together.

Using the Source Monitor

The Source Monitor is the main place you'll go when you want to check your assets before including them in a sequence.

When you view video clips in the Source Monitor, you watch them in their original format. They will play back with their frame rate, frame size, field order, audio sample rate, and audio bit depth exactly as they were recorded.

When you add a clip to a sequence, Adobe Premiere Pro conforms it to match the sequence settings. This means the frame rate, frame size, and audio type might all be adjusted so that everything plays back the same way.

As well as being a viewer for multiple file types, the Source Monitor provides important additional functions. You can use two special kinds of markers, called In and Out points, to select just part of the clip for inclusion in your sequence. You can also add comments to other kinds of markers to refer to later or remind yourself about important facts relating to a clip. You might include a note about part of a shot you don't have permission to use, for example.

Loading a clip

To load a clip do the following:

1   Browse to the Double Identity bin. With the default preferences, you can double-click the bin in the Project panel while holding the Control (Windows) or Command (Mac) key. The bin will open in the existing frame. To navigate back to the Project panel contents, click the Navigate Up button ⬚.

2   Double-click a video clip, or drag and drop a clip into the Source Monitor.

    Either way, the result is the same: Adobe Premiere Pro displays the clip in the Source Monitor, ready for you to watch it and add markers.

3   Position your mouse pointer so that it is over the Source Monitor, and press the ` (grave) key. Press the ` (grave) key again, to restore the Source Monitor to its original size.

> **Tip:** Notice that the active frame has an orange outline. It's important to know which frame is active because menus sometimes update to reflect your current selection. If you press Shift+` (grave), the currently selected frame will toggle to full-screen, rather than the frame your mouse is over.

Viewing video on a second monitor

If you have a second monitor connected to your computer, Adobe Premiere Pro can use it to display full-screen video.

Choose Edit > Preferences > Playback (Windows) or Premiere Pro > Preferences > Playback (Mac), and select the checkbox for the monitor you would like to use for full-screen playback.

You also have the option of playing video via a DV device if you have one connected.

Loading multiple clips

Next you'll create a selection of clips to work with in the Source Monitor.

1   Click the recent items menu at the top left of the Source Monitor, and choose Close All.

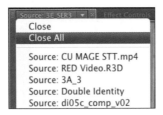

2   Click the List View button on the Double Identity bin, and make sure the clips are displayed in alphabetical order by clicking the Name heading.

3   Select the first clip, 3_4, and then hold down the Shift key and click the clip 16_6B.

This makes a selection of multiple clips in the bin.

4   Drag the clips from the bin to the Source Monitor.

Now just the clips selected will be displayed in the Source Monitor Recent Items menu. You can use the menu to choose which clip to view.

Source Monitor controls

As well as playback controls, there are some important additional buttons in the Source Monitor.

- **Add Marker:** Adds a marker to the clip at the current time of the playhead. Markers can provide a simple visual reference or store comments.

- **Mark In:** Marks the beginning of the part of the clip you intend to use in a sequence. You can have only one In point. A new In point will automatically replace the existing one.

- **Mark Out:** Marks the end of the part of the clip you intend to use in a sequence. You can only ever have one Out point. A new Out point will automatically replace the existing one.

- **Go to In:** Moves the playhead to the clip In point.

- **Go to Out:** Moves the playhead to the clip Out point.

- **Insert:** Adds the clip to the sequence currently displayed in the Timeline panel using the insert edit method (see "Essential editing commands" later in this chapter).

- **Overwrite:** Adds the clip to the sequence currently displayed in the Timeline panel using the overwrite edit method (see "Essential editing commands" later in this chapter).

Selecting a range in a clip

Sometimes you want to select only a specific range within a clip.

1 Use the recent items menu to select the clip 3D_SER1. It's a shot of a lady looking nervous as she walks.

2 Play the clip to get an idea of the action.

There's a moment, about a third of the way through the clip, where the director tells the actress to turn her head. She does, and she looks nervous. It's a nice dramatic moment.

▶ **Tip:** To help you find your way around your footage, Adobe Premiere Pro can display timecode numbers on the time ruler. Toggle this option on and off by clicking the Settings button ▧ and choosing Time Ruler Numbers.

3 Position the playhead a couple of seconds before the actress turns her head, while she's still looking forward. Something around 00:00:07:00 is about right.

▶ **Tip:** If your keyboard has a separate numerical keypad, you can use it to enter timecode directly. For example, if you type *700*, Adobe Premiere Pro will position the playhead at 00:00:07:00. There's no need to enter the leading zeros. Also, be sure to use the numerical keypad and not the numbers along the top of your keyboard.

4 Click the Mark In button. You can also press the I key on your keyboard.

Adobe Premiere Pro highlights the section of the clip that is selected. You have excluded the first part of the clip, but you'll be able to reclaim this part later if you need to do so—that's the wonderful freedom of nonlinear editing.

5 Position the playhead just after she leaves the shot. Around 00:00:13:00 is perfect.

6 Press the O key on your keyboard to add an Out point.

▶ **Tip:** The tooltip that pops up if you hover your mouse over a button tells you the keyboard shortcut key in brackets after the name of the button.

In and Out points added to clips are persistent. That is, they will still be present if you close and open the clip again. Let's add In and Out points for the following two clips as well.

7 For 3E_SER3, add an In point about ten frames from the start of the shot, just before the stalker flicks the knife (00:00:00:10).

8 Add an Out point around 1 second and 20 frames from the start of the shot, just after the stalker flicks the knife (00:00:01:20).

9 For 3B_SER4, add an In point around eight seconds from the start of the shot, as the lady runs past the camera (00:00:08:00).

10 Add an Out point around 16 seconds from the start of the shot, when the car has nearly left the screen (00:00:16:00).

As you gain experience as an editor, you may find you prefer to go through all of your available clips, adding In and Out points as required, before building your sequences. Some editors prefer to add In and Out points only as they use each clip.

Creating subclips

If you have a very long clip—perhaps even the entire contents of a video tape—there might be several parts you would like to use in your sequence, and it would be useful to have a way of preseparating the parts so they could be organized prior to building your sequence.

This is exactly the situation subclips were created for. Subclips are partial copies of clips. They are commonly used when working with very long clips, especially when there are several parts of the same original clip that might be used in a sequence.

- They can be organized in bins, just like regular clips (they have a different icon ![3C_2-2]).

- They have a limited duration—based on the In and Out points used to create them (this makes it easier to view their contents when compared with viewing potentially much longer original clips).

- They share the same media files as the original clips they are based on.

Let's make a subclip:

1 While viewing the contents of the Double Identity bin, click the New Bin button at the bottom of the panel to create a new bin. The new bin will appear inside the existing Double Identity bin.

2 Name the bin *DI Subclips*, and open it to see the contents; consider holding the Control (Windows) or Command (Mac) key while double-clicking the bin to have it open in the same frame, rather than floating as an independent frame.

3 In the recent items menu at the top of the Source panel, choose the clip 3C_2-2. It's a shot of the stalker's feet walking. He's walking in the wrong direction, but we'll be able to fix that easily later with a special effect.

4 Place an In point around six seconds from the start of the clip.

5 Place an Out point around eight seconds from the start of the clip.

6 To create a subclip from the partial selection, between your In and Out point, do one of the following:

- Right-click inside the picture display of the Source monitor, and choose Make Subclip. Give the subclip the name *Footsteps*, and click OK.

- Click the Clip menu, and choose Make Subclip. Name the subclip *Footsteps*, and click OK. The new subclip is added to the DI Subclips bin.

Using a keyboard shortcut to make subclips

By default, Adobe Premiere Pro does not have a keyboard shortcut assigned for making subclips. If you expect to make lots of subclips, it makes sense to use the keyboard for this purpose; keyboard shortcuts are often faster than using the mouse.

1   Click the Edit menu and choose Keyboard Shortcut (Windows) or click the Adobe Premiere Pro menu and choose Keyboard Shortcuts (Mac).

2   In the Keyboard Shortcuts dialog, expand the Clip category of shortcuts, and double-click the Make Subclip entry.

3   Press the keyboard shortcut you would like. Adobe Premiere Pro will warn you if you use an existing shortcut. Shift+Alt+S is available by default.

4   Click OK.

Navigating the Timeline

If the Project panel is the heart of your project, then the Timeline panel is the canvas. The Timeline is where you will add clips to your sequences, make editorial changes to them, add visual and audio special effects, mix soundtracks, and add titles and graphics.

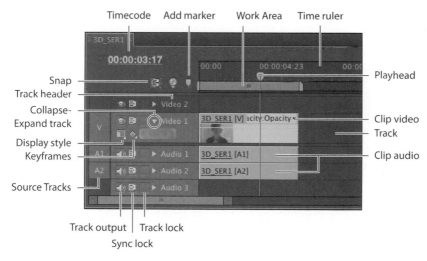

Here are a few facts about the Timeline panel:

- You view and edit sequences in the Timeline panel.

- You can open multiple sequences at the same time, and each will be displayed in its own Timeline panel.

- The names Sequence and Timeline are often used interchangeably as "in the Sequence" or "on the Timeline."

- You can have up to 99 video tracks and upper video tracks play "in front" of lower ones.

- You can have up to 99 audio tracks that all play at the same time to create an audio mix (audio tracks can be mono, stereo, 5.1, or adaptive—with up to 16 channels).

- Each track has a set of controls that change the way it functions.

- Time is displayed on the Timeline, always moving from left to right.

- The Program Monitor shows you the contents of the currently displayed sequence.

- For most operations on the Timeline, you will use a standard selection tool. However, there are a series of other tools for dedicated purposes. If in doubt, press the V key. This is the keyboard shortcut for the selection tool.

What is a sequence?

A *sequence* is a container for a series of clips that play, one after another, sometimes with multiple blended layers, and often with special effects, titles, and audio, to produce a completed film.

You can have as many sequences as you like in a project.

Conforming

Sequences have a frame rate, frame size, and audio mastering format (mono or stereo, for example). They *conform*, or adjust, any clips you add to match these settings.

You can choose whether clips should be scaled visually to match your sequence frame size or not. For example, if you have a sequence with a frame size of 720 x 480 (standard-definition NTSC-DV) and a video clip that is 1920 x 1080 (high definition), you might decide to automatically scale the high-resolution clip down to match your sequence resolution or leave it as it is, viewing only part of the picture in the reduced "window" of the sequence.

When clips are scaled, the vertical and horizontal sizes are scaled equally to keep the original aspect ratio. This means if a clip has a different aspect ratio than your sequence, it may not completely fill the frame of your sequence when it is scaled. For example, if your clip had a 4 x 3 aspect ratio and you added it, scaled, to a 16 x 9 sequence, you'd see gaps at the sides.

Using Motion controls (see Chapter 9, "Putting Clips in Motion"), you can animate which part of the picture you see, creating a dynamic pan-and-scan effect.

Let's make a new sequence for our Double Identity drama:

1   In the Double Identity bin, drag the clip 3D_SER1 onto the New Item button at the bottom of the panel.

    This is a shortcut to make a sequence that perfectly matches your media. Adobe Premiere Pro creates a new sequence that shares the name of the clip you selected.

● **Note:** You may need to click the Navigate Up button to see the Double Identity bin.

2. The sequence is highlighted in the bin, and it would be a good idea to rename it right away. Right-click the sequence in the bin, and choose Rename. Call the sequence *Double Identity*.

The sequence is automatically open, and it contains the clip you used to create it. This works for our purposes, but if you had used a random clip to perform this shortcut, you could always just select it in the sequence and delete it now (with the Delete key).

Close the sequence by clicking the *x* on its name tab in the Timeline panel.

Opening a sequence in a Timeline panel

Tip: You can also open a sequence into the Source Monitor to use it as if it were a clip. Be careful not to drag a sequence into the Timeline panel to open it. You'll add it to your current sequence as a clip instead.

To open a sequence in the Timeline panel, do *one of the following:*

* Double-click the sequence in a bin.
* Right-click the sequence in a bin, and choose Open in Timeline.

Open the Double Identity sequence now, and take a look at it in the Timeline panel.

Understanding tracks

Much in the way that railway tracks keep trains in line, sequences have video and audio tracks that constrain the positions of clips you add to them. The simplest form of sequence would have just one video track and perhaps one audio track. You add clips to tracks, one after another, from left to right, and they play in the order you position them.

Sequences can have additional video and audio tracks. These become layers of video and additional audio channels. Since the higher video tracks appear in front of lower ones, you can use them to creatively produce layered compositions.

You might use an upper video track to add titles to a sequence or to blend multiple layers of video using special effects.

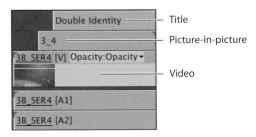

You might use multiple audio tracks to create a complete audio composition for your sequence, with original source dialogue, music, spot audio effects like gunshots or fireworks, atmospheric sound, and voice-over.

Targeting tracks

Track headers are more than name plates. They also act as enable/disable buttons for the tracks when editing new clips into a sequence. By turning off a track, you can prevent a clip, or part of a clip, from being placed on it when applying an edit with keyboard shortcuts or on-screen buttons. If you drag and drop clips into a sequence, the track headers are ignored.

To the left of the track headers, you'll see an extra set of buttons that represent the available tracks for the clip currently displayed in the Source Monitor. These are the source track indicators.

Just as with the track headers, if you drag and drop a clip into a sequence, the source track indicators are ignored. However, when you use the keyboard or the buttons on the Source Monitor to add a clip to a sequence, source track indicators are very important.

In the previous example, the position of the source track indicators means a clip would be added to the Video 1, Audio 1, and Audio 2 tracks on the Timeline.

In the following example, the source track indicators have been moved, by dragging and dropping. In this example, the clip would be added to the Video 2, Audio 3, and Audio 4 tracks on the Timeline.

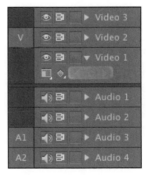

The source track indicators enable or disable the video and audio channels of your source clips, while the track headers enable or disable targeting for your sequence tracks. You can make more advanced edits by carefully positioning the source track indicators and selecting which tracks you have on or off.

In and Out points

The In and Out points used in the Source Monitor define the part of a clip you would like to add to a sequence. The points you use on the Timeline have two primary purposes:

- Use them to tell Adobe Premiere Pro where a clip should be positioned when it is added to a sequence.

- Use them to select parts of a sequence you would like to remove. In combination with the track headers, you can make very precise selections to remove whole clips, or parts of clips, from multiple tracks.

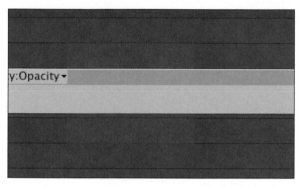

The light blue highlight indicates the selected part of the sequence.

Setting In and Out points

Adding In and Out points on the Timeline is almost the same as adding them in the Source Monitor. One key difference is that, unlike the controls in the Source Monitor, the controls on the Program Monitor also apply to the Timeline.

To add an In point to the Timeline, make sure the Timeline panel is active, and press the I key, or click the Mark In button on the Program Monitor.

To add an Out point to the Timeline, make sure the Timeline panel is active, and press the O key, or, click the Mark Out button on the Program Monitor.

▶ **Tip:** There's also a shortcut to adding In and Out points to your Timeline based on the duration of a clip in your sequence. Try it now: Position the Timeline playhead so that it is over an existing clip segment in your sequence, and press Shift + /.

Clearing In and Out points

If you open a clip that has In and Out points already that you would like to remove or In and Out points on the Timeline that are cluttering up your view, it's easy to remove them. You use the same techniques to remove In and Out points on the Timeline, in the Program Monitor, and in the Source Monitor.

Let's try it:

1 Open the clip 3C_2-2, in the Double Identity bin.

This clip already has marks because we added them when we created a subclip from it.

2 Right-click the time ruler at the bottom of the Source Monitor, and take a look at the menu.

3 Select the option you need in this menu, or use one of the following keyboard shortcuts:

```
Clear In
Clear Out
Clear In and Out
```

- **Alt+I:** Remove In Point

- **Alt+O:** Remove Out Point

- **Alt+X:** Remove In Point and Out Point

That last option, Alt+X, is particularly useful. It's easy to remember and quickly removes both points.

Using time rulers

The time rulers at the bottom of the Source Monitor and the top of the Timeline all serve the same purpose. They allow you to navigate through your clips or your sequences in time. Time always goes from left to right, and the location of the play-head gives you a visual reference in relation to your clips.

Click the Timeline time ruler now, and drag left and right. The playhead moves to follow your mouse. As you drag across the 3D_SER1 clip, you see the contents of the clip in the Program Monitor. Dragging through your content in this way is called *scrubbing*.

Notice that the Source Monitor, Program Monitor, and Timeline all have zoom bars at the bottom of the panel. You can zoom the time ruler and navigate through the duration of the clip using these bars.

The zoom bar on the Program Monitor

Understanding the Work Area

The Work Area is an important part of the Timeline. It allows you to identify sections of your sequence you would like to render when working with special effects or export when creating a new video and/or audio file based on your sequence.

The functions of the Work Area can be performed by In and Out points on the Timeline if you prefer. To turn off the Work Area, click the Panel menu for the Timeline and choose Work Area bar to disable it (and again, to turn it back on).

The Work Area bar automatically extends as you add new clips to your sequence.

Essential editing commands

Adobe Premiere Pro gives you two ways of editing clips into a sequence. Whether you use the mouse to drag and drop a clip into a sequence, use a button on the Source Monitor, or use a keyboard shortcut, you'll be using an insert edit or an overwrite edit.

When you add a clip to a sequence that has existing clips where you want to position the new clip, these two choices—Insert or Overwrite—will have markedly different effects.

Insert edit

To perform an insert edit in the Adobe Premiere Pro Timeline, do the following:

● **Note:** If you add an In point or an Out point to the Timeline, Adobe Premiere Pro will use it in preference to the location of the playhead.

1   Drag the Timeline playhead so that it is positioned over the 3D_SER1 clip just after the lady turns her head (around 00:00:02:10).

    When you make an edit using a shortcut key or using the buttons on the Source monitor, Adobe Premiere Pro uses the location of the Timeline playhead as the In point for the new clip in the sequence.

2   Open clip 3E_SER3 in the Source Monitor. You already added In and Out marks for this clip, so it's ready to edit into the sequence.

3 Check that your Timeline has the Source track indicators lined up as in the following example.

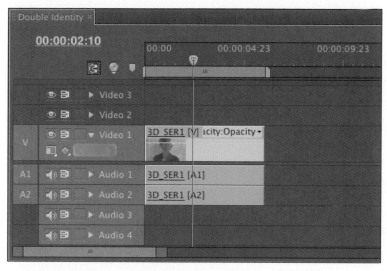

Note that the clips are green because you changed them from the default label color.

4 Click the Insert button 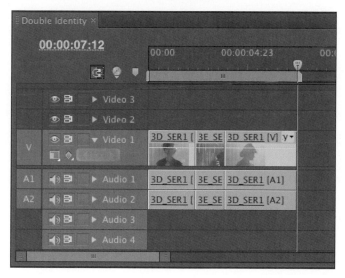 on the Source Monitor.

Congratulations! You have completed an insert edit. The clip 3D_SER1 already in the sequence has been split, with the part after the playhead moved later to accommodate the new clip 3E_SER3.

5 Position the playhead at the beginning of the sequence, and play through your edit. You can use the Home key on your keyboard to jump to the beginning, drag the playhead with the mouse, or press the up arrow key to jump the playhead between edits (the down arrow key jumps to later edits).

6 Open the clip 3B_SER4 in the Source Monitor. Once again, this clip already has In and Out points.

▶ Tip: Hold the Shift key while you scrub to have the playhead snap to edits on the Timeline.

7 Position the Timeline playhead at the end of the sequence—on the end of the 3D_SER1 clip.

8 Click either the Insert or Overwrite button on the Source Monitor. Since the Timeline playhead is at the end of the sequence, there are no clips in the way, and it makes no difference which kind of edit you perform.

Let's insert one more.

9 Position the Timeline playhead just before the last shot in the sequence, between 3D_SER1 and 3B_SER4.

10 Open the clip 3A_3 in the Source Monitor, and, using In and Out points, choose a part you think would go well between those last two shots in the sequence.

Note: When you use an insert edit, it makes your sequence longer. More specifically, it makes the contents of the selected track longer.

11 Edit the clip into the sequence using an insert edit.

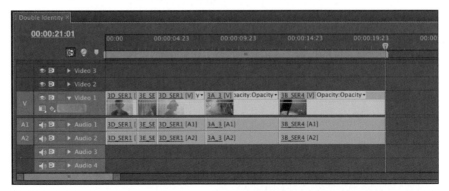

The timing of the edit may not be perfect, but that's OK. The beauty of working with a nonlinear editing system like Adobe Premiere Pro is that you can change your mind about the timing later. The important thing, to begin with, is to get the order of the clips right.

Overwrite edit

Let's use an overwrite edit to add a shot of our hero as the lady gets into the car.

1 Open the shot di05c_comp_v02 in the Source Monitor.

● **Note:** The names *shot* and *clip* are often used interchangeably.

2 You'll need to set up the Timeline carefully for this edit. Position the Timeline playhead just after the car door opens in the last sequence clip. There's a moment when the lady is looking back at the stalker, and we want the playhead just before that, around 00:00:16:00.

3 Though the new clip has an audio track, it's actually silent. We'll keep the audio on the Timeline. Click the Timeline header buttons for Audio 1 and Audio 2 to turn them off. The difference is subtle, but they turn a darker gray when they're switched off.

4 Click the Overwrite button on the Source Monitor.

The clip is added to the Timeline, but only on the Video 1 track. Once again, the timing might not be perfect, but you're building a nice dramatic scene!

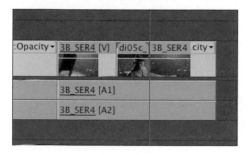

● **Note:** Notice that the sequence does not get longer when you perform an overwrite edit.

By default, when you drag and drop a clip into a sequence using the mouse, you perform an overwrite edit. You can change it to an insert edit by holding down the Control (Windows) or Command (Mac) key.

Three-point editing

To perform an edit, Adobe Premiere Pro needs to know the duration you'll work with in both the Source Monitor and the Timeline. The duration of one can be worked out from the other, so you need only three points, not four. For example, if you choose four seconds of a clip in the Source Monitor, Adobe Premiere Pro automatically knows it will take four seconds of time in your sequence.

In your last edit, you didn't add an In or Out point, so Adobe Premiere Pro used the entire duration of the clip. You also didn't add an In point to the Timeline, so Adobe Premiere Pro used the Timeline playhead as an In point.

When you made the edit, Adobe Premiere Pro aligned the presumed In point from the clip (the start of the clip) with the presumed In point on the Timeline (the playhead).

The result is that you are still performing a three-point edit, with the duration calculated from the Source Monitor clip.

What happens if you use four points?

You can use four points to make an edit. If the clip duration you select matches the sequence duration, the edit will take place as usual. If they are different, Adobe Premiere Pro will invite you to choose what you would like to happen. You can stretch or compress the playback speed or selectively ignore one of your In or Out points.

If you add an In point to the Timeline, Adobe Premiere Pro ignores the position of the playhead (though the visible frame in the Program panel will still reflect the position of the playhead and won't visually indicate the edit In point).

You can achieve a similar result by adding just an Out point to the Timeline. In this case, Adobe Premiere Pro will align the Out point of the clip with the Out point on the Timeline when you perform the edit. You might choose to do this if you have a piece of timed action like a door closing at the end of a clip in the sequence and your new clip needs to line up in time with it.

● **Note:** You might apply an edit where some of your track headers are turned on without having source video or audio targeting them. In this case, the edit will still be applied to those tracks, but blank space will be added to the Timeline on those tracks.

Storyboard editing

The term *storyboard* usually describes a series of drawings that show the intended camera angles and action for a film. Storyboards are often quite similar to comic strips, though they usually include more technical information such as intended camera moves, lines of dialogue, and sound effects.

You can use clip thumbnails in a bin as storyboard images. Arrange the thumbnails by dragging and dropping them in the order you would like the clips to appear in your sequence, from left to right and from top to bottom. Then drag and drop them into your sequence or use a special automated edit feature to add them to your sequence with transition effects.

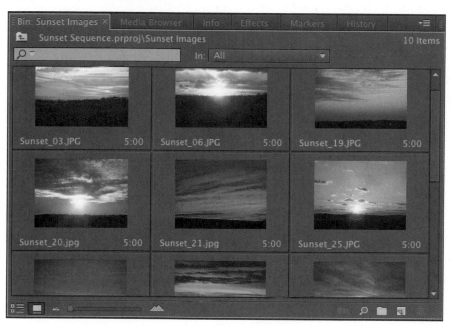

Using a storyboard to build an assembly edit

An assembly edit is a sequence where the order of the clips is correct but the timing has yet to be worked out. It is common to build sequences as an assembly first, just to make sure the structure works, and then adjust the timing later.

You can use storyboard editing to quickly get your clips in the right order.

1 Save the current project.

2 Open Sunset Sequence.prproj in the Chapter 05 folder.

This project has a Sunset Montage sequence that already has music. We'll add some shots of beautiful sunsets to the sequence.

Arranging your storyboard

Double-click the Sunset Images bin to open it. There are a series of JPEG images in this bin. The interpretation of the pixel aspect ratio has already been changed so that the images more closely match the aspect ratio of the sequence.

1 Click the Icon View button ▣ on the bin to see thumbnails for the clips.

2 Drag and drop the thumbnails in the bin to position them in the order you would like them to appear in the sequence.

Setting the duration for still images

Since these are still images, it's not too important to add In or Out points to them. If they were video clips, you could add In and Out points before creating the storyboard edit. These In and Out points are used automatically when adding the clips to your sequence.

Graphics and photos have any duration when you add them to the Timeline. However, they have a default duration that is set as you import them. The default duration can be changed in the Adobe Premiere Pro preferences.

Choose Edit > Preferences > General (Windows) or Adobe Premiere Pro > Preferences > General (Mac), and change the duration in the Still Image Default Duration box.

3 Make sure the Sunset Images bin is selected. Select all of the clips in the bin by pressing Control+A (Windows) or Command+A (Mac).

4   Drag and drop the clips into the sequence, positioning them on the Video 1 track right at the beginning of the Timeline, above the music clip.

5   Play through your sequence to see the result.

Automating your storyboard to a sequence

As well as dragging and dropping your storyboard edit into the Timeline, you can use the special Automate to Sequence option.

1   Undo your edit by pressing Control+Z (Windows) or Command+Z (Mac), and position your Timeline playhead at the very beginning of the Timeline.

2   In the bin, with your clips still selected, click the Automate to Sequence button.

Automate to Sequence, as the name suggests, automatically adds your clips to the currently displayed sequence. Here are the options:

- **Ordering:** This positions clips in your sequence in the order they appear in the bin or in the order you click them to select them.

- **Placement:** By default, the clips will be added one after another. If you have markers on the Timeline (perhaps in time with the beat of your music), clips can be added wherever there is a marker.

- **Method:** Choose between Insert edit and Overlay (an overwrite).

- **Clip Overlap:** Automatically overlaps the clips to allow for a special-effect transition.

- **Transitions:** Choose to have a video or audio transition automatically added between each clip.

- **Ignore Options:** Choose to exclude the video or audio parts of your clips.

3 Set up the Automate to Sequence dialog so that the settings match the figure, and click OK.

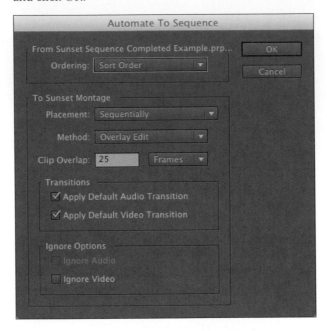

This time, the clips are overlapping with a special-effect dissolve. Note that the overlap decreases the total duration for the sequence.

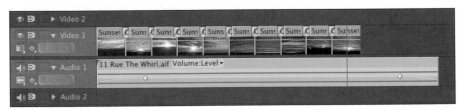

Review questions

1 What do In and Out points do?

2 How do subclips help you stay organized?

3 Is the Video 2 track in front of the Video 1 track or behind it?

4 When would you use the Work Area?

5 What is the difference between an overwrite edit and an insert edit?

6 How much of your source clip will be added to a sequence if you don't use an In or Out point?

Review answers

1 In the Source Monitor, In and Out points define the part of a clip you would like to use in a sequence. On the Timeline, In and Out points are used to define parts of your sequence you would like to remove. They can also be used to define parts of your sequence you would like to render when working with effects and parts of your Timeline you would like to export to create a new video file.

2 Though subclips make little difference to the way Adobe Premiere Pro plays back video and sound, they make it easier for you to divide up your footage into different bins. For larger projects with lots of longer clips, it can make a big difference to be able to divide up content this way.

3 Upper video tracks are always in front of lower ones.

4 You would not generally use the Work Area during normal editing. Instead, you'll use it to define parts of your sequence you would like to render when working with effects or parts of your sequence you would like to export to make a file you can share.

5 Clips added to a sequence using an overwrite edit replace any content already in the sequence where they are placed. Clips added to a sequence using an insert edit displace existing clips, pushing them later (to the right).

6 If you don't add In or Out points to your source clip, Adobe Premiere Pro will use the entire clip when you add it to a sequence. Just using one of the two marks will limit the part used.

6 WORKING WITH CLIPS AND MARKERS

Lesson overview

In this lesson, you'll learn about the following:

- Comparing the Program Monitor with the Source Monitor

- Using markers

- Applying sync locks and track locks

- Selecting items in a sequence

- Moving clips in a sequence

- Removing clips from a sequence

 This lesson will take approximately 60 minutes.

Adobe Premiere Pro CS6 makes it easy to fine-tune your edits with markers and advanced tools for syncing and locking tracks when you're editing clips in your video sequence.

Once you have some clips in a sequence, you're ready for the next stage of fine-tuning. You'll move clips around inside your edit and remove the parts you don't want. You can also use special markers to add helpful information to clips and sequences, which can be useful during your edit or when you send your sequence to other components in the Adobe Creative Suite CS6 family, such as Adobe After Effects or Adobe Encore.

Getting started

The art and craft of video editing is perhaps best demonstrated during the phase *after* your assembly edit. Once you've chosen your shots and put them in approximately the right order, the process of carefully adjusting the timing of your edits begins.

In this lesson, you'll learn about additional controls in the Program Monitor and discover how markers help you stay organized during your edit.

You'll also learn about working with clips that are already on the Timeline—the "nonlinear" part of nonlinear editing with Adobe Premiere Pro.

Before you begin, make sure you are using the default Editing workspace.

1   Choose Window > Workspace > Editing.

2   Choose Window > Workspace > Reset Workspace.

    The Reset Current Workspace dialog opens.

3   Click Yes.

Program Monitor controls

The Program Monitor is almost identical to the Source Monitor, so you should feel in familiar territory already, and you could be forgiven for thinking it does exactly the same thing. However, there are a small number of very important differences.

Let's take a look. For this lesson, open Lesson 06.prproj.

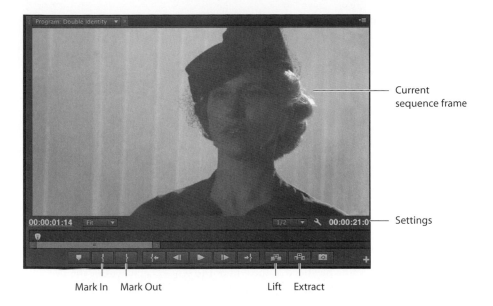

Current sequence frame

Settings

Mark In   Mark Out   Lift   Extract

The Program Monitor vs. the Source Monitor

The key differences between the Program Monitor and the Source Monitor are as follows:

- While the Source Monitor shows the contents of a clip, the Program Monitor shows the contents of whichever sequence is currently displayed in the Timeline panel.

- The Source Monitor has Insert and Overwrite buttons for adding clips (or parts of clips) to sequences. The Program Monitor has equivalent Extract and Lift buttons for removing clips (or parts of clips) from sequences.

- While both monitors have a time ruler, the playhead on the Program Monitor is the playhead in the sequence you're currently working on (the sequence is identified in the top left of the Program panel by name). As one moves, so does the other, allowing you to use either panel to change the currently displayed frame.

- When you work with special effects in Adobe Premiere Pro, you'll preview them (and see the results) in the Program Monitor.

- The Mark In and Mark Out buttons on the Program Monitor work in the same way as the ones on the Source Monitor. However, In and Out marks are added to the currently displayed sequence when you add them to the Program Monitor.

The Program Monitor displays the contents of your sequence. The sequence in the Timeline panel shows the clip segments and tracks, while the Program Monitor shows the resulting video output. The Program Monitor time ruler is a miniature version of the Timeline.

Adding clips to the Timeline with the Program Monitor

You've already learned how to make a partial clip selection with the Source Monitor and then add the clip to a sequence by pressing a key, clicking a button, or dragging and dropping.

In fact, you can also drag and drop a clip directly into the Program Monitor to add it to the Timeline.

1   In the Sequences bin, open the Double Identity sequence. This is the scene you have already been editing.

2   Position the Timeline playhead at the end of the sequence, just after the last frame of clip 3B_SER4. You can hold the Shift key to snap the playhead to edits, or you can press the up-arrow and down-arrow keys to navigate between edits.

3   Open the clip 3A_3 from the Double Identity bin in the Source Monitor. This is a clip that has already been used in the sequence, but we want a different part.

4   Add an In point to the clip around 00:00:22:15, just before the car leaves the shot, and add an Out point around 00:00:28:00, when the man is still watching it offscreen.

5   Drag the clip from the Source Monitor directly into the Program Monitor.

A large Overwrite icon appears in the middle of the Program Monitor. When you release the mouse button, Adobe Premiere Pro adds the clip at the end of the sequence, and your edit is complete.

Insert editing with the Program Monitor

Let's try an insert edit using the same technique.

1 Position the Timeline playhead at around 00:00:01:00, about halfway through the clip.

2 Open the clip 3C_2-2 from the Double Identity bin in the Source Monitor.

3 Add a new In point and an Out point to the clip, selecting about two seconds in total. You can see the selected duration at the bottom-right corner of the Source Monitor (`00:00:02:00`), displayed in white numbers.

4 While you hold down the Control (Windows) or Command (Mac OS) key, drag the clip from the Source Monitor into the Program Monitor. When you release the mouse button, the clip is inserted into your sequence.

● **Note:** By default, when you drag a clip into your sequence using the mouse, Adobe Premiere Pro adds both the video and audio parts of the clip. Also note that, in both cases, your clips are added to the sequence based on your *track patching*—the position of the source channel selection buttons in relation to the Timeline track headers.

Choosing content

You may have noticed that the clip you just added, 3C_2-2, has a continuity problem. The man is walking in the opposite direction compared to the other shots. This is easy to fix using the Horizontal Flip special effect (see Lesson 13, "Adding Video Effects," to learn about adding effects).

This shot is an example of the kind of problem that can be easy to fix in post. The only way to know for sure is to try the effect and see whether everything fits together.

● **Note:** The track patching controls are ignored when dragging clips into the Timeline panel with the mouse. They apply only when using a keyboard shortcut or the Insert/Overwrite buttons on the Source Monitor or when dragging directly into the Program Monitor.

If you prefer to use the mouse for editing in this way, rather than the keyboard shortcuts or the Insert/Overwrite buttons on the Source Monitor, there is a way to bring in just the video or audio part of a clip.

Let's try a combination of techniques. You'll set up your Timeline track headers and then drag and drop into the Program Monitor:

1   Position the Timeline playhead at around 00:00:08:00, just before the lady leaves the shot.

2   Turn off Timeline track Video 1, and make sure track Video 2 is turned on. For the technique you're about to use, the lowest track that is turned on receives the clip.

Your Timeline track headers should look like this.

3   Look at the clip 3C_2-2 in the Source Monitor. About 12 seconds in, the man leaves the shot. Mark an In point there, at 00:00:12:00.

4   Add an Out point at about 00:00:14:00. Only the man's shadow remains on-screen at this point—a pretty dramatic end to the shot.

At the bottom of the Source Monitor, you'll see the Drag Video Only and Drag Audio Only icons (▤ ⊹).

These icons serve two purposes:

•   They tell you whether your clip has video and/or audio. If there is no video, for example, the filmstrip icon is dimmed. If there is no audio, the waveform is dimmed.

•   You can drag them with the mouse to selectively edit video or audio into your sequence.

● **Note:** When using this technique, the track patching is ignored.

5   Drag the filmstrip icon from the bottom of the Source Monitor into the Program Monitor. You'll see a familiar Overwrite icon in the Program Monitor. When you release the mouse button, just the video part of the clip is added to the Video 2 track on the Timeline.

6   Play your sequence from the beginning.

The timing needs a little work, but there's a nice dramatic tension. The clip you just added plays in front of the 3D_SER1 clip, and the start of the 3A_3 clip, changing the timing. Because Adobe Premiere Pro is a nonlinear editing system, it's fine if the timing needs adjusting later. You'll learn how to do this in Lesson 8, "Advanced Editing Techniques."

Why are there so many ways to edit clips into a sequence?

This method may seem like yet another way to achieve the same thing, so what's the benefit? It's simple: As screen resolution increases and buttons get smaller, it's an increasingly delicate maneuver to aim and click in the right place.

If you prefer to use the mouse to edit (rather than the keyboard), the Program Monitor represents a conveniently large drop zone for you to add clips to the Timeline. It gives you accurate placement of clips, using the track header controls and the position of the playhead (or your In and Out marks), while still flowing naturally as a mouse operation.

Controlling resolution

The powerful Mercury Playback Engine enables Adobe Premiere Pro to play multiple media types, special effects, and more in real time. Mercury uses the power of your computer hardware to boost performance. This means the speed of your CPU, the amount of RAM you have, and the speed of your hard drives are all factors that impact playback performance.

If your system has difficulty playing back every frame of video in your sequence (in the Program Monitor) or in your clip (in the Source Monitor), Adobe Premiere Pro can lower the playback resolution to make it easier. When you see your video playback stuttering, stopping, and starting, it usually indicates that your system is unable to play the file because of CPU speed or hard drive speed.

Though reducing the resolution means you won't see every pixel in your pictures, it can dramatically improve performance, making creative work much easier. Also, it's common for video to have a much higher resolution than is being displayed, simply because your Source and Program Monitors are smaller. This means you may not actually see a difference in the display when you lower the playback resolution.

Playback resolution

Let's try this:

1   Open the clip 16_6B from the Double Identity bin. By default, the clip should be displayed at full quality in the Source Monitor.

At the bottom right of the Source Monitor and Program Monitor, you'll see the Select Playback Resolution menu.

2   Play the clip a little to get a sense of the quality when set to full resolution.

3   Change the resolution to 1/2, and play it again to compare.

Now let's try this with something bigger.

4   Import the file RED Video.R3D from the Lesson 04 folder. This clip has a much higher picture resolution than the Double Identity media.

5   Open the RED Video.R3D clip in the Source Monitor, set the playback resolution to Full, and try to play it.

There is a good chance that your computer will not be able to play the clip without dropping frames. This is partly because files of this kind need a much faster hard drive than most computers have.

6   Try dropping the playback resolution to 1/8, and play the clip again.

There's a good chance the clip will play just fine this time. You might find 1/4 resolution works fine too.

● **Note:** There are some resolutions you cannot select in some sequence settings. These are reserved for very high-resolution media like 4K video.

● **Note:** The playback resolution controls are exactly the same on the Source Monitor and the Program Monitor.

Paused resolution

You can also change the playback resolution using the Panel menu for the Source and Program Monitors.

If you look in that menu, you'll find a second option related to display resolution: Paused Resolution.

This menu works in the same way as the playback resolution, but as you might have guessed, it changes the resolution you see only when the video is paused.

Most editors choose to leave Paused Resolution set to Full. This way, during playback you may see lower-resolution video, but when you pause, Adobe Premiere Pro reverts to showing you full resolution.

If you work with third-party special effects, it is possible you'll find they do not make use of your system hardware as efficiently as Adobe Premiere Pro does. As a consequence, it might take take a long time to update the picture when you make changes to the effect settings. You can speed things up by lowering the paused resolution.

Using markers

Sometimes it can be difficult to remember where you saw that useful shot or what you intended to do with it. Wouldn't it be useful if you could mark clips with comments and flag areas of interest for later?

What you need are markers.

Markers allow you to identify specific times in clips and sequences and add comments to them. These temporal (time-based) markers are a fantastic aid to help you stay organized and share your intentions with co-editors.

You can use markers for personal reference or for collaboration. They can be based on clips or on the Timeline.

When you add a marker to a clip, it is included in the metadata for the original media file. This means you can open the clip in another Adobe Premiere Pro project and see the same markers.

Open the sequence Double Identity 02 in the Sequences bin.

Types of markers

More than one type of marker is available:

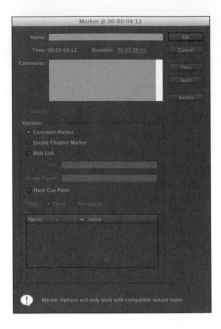

- **Marker:** A general marker you can assign a name, duration, and comments.

- **Encore chapter marker:** A special kind of marker that Adobe Encore can convert into a regular chapter marker when making a DVD or Blu-ray disc.

- **Web link:** A special kind of marker that supported video formats such as QuickTime can use to automatically open a web page while the video plays. When you export your sequence to create a supported format, web link markers are included in the file.

- **Flash cue point:** A marker used by Adobe Flash. By adding these cue points to the Timeline in Adobe Premiere Pro, you can begin to prepare your Flash project while still editing your sequence.

Sequence markers

Let's add some markers.

1 Open the sequence Double Identity 02 in the Sequences bin.

Around four seconds into the sequence, you can hear the director tell the actress to "turn back." Let's leave a marker as a reminder to remove that audio.

2 Set the Timeline playhead to the moment where the director speaks, around 00:00:03:22.

● **Note:** You can right-click and choose to add a marker on the time ruler for the Timeline, Source Monitor, or Program Monitor.

3 Click the Add Marker button on the Timeline, or right-click the Timeline time ruler and choose Add Marker.

A green marker is added to the Timeline, just above the playhead. You can use this as a simple visual reminder or go into the settings and change it into a different kind of marker.

You'll do that in a moment, but first let's look at this marker in the Markers panel.

4 Open the Markers panel. By default, this is grouped with the Project panel. If you don't see it there, go to the Window menu and choose Markers.

The Markers panel shows you a list of markers, displayed in time order. The same panel shows you markers for a sequence or for a clip, depending on whether the Timeline panel or the Source Monitor is active.

▶ **Tip:** You may need to click the Timeline panel to make it active before your current Timeline markers are shown in the Markers panel.

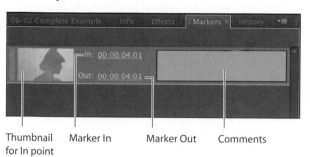

Thumbnail   Marker In   Marker Out   Comments
for In point

5 Double-click the thumbnail for the marker in the Markers panel. This displays the Marker panel.

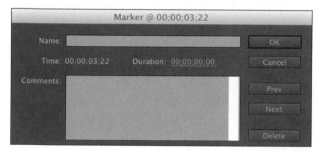

6 Click the Duration and type **400**. Adobe Premiere Pro will automatically add punctuation, turning this into 00:00:04:00 (4 seconds).

7 Click into the Comments box and type a comment, such as **Check the sound**. Then click OK.

Notice that the marker now has a duration on the Timeline, and if you zoom in a little, you can see the comment you added. It's also displayed in the Markers panel.

▶ **Tip:** Notice that the entries in the Marker menu all have keyboard shortcuts. Working with markers using the keyboard is generally much faster than using the mouse.

Clip markers

● **Note:** Markers can be added using a button or a keyboard shortcut. If you use the keyboard shortcut, it's easy to add markers that match the beat of your music, because you can add them during playback.

Let's look at markers on a clip.

1 Open the clip Seattle_Skyline.mov from the Further Media bin in the Source Monitor.

2 Play the clip, and while it plays, press the M key several times to add markers.

3 Look in the Markers panel. Every marker you added is listed. When clips with markers are added to a sequence, they retain their markers.

▶ **Tip:** You can use markers to quickly navigate your clips and sequences. If you double-click a marker, you'll access the options for that marker. If you single-click it instead, Adobe Premiere Pro will take the playhead to the location of the marker—a fast way to find your way around.

▶ **Tip:** You can get to the same option to remove all markers—or a current marker—by right-clicking in the Source Monitor or on the Timeline and choosing Clear All Markers.

4 Make sure the Source Monitor is active by clicking it. Go to the Adobe Premiere Pro Marker menu and choose Clear All Markers.

```
Clear Current Marker
Clear All Markers
```

Adobe Premiere Pro removes all the markers from the clip in the Source panel.

Interactive markers

Adding an interactive marker is as easy as adding a regular marker:

1 Position the playhead anywhere you would like a marker on the Timeline and click the Add Marker button or press M. Adobe Premiere Pro adds a regular marker.

2 Double-click the marker you have added, either on the Timeline or in the Markers panel.

3 Change the marker type to Flash Cue Point and add the Name and Value details you need by clicking the + button at the bottom of the Marker panel.

Adding markers with Adobe Prelude

Adobe Prelude is a logging and ingest application included with Creative Suite Production Premium. Prelude provides excellent tools for managing enormous quantities of footage and can add markers to clips that are fully compatible with Adobe Premiere Pro.

Markers are added to clips in the form of metadata, and like the markers you add in Adobe Premiere Pro, they will travel with your media into other applications.

If you add markers to your footage using Adobe Prelude, those markers will automatically appear in Adobe Premiere Pro when you view the clips. No conversion is necessary because the markers Adobe Prelude adds are designed to be compatible with Adobe Premiere Pro.

In fact, you can even copy and paste a clip from Adobe Prelude into your Adobe Premiere Pro project, and the markers will automatically come too.

Automated editing to markers

In the previous lesson, you learned how to automate editing clips into a sequence from a bin. One of the options in that workflow is to automatically add clips to a sequence where you have markers. Let's take a look at that.

1   Open the sequence Sunset Montage in the Sequences bin.

    This is the sequence you worked on earlier, with music already on the Timeline but no clips added yet.

2   Set the Timeline playhead at the beginning and play the sequence; then press the M key to add an initial marker.

3   Play the sequence, and as it plays, press the M key to the music. You should be adding markers about two seconds apart.

4   Set your Timeline playhead to the start of the sequence. Then click into the Sunset Images bin and select all of the clips.

5   Click the Automate To Sequence button at the bottom of the bin. Choose settings to match this example, and click OK.

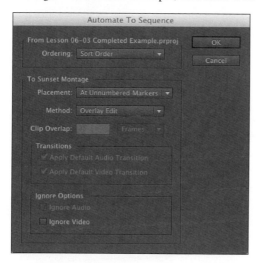

The clips are added to the sequence, with the first frame of each clip lined up to a marker, starting with the position of the playhead.

This is a very fast way of building a montage if you have music or sound effects you'd like to synchronize with your pictures.

Using Sync Lock and Track Lock

There are two very distinct ways to lock tracks on the Timeline:

- You can lock clips in sync, so when you use an insert edit to add a clip, everything stays together in time.

- You can lock a track so that no changes can be made to it.

Toggle Sync Lock   Toggle Track Lock

Using Sync Locks

Sync is not just for speech! It's helpful to think of sync as any two things that are meant to happen at the same time. You might have a musical event that happens at the same time as some climatic action or something as simple as a lower-third title that identifies a speaker. If it happens at the same time, it's synchronized.

Open your original Double Identity sequence in the Sequences bin.

We could use a little more of the footsteps in this sequence. Right now, we just get the end of the shot, and it might make more sense if we saw a little more walking first.

1 Open the shot 3C_2-2 in the Source Monitor. Add an In point around 00:00:06:00, and add an Out point around 00:00:08:00.

2 You want to add the clip to the sequence just after the lady turns her head back, at 00:00:06:22. Position the Timeline playhead at that time.

3 Switch off the Sync Lock for the Video 2 track, and turn the track off. Check that your Timeline is configured as in the following example.

Note that Video 1 is turned on, while the other video tracks are turned off.

● **Note:** You may need to zoom out to see the other clips in the sequence.

4 Notice the position of the cutaway clip on the Video 2 track. It's just over the cut between the clips 3D_SER1 and 3A_3. Insert the source clip into the sequence, and take another look at the location of the 3C_2-2 clip.

The clip 3C_2-2 stays where it is, while the other clips move to the right to accommodate the new clip. This is a problem, because the cutaway is now out of position with the clips to which it relates.

5 Undo by pressing Control+Z (Windows) or Command+Z (Mac OS), and let's try that again with Sync Lock turned on.

6 Turn on Sync Lock for the track Video 2, and perform the insert edit again.

This time, the cutaway moves along with the other clips on the Timeline, even though nothing is being edited onto the Video 2 track. This is the power of sync locks—they keep you in sync!

If your Video 2 track had been turned on, you would not have needed its Sync Lock. They help you when you forget.

● **Note:** Overwrite edits do not change the duration of your sequence, so they are not affected by Sync Locks.

Using Track Locks

Track locks prevent you from making changes to a track. They are an excellent way to avoid making any kind of accidental changes to your sequence or a way of fixing specific tracks while you work creatively.

For example, you could lock your music track while you insert different video clips. By locking the music track, you can simply forget about it while editing, because no changes can be made to it.

Lock and unlock tracks by clicking the Toggle Track Lock button.

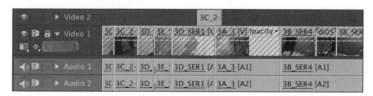

Clips on a locked track are highlighted with diagonal lines.

Finding gaps in the Timeline

Until now, you have been adding clips to a sequence. Part of the power of nonlinear editing is in being able to move clips around and remove the parts you don't want.

Let's learn a little more about working with clips on the Timeline. You'll continue working with the Double Identity sequence.

Selecting clips

Selection is an important part of working with Adobe Premiere Pro. Depending on the panel you have selected, different menu options will be available. You'll want to select clips in your sequences carefully before applying any adjustments to them.

When working with clips that have video and audio, you'll have two or more segments for each clip. You'll have one video segment and at least one audio segment.

When the video and audio clip segments come from the same original camera recording, they are automatically linked. Click one, and the other is automatically selected.

When selecting clips on the Timeline, it's useful to think in terms of two approaches:

- Making selections in time using In and Out points
- Making selections by choosing clip segments

Selecting a clip or range of clips

The simplest way to select a clip in a sequence is to click it. Be careful not to double-click, because this will open the clip in the Source Monitor, ready for you to adjust the In or Out points.

When making selections, you'll want to use the default Timeline tool—the Selection tool (▶). This tool has the keyboard shortcut V.

If you hold the Shift key while you click, you can select, or deselect, additional clips.

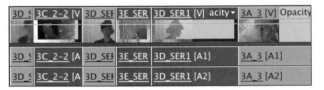

You can also lasso to select multiple clips. Begin by clicking an empty part of the Timeline and then drag to create a selection box. Any clip you drag over with the selection box will be selected.

Selecting all the clips on a track

If you want to select every clip on a track, there's a handy tool to do just that: the Track Select tool (▦), which has the keyboard shortcut A.

Try it now. Choose the Track Select tool and click any clip on the Video 1 track.

Every clip on that track from the one you select until the end of the sequence is selected. Notice that the audio for those clips is also selected because they are linked.

If you hold the Shift key while using the Track Select tool, you'll select clips on every track from the one you select until the end of the sequence, which is useful if you want to add a gap to your sequence to make space for more clips.

Selecting audio or video only

It is common to add a clip to a sequence and later realize you don't need the audio or video part of the clip. You'll want to remove one or the other, and there is an easy way to make the correct selection.

Try clicking some clip segments on the Timeline by using the Selection tool while holding the Alt (Windows) or Option (Mac OS) key. When using the Alt (Windows) or Option (Mac OS) key, the link between video and audio parts of your clips is ignored. You can even lasso in this way.

Splitting a clip

It is also common to add a clip to a sequence and then realize you need it in two parts. Perhaps you want to take just a section of a clip and use it as a cutaway, or maybe you want to separate the beginning and the end to make space for new clips.

You can split clips in three ways:

- Use the Razor tool (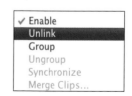), with the keyboard shortcut C. If you hold the Shift key while clicking with the Razor tool, you'll add an edit to clips on every track.

- Go to the Sequence menu and choose Add Edit. An edit is added at the location of your playhead to clips on any tracks that are turned on. If you choose Add Edit to All Tracks, an edit is added to clips on all tracks, regardless of whether they are turned on.

- Use the Add Edit keyboard shortcuts. Press Control+K (Windows) or Command+K (Mac OS) to add an edit to selected tracks, or press Shift+Control+K (Windows) or Shift+Command+K (Mac OS) to add an edit to all tracks.

Try it with this sequence now, but be sure to undo to remove the new cuts.

Linking and unlinking clips

The link between connected video and audio segments can be switched off and on very easily. Just select the clip or clips you want to change, right-click one of them, and choose Unlink. You can also use the Clip menu.

You can link a clip with its audio again by selecting both, right-clicking one of the segments, and choosing Link. There's no harm in linking or unlinking clips—it won't change the way Adobe Premiere Pro plays your sequence. It's just a question of giving you the flexibility to work with clips the way you want.

Moving clips

Insert edits and overwrite edits add new clips to sequences in dramatically different ways. Insert edits push existing clips out of the way, while overwrite edits simply replace them. This theme of having two ways of working with clips extends to the techniques you'll employ to move clips around the Timeline and to remove clips from the Timeline.

When moving clips using the Insert mode, you may want to ensure you have the sync locks on for your tracks to avoid any possible loss of sync.

Let's try a few techniques.

Dragging clips

At the top left of the Timeline panel, you'll see the Snap (▣) button. When this is on, clip segments will snap automatically to the edges of each other. This simple but tremendously useful feature will help you accurately position clip segments.

1 Click the last clip on the Timeline, 3A_3, and drag and drop it a little to the right.

   Because there are no clips after this one, you simply introduce a gap before the clip. No other clips are affected.

2 Drag the clip back to its original position. If you move the mouse slowly and if Snap mode is on, you'll notice the clip segment slightly jumps into position. When this happens, you can be confident it is perfectly positioned.

3 Drag the clip to the left so it's positioned earlier in the Timeline. Slowly drag the clip until it snaps to the beginning of the clip before. When you release the mouse button, the clip simply replaces the earlier clip.

   When you drag and drop clips, the default mode is Overwrite.

4 Undo to restore the clip to its original position.

Rearranging clips in a sequence

If you hold the Control (Windows) or Command (Mac OS) key while you drag clips on the Timeline, Adobe Premiere Pro uses Insert mode.

The third clip in our sequence shows the lady reacting and turning around, followed by a shot of the man flicking his knife. It might be more dramatic if these two clips swapped places. Let's try it:

▶ **Tip:** You may need to zoom in to the Timeline to see the clips clearly and move them easily.

1 Drag and drop the fourth clip on the Timeline, 3E_SER3, to the left of the third clip, 3D_SER1. Once you have begun dragging, hold the Control key (Windows) or Command key (Mac OS), releasing the key after you have dropped the clip.

▶ **Tip:** Be careful when dropping the clip into position. The ends of clips snap to edges just as the beginnings do.

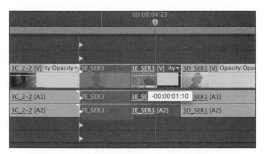

2 Play through the result. This creates the edit you want, but it introduces a gap where the clip 3E_SER3 used to be.

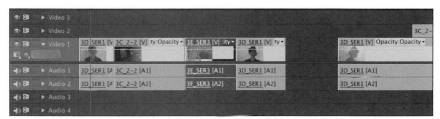

Let's try that again with an additional modifier key.

3 Undo to restore the clips to their original positions.

4 Holding Control+Alt (Windows) or Command+Alt (Mac OS), drag and drop the fourth clip on the Timeline, 3E_SER3, before the third clip, 3D_SER1.

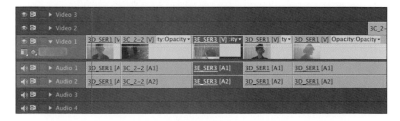

This time, no gap is left in the sequence. Play through the edit to see the result.

Using the clipboard

You can copy and paste clip segments on the Timeline just as you might copy and paste text in a word processor.

1 Select any clip segment (or segments) you want to copy and then simply press Control+C (Windows) or Command+C (Mac OS) to add them to the clipboard.

2 Position your playhead where you would like to paste the clips you copied, and press Control+V (Windows) or Command+V (Mac OS).

Adobe Premiere Pro adds copies of the clips to your sequence based on the tracks you enable. The lowest enabled track receives the clip (or clips).

Extracting and deleting segments

Now that you know how to add clips to a sequence and how to move them around, you just need to learn how to remove them. Once again, you'll be operating in Insert or Overwrite mode.

There are two ways of selecting parts of a sequence you want to remove. You can use In and Out points, combined with track selections, or you can select clip segments.

Lift

Open the sequence Double Identity 03 in the Sequences bin.

This sequence has some unwanted extra clips. Earlier, you changed the label colors for the Double Identity clips from the default, Iris, to Forest. These clips have been restored to the default so they are easier to see on the Timeline.

A lift edit will remove the selected part of a sequence, leaving blank space. It's a similar kind of edit to an overwrite edit but in reverse.

You'll need to set In and Out points on the Timeline to select the part that will be removed. You can do this by positioning the playhead and pressing I or O. You can also use a handy shortcut.

1 Position the playhead so that it is over the clip 16B_6B.

2 Make sure the Video 1 track header is turned on, and press Shift+/.

Adobe Premiere Pro automatically adds an In point and an Out point that matches the beginning and end of the clip. You should see a blue highlight that shows the selected part of the sequence.

All of the tracks are already selected, so there's no need to do anything else to prepare for the lift edit.

3 Click the Lift button (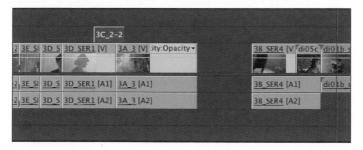) at the bottom of the Program Monitor, or press the ; key.

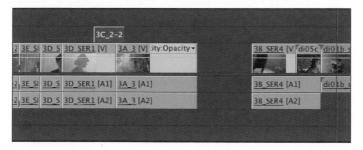

Adobe Premiere Pro removes the part of the sequence you selected, leaving a gap behind. This might be fine on another occasion, but we don't want the gap. You could right-click inside the gap and choose Ripple Delete, but let's use Extract instead, try using an extract edit.

Extract

An extract edit removes the selected part of your sequence and does not leave a gap. It's similar to an insert edit, but in reverse.

1 Undo the last edit.

2 Click the Extract button (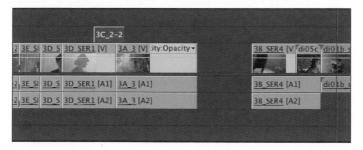) at the bottom of the Program Monitor, or press the ' key.

This time, Adobe Premiere Pro removes the selected part of the sequence and doesn't leave a gap.

Delete and Ripple Delete

There are also two ways of removing clips by selecting segments: Delete and Ripple Delete.

Click the second unwanted clip, di01b_ser1_comp, and try these two options:

- Pressing the Delete key removes the selected clip (or clips), leaving a gap behind. This is the same as a lift edit.

- Pressing Shift+Delete removes the selected clip (or clips) without leaving a gap behind. This is the same as an extract edit. If you're using a Mac keyboard without a dedicated Delete key, use the Function key to convert the Backspace key into a Delete key.

Disabling a clip

Just as you can turn a track output off or on, you can also turn off and on individual clips. Clips that you disable are still in your sequence, but they cannot be seen or heard.

This is a useful feature for selectively hiding parts of a complex, multilayered sequence when you want to see background layers.

Try this on the cutaway shot of the man's shadow.

1   Right-click the clip 3C_2-2 on the Video 2 track, and choose Enable.

This disables the clip by deselecting the Enable option. Play through that part of the sequence, and you'll notice that the clip is present but you can no longer see it.

2   Right-click the clip again, and choose Enable. This reenables the clip.

Review questions

1 When dragging clips into the Program Monitor, what modifier key (Control/Control, Shift, or Alt) do you use to make an insert edit rather than an overwrite edit?

2 How do you drag and drop just the video or audio part of a clip into a sequence?

3 How do you reduce the playback resolution in the Source or Program Monitor?

4 How do you add a marker to a clip or sequence?

5 What is the difference between an extract edit and a lift edit?

6 What is the difference between the Delete and Ripple Delete functions?

Review answers

1 Hold the Control (Windows) or Command (Mac OS) key when dragging a clip into the Program Monitor to make an insert edit rather than an overwrite edit.

2 Rather than grabbing the picture in the Source Monitor, drag and drop the filmstrip icon or the audio waveform icon to select only the video or audio part of the clip.

3 Use the Select Playback Resolution menu at the bottom of the monitor to change the playback resolution.

4 To add a marker, click the Add Marker button at the bottom of the monitor or on the Timeline or press the M key or use the Marker menu.

5 When you extract a section of your sequence using In and Out points, no gap is left behind. When you lift, a gap remains.

6 When you delete a clip, a gap is left behind. When you ripple delete a clip, no gap is left.

7 ADDING TRANSITIONS

Lesson overview

In this lesson, you'll learn about the following:

- Understanding transitions
- Understanding edit points and handles
- Adding video transitions
- Modifying transitions
- Fine-tuning transitions
- Applying transitions to multiple clips at once
- Using audio transitions

 This lesson will take approximately 60 minutes.

Transitions can help create a seamless transition between two video or audio clips. Video transitions are often used to signify a transition in time or location. Audio transitions are a useful way to avoid abrupt edits that jar the listener.

Getting started

In this lesson, you'll learn to use transitions between video and audio clips. Transitions are a common practice when editing video because they can be used to help the overall project flow more smoothly. You'll learn best practices for choosing transitions selectively.

For this lesson, you'll use a new project file.

1 Start Adobe Premiere Pro CS6, and open the project Lesson 07.prproj.

The sequence 01 Transitions should already be open.

2 Choose Window > Workspace > Effects.

This changes the workspace to the preset that the Adobe Premiere Pro development team created to make it easier to work with transitions and effects.

3 If necessary, click the Effects panel to make it active.

What are transitions?

Adobe Premiere Pro offers several special effects and animations to help you bridge neighboring clips in the Timeline. These transitions—such as dissolves, page wipes, spinning screens, and the like—provide a nice way to ease viewers from one scene to the next. Occasionally, a transition can also be used to grab the viewer's attention to help them notice a major jump in the story.

Adding transitions to your project is an art, though. Applying them starts simply enough; it's a mere drag-and-drop process. The skill comes in their placement, length, and parameters, such as direction, motion, and start/end locations.

Most transition work takes place in the Effect Controls panel. In addition to the various options

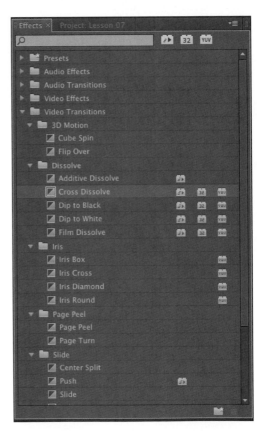

unique to each transition, that panel displays an *A/B timeline*. This feature makes it easy to move transitions relative to the edit point, change the transition duration, and apply transitions to clips that don't have sufficient head or tail frames. With Adobe Premiere Pro, you can also apply a transition to a group of clips.

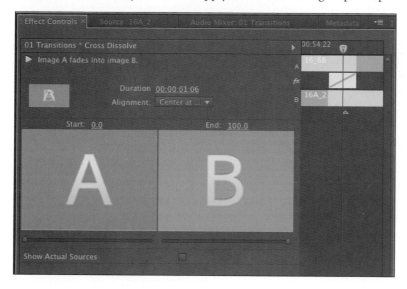

When to use transitions

Transitions are most effective when you need to remove a distracting edit that makes your sequence appear jarring when viewed. For example, you may switch from indoors to outdoors in a video, or you may jump forward in time by several hours. An animated transition or a dissolve helps the viewer understand that there has been a passing of time or a notable change in location.

Transitions have become part of the standard narrative used in video editing. For many years, viewers have gotten used to seeing transitions applied in standard ways, such as the changing of one section to another in a video or the slow fade to black at the end of a scene. The key with transitions is to use restraint.

Best practices with transitions

Many users have a tendency to overuse transitions. Some come to rely on them as a crutch and think that they add visual interest. Once you discover the many options Adobe Premiere Pro offers, you may be tempted to use them for every edit. Don't!

Transitions should be thought of as seasoning or spice. When added in small amounts and at the right time, they can make a meal tastier and more enjoyable. When overdone, they can quickly ruin that meal. It is highly recommended that you exercise restraint with transitions.

Watch some TV news stories. Most use cuts-only edits. It's unlikely you'll see any transitions. Why? Time is a factor, but most stations these days have ready access to nonlinear editors (NLEs) such as Adobe Premiere Pro, and it takes almost no time to add a transition when using an NLE.

● **Note:** Transitions are fun and interesting to add to your project. However, overusing them is the giveaway of an amateur video. When choosing a transition, make sure it adds meaning to your project rather than showing off how many editing tricks you know. Watch your favorite movies and TV shows to learn how the pros use transitions.

The principal reason for the lack of transitions is that they can be distracting. If a TV news editor uses one, it's for a purpose. Their most frequent use in newsroom editing bays is to take what would have been a jarring or abrupt edit—often called a *jump cut*—and make it more palatable.

That's not to say transitions don't have their place in carefully planned stories. Consider the *Star Wars* movies with all their highly stylized transitions, such as obvious, slow wipes. Each of those transitions has a purpose. George Lucas purposely created a look reminiscent of old serialized movies and TV shows. Specifically, they send a clear message to the audience: "Pay attention. We're transitioning across space and time."

Edit points and handles

Two crucial concepts to understand with transitions are edit points and handles. An edit point is the point in your Timeline where one clip ends and the next begins. These are easy to see because Adobe Premiere Pro draws vertical lines to show where one clip ends and another begins (much like two bricks next to each other).

A handle is the trickier item to understand. During the process of editing, you'll end up with portions of clips that you won't use in your project. When you first edited a clip into your Timeline, you set In and Out points to define each shot. The handle between a clip's Media Start time and In point is called the *head* material, and the handle between a clip's Out point and Media End time is called the *tail* material.

If you see a little triangle in the upper-right or upper-left corner of a clip, it means you've reached the end of that clip. There are no additional frames past the beginning or the end of the clip. For transitions to work smoothly, you need handles. When your clip has handles, there are no triangles displayed in the upper corners of the clip.

A. Media start
B. Handle
C. In point
D. Out point
E. Handle
F. Media end

A video clip with handles. The ghosted area in the Timeline simulates the handle area and would not be visible normally.

Portions of a clip that are not normally visible will be used when you apply a transition. Essentially, the outgoing clip is overlapped with the incoming clip to create an area for transitions to occur. For example, if you apply a two-second, Cross Dissolve transition centered between two video clips, you'd need a two-second handle on both clips (one additional second that would normally be invisible in the Timeline panel).

Adding video transitions

Adobe Premiere Pro contains several video transitions (plus three audio transitions). You'll find two types of video transitions inside Adobe Premiere Pro. The most commonly used transitions are those in the Video Transitions group. These are organized into six categories based on style. You'll also find additional transitions in the Video Effects group in the Effects panel. These are meant to be applied to an entire clip and can be used to reveal the footage (typically between its In and Out points). This second category works well for superimposing text or graphics.

● **Note:** If you need more transitions, check the Adobe website. Just visit *www.adobe. com/products/premiere/ extend.html* and click the Plug-in tab. There, you'll find several third-party effects to explore.

Applying a single-sided transition

The easiest transition to understand is one that applies to only a single clip. This could be the first or last clip in a sequence that you want to apply a dissolve to (creating a fade from or to black). You might also use a single-sided transition when you fade on a superimposed graphic such as a lower-third or title.

Let's give it a try.

1   Use the opened sequence named 01 Transitions.

This sequence has four video clips inserted. The clips have adequate handles for transitions.

2   The Effects panel should be docked with the Project panel. In the Effects panel, open the Video Transitions > Dissolve bin. Find the Cross Dissolve effect.

You can use the Search field to locate it by name or open folders of presets.

3   Drag the effect onto the start of the first video clip. You can set the effect only to Start At Cut for the first clip.

The Start at Cut icon is displayed to indicate that this is a single-sided transition.

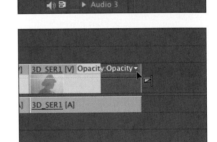

4   Drag the Cross Dissolve effect onto the end of the last video clip. You can set the effect to End At Cut for only the last clip.

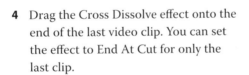

The End at Cut icon clearly shows that the effect will start before the end of the clip and complete by the time it reaches the clip's end. In this case, it clearly shows that the Cross Dissolve transition will fade out the clip without extending the duration of the last clip.

5   Review the transitions by playing the sequence back a few times.

You should see a simple fade-up at the start of the sequence and a fade to black at the end. This is a common way to start and end a video segment.

● **Note:** You can copy a transition from one part of a sequence to another. Just select the transition using your mouse and choose Edit > Copy. Then move the playhead to another edit point where you want the transition, and choose Edit > Paste.

Applying a transition between two clips

Applying a transition between two clips starts with a simple drag-and-drop process. Let's try creating an animation between several clips. For purposes of exploration, we'll break the rules and try a few different options.

1 Continue working with the previous sequence named 01 Transitions.

To make the transition you are about to apply easier to see, you need to zoom in closer to the Timeline.

2 Put the playhead at the edit point between clip 1 and clip 2 on the Timeline, and then press the equal (=) sign three times to zoom in fairly close.

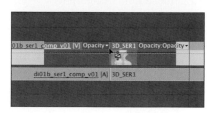

3 Drag the Dip to White transition from the Dissolve category onto the edit point between clip 1 and clip 2.

Let's continue exploring available effects.

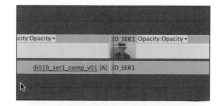

4 Drag the Push transition from the Slide category onto the edit point between clip 2 and clip 3, making sure the transition is selected.

In the Effect Controls panel, change the direction of the clip from West to East.

5 Drag the Flip Over transition from the 3D Motion category onto the edit point between clip 3 and clip 4.

6 Review the sequence by playing it back from beginning to end a few times.

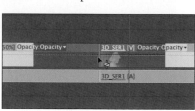

Now do you understand the suggestion to use transitions with restraint? Let's try replacing an existing effect.

7 Drag the Split transition from the Slide category onto the existing effect between clip 2 and clip 3.

Note: When you drag a new video or audio transition from the Effects panel on top of an existing transition, it will replace the existing effect. It also preserves the alignment and duration of the previous transition. This is an easy way to swap out transitions and experiment.

8 In the Effect Controls panel, set Border Width to 7 and Anti-aliasing Quality to Medium to create a thin black border that accompanies the edge of the wipe.

The anti-aliasing method reduces any potential flicker when the line animates.

9 Watch the sequence play back to see the change in the transition.

Each transition has a 30-frame duration by default. In the case of this sequence, this was slightly problematic. The material being edited is a 24p sequence, so a 30-frame transition is 1.25 seconds long. The default can be changed to match your sequence settings by opening the General tab of the Preferences and entering a new default value.

10 Choose Edit > Preferences > General (Windows) or Premiere Pro > Preferences > General (Mac OS).

11 If you want your transitions to default to one second, enter a value of **24** frames for Video Transition Default Duration and click OK.

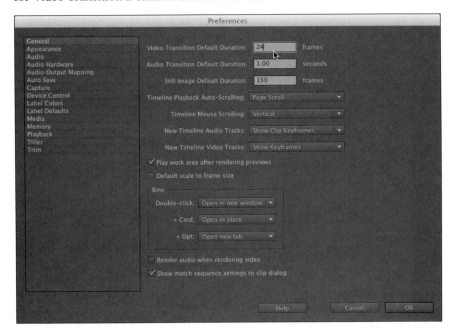

The existing transitions already applied stay the same, but any future ones you add will be the new duration. Be sure to update this value to match your specific needs if you're using 25, 30, or 60 fps sequence settings, keeping in mind that few transitions employed by professional editors are actually a full second in duration. You'll learn how to customize transitions more later in the lesson.

Applying transitions to multiple clips at once

So far, you've been applying transitions to video clips. However, you can also apply transitions to still images, graphics, color mattes, and even audio, as you will see in the next section of this lesson.

A common project that editors encounter is the photo montage. Often these montages look nice with transitions between photos. Applying transitions one at a time for 100 images would not be fun. Adobe Premiere Pro makes it easy to automate this process by allowing the default transition (that you define) to be added to any group of contiguous or noncontiguous clips:

1 In the Project panel, double-click to load the sequence 02 Slideshow.

   This sequence has several images edited sequentially.

2 Play the Timeline by pressing the spacebar.

   You'll notice that there is a cut between each clip.

3 Press the backslash (\) key to zoom out the Timeline to make the whole sequence visible.

4 With the Selection tool, draw a marquee around all the clips to select them.

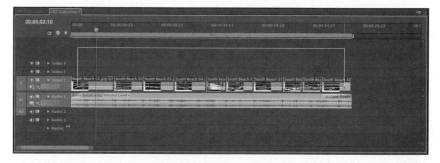

5 Choose Sequence > Apply Default Transitions to Selection.

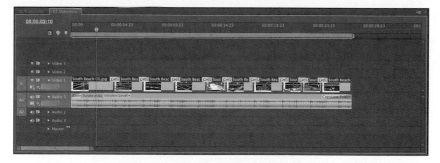

This will apply the default transition between all of the clips currently selected. The standard transition is a one-second Cross Dissolve effect. However, you can change the default transition by right-clicking an effect in the Effects panel and choosing Set Selected as Default Transition.

Sequence display changes

When you add a transition to a sequence, a short red horizontal line may appear above that transition. The red line means that this portion of the sequence must be rendered before you can record it to tape or create a file of your finished project.

Rendering happens automatically when you export your project, but you can choose to render selected portions of your sequence to make those sections display more smoothly on slower computers. To do that, slide the handles of the Work Area bar (shown here) to the ends of the red rendering line (they will snap to those points). You can also use the Sequence > Apply Video Transition or Sequence > Apply Audio Transition command.

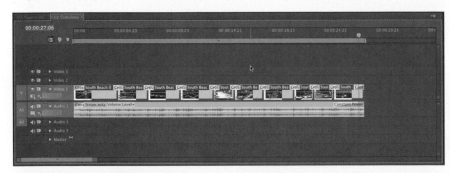

Press Enter (Windows) or Return (Mac OS) to start the render.

Adobe Premiere Pro will create a video clip of that segment (tucked away in the Preview Files folder) and will change the line from red to green.

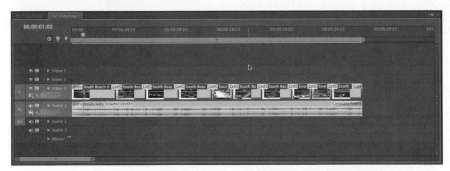

6 Add a Cross Dissolve effect to the start and end of the sequence.

7 Play the Timeline, and notice the difference a Cross Dissolve transition makes between images in a photo montage.

Using A/B mode to fine-tune a transition

The Effect Controls panel's A/B editing mode splits a single video track into two subtracks. What would normally be two consecutive and contiguous clips on a single track are now displayed as individual clips on separate subtracks, giving you the option to apply a transition between them, to manipulate their head and tail frames (or handles), and to change other transition elements.

Changing parameters in the Effect Controls panel

All transitions in Adobe Premiere Pro can be customized. Some effects have very few customizable properties (such as duration or starting point). Other effects offer more options for direction, color, border, and so on. The major benefit of the Effect Controls panel is that you can see the outgoing and incoming footage. This makes it easy to adjust the positioning of an effect or even to trim sources.

Let's modify a transition.

1 Switch back to the sequence 01 Transitions.

2 Double-click the Dip to White transition you added between clips 1 and 2.

The Effect Controls panel opens with the transition loaded.

3 If necessary, select the Show Actual Sources option to view frames from the actual clips.

● **Note:** If you're working with clips that have audio and video linked, you can select just the video or audio portions. Simply Alt+drag (Windows) or Option+drag (Mac OS) with the Selection tool to select just the audio or video clips that you want to affect. Then choose Sequence > Apply Default Transitions to Selection. The command works only with double-sided transitions, however.

It's now easier to judge changes you make to the transition's source clips.

4 Click the alignment menu and switch the effect to Start at Cut.

The transitions icon switches to show the new position.

5 Click the Play the Transition button to play back the transition in the panel.

6 Click the duration field and enter **1:12** for a 1.5-second duration effect.

Play back the transition to see the changes. Let's customize the next effect.

7 Click the transition between clip 2 and clip 3 in the Timeline.

8 In the Effect Controls panel, hover the pointer over the edit line at the center of the transition rectangle.

● **Note:** You might need to expand the width of the Effect Controls panel to make the Show/Hide Timeline View button available. Also, the Effect Controls Timeline may already be visible. Clicking the Show/Hide Timeline View button in the Effect Controls panel toggles it on and off.

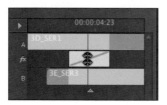

That's the edit point between the two clips, and the pointer that appears there is the Rolling Edit tool. This tool lets you reposition the effect.

9 Drag the Rolling Edit tool left and right, and note how the changing Out point of the left clip and the changing In point of the right clip show up in the Program Monitor. This is also called *trimming*, and you'll explore it more in Chapter 8, "Advanced Editing Techniques."

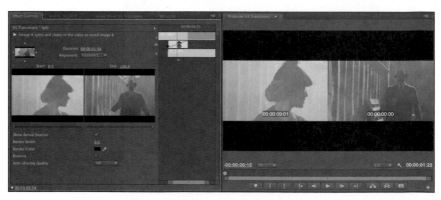

10 Move the pointer slightly to the left or right of the edit line, and notice that it changes to the Slide tool.

Using the Slide tool changes the start and end points of the transition without changing its overall length (the default duration is one second). The new start and end points show up in the Program Monitor, but unlike using the Rolling Edit tool, moving the transition rectangle by using the Slide tool does not change the edit point between the two clips.

11 Use the Slide tool to drag the transition rectangle left and right.

12 Continue to experiment with the controls for the remaining effects.

Dealing with inadequate (or nonexistent) head or tail handles

If you try to extend a transition for a clip that doesn't have enough frames as handle, the transition appears but has diagonal warning bars through it. This means Adobe Premiere Pro is using a freeze frame to extend the duration of the clip, which is usually undesirable.

You can adjust the duration and position of the transition to resolve the issue.

1 In the Project panel, double-click the sequence 03 Handles.

2 Locate the first edit in the sequence.

Notice that the two clips on the Timeline have no "heads or tails." You can tell this because of the little triangles in the corners of the clips; the triangles indicate the very ends of the clips.

3 Using the Ripple Edit tool, drag the right edge of the first clip to the left. Drag approximately 2:00 to shorten the first clip and then release.

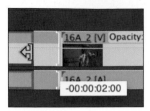

The clip after the edit point ripples to close the gap. Notice that the little triangle at the end of that clip is no longer visible.

4 Drag a Cross Dissolve effect onto the edit point between the two clips.

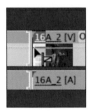

You can only drag the transition to start at the edit point because the handle is insufficient to create a dissolve into the incoming clip without using freeze frames.

5 With the standard Selection tool, click the transition to load it in the Effect Controls panel. You may need to zoom in to make it easier to select a transition.

6 Set the duration of the effect to 2:00.

7 Change the alignment of the transition to Center at Cut.

In the Effect Controls panel, note that the transition rectangle has parallel diagonal lines running through it, indicating the lack of head frames.

8 Drag the playhead slowly through the entire transition, and watch how it works:

- For the first half of the transition (up to the edit point), the B clip is a freeze frame, while the A clip continues to play.

- At the edit point, the A clip and the B clip start to play.

9 You have several ways to fix the issue:

- You can change the duration or alignment of the effect.

- You can use the Rolling edit tool to reposition the transition.

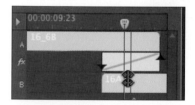

● **Note:** Using the Rolling Edit tool lets you move the left or right but does not change the overall length of the sequence.

- You can use the Ripple edit tool to shorten a clip.

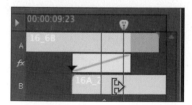

You'll learn more about the Ripple Edit and Rolling Edit tools in the next lesson.

Adding audio transitions

The use of audio transitions can improve a sequence's soundtrack by removing unwanted audio pops or abrupt edits. The use of a crossfade transition at the end of (or between) audio clips is a fast way to add a fade-in, fade-out, or fade between your audio clips.

Creating a crossfade

Because all audio is different, you'll find three styles of crossfades to choose from. The subtle differences between the types are important to understand if you want to achieve a professional mix.

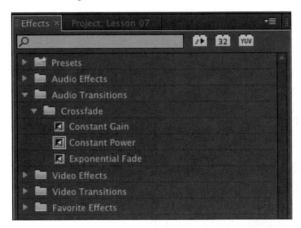

- **Constant Gain:** The Constant Gain crossfade (as its name implies) transitions audio by using a constant audio gain (volume) between the clips. Some find this transition type useful. It can, however, create a very sudden transition in the audio as the sound of the outgoing clip fades out and the incoming clip then fades in at an equal gain. The Constant Gain crossfade is most useful in situations where you do not want much blending between two clips but rather more of a dip out and in between the clips.

- **Constant Power:** The default audio transition in Adobe Premiere Pro creates a smooth, gradual transition between two audio clips. The Constant Power crossfade is very similar to how a video dissolve works. When applied, the outgoing clip at first slowly fades out and then fades out at a faster rate toward the end of the clip. On the incoming clip, the opposite occurs. The audio level increases quickly at the start of the incoming clip and slower toward the end of the transition. This crossfade is useful in most situations where you want a blending between clips.

- **Exponential Fade:** This effect is similar to the Constant Power crossfade. The Exponential Fade transition is a fairly smooth fade between clips. It uses a logarithmic curve to fade out and fade up audio. This results in very good natural blending between audio clips. Some prefer the Exponential Fade transition when performing a single-sided transition (such as fading in a clip from silence at the start or end of a program).

Applying audio transitions

There are several ways to apply an audio crossfade to a sequence. You can, of course, drag and drop a transition, but there are also useful shortcuts for speeding up the process. Let's take a look at the three available methods.

1 Double-click to load the sequence 04 Audio.

The sequence has several different audio clips in a Timeline.

2 In the Audio Transitions bin in the Effects panel, open the Crossfade bin.

3 Drag the Exponential Fade transition to the start of the first audio clip.

4 Move to the end of the sequence.

5 Right-click the final edit point in the Timeline and choose Apply Default Transitions.

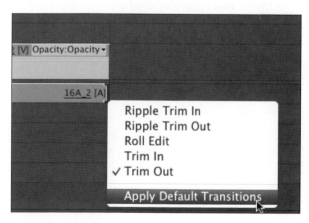

Adobe Premiere Pro adds a new video and audio transition. To add only an audio transition, hold down the Alt (Windows) or Option (Mac OS) key when right-clicking.

The Constant Power transition is added to the end audio clip as a transition to create a smooth blend as the audio ends.

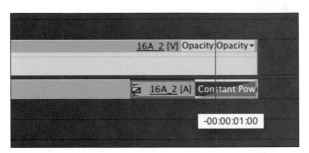

Note: Another way to change the duration of the transition is to drag the edge of the transition on the Timeline. Drag the right edge of the transition left and right with the standard Selection tool to adjust its length.

6 Drag the length of the audio transition to be longer or shorter, and listen to the effect when you play the Timeline.

7 To polish the project, add a Video Cross Dissolve transition to the beginning and end of the sequence by moving the playhead near the beginning and pressing Control+D (Windows) or Command+D (Mac OS) to add the default video transition.

Repeat this for the end of the clip. This will create a fade from black at the beginning and a fade to black at the end. Now let's add a series of short audio dissolves to smooth out the background sound.

8 With the Selection tool, hold down the Alt (Windows) or Option (Mac OS) key and lasso all of the audio clips on track Audio 1. The Alt (Windows) or Option (Mac OS) key lets you temporarily unlink the audio clips from the video clips to isolate the transitions.

Note: The selection of clips does not have to be contiguous. You can Shift+click clips to select only a portion of the clips on the Timeline.

9 Choose Sequence > Apply Default Transitions to Selection.

10 Play back the Timeline and evaluate the changes you made.

▶ **Tip:** Shift+Command+D (Mac OS) or Shift+Ctrl+D (Windows) is the keyboard shortcut for adding the default audio transition to the edit point near the playhead on the selected audio track—a very fast way to add a fade-in or fade-out to an audio track.

Review questions

1 How can you apply the default transition to multiple clips?

2 How do you track down a transition by name?

3 How do you replace a transition with another one?

4 Explain three ways to change the duration of a transition.

5 What is an easy way to fade audio at the beginning or end of a clip?

Review answers

1 Select clips already on the Timeline and choose Sequence > Apply Default Transitions to Selection.

2 Start typing the transition name in the Contains textbox in the Effects panel. As you type, Adobe Premiere Pro displays all effects and transitions (audio and video) that have that letter combination anywhere in their names. Type more letters to narrow down your search.

3 Drag the replacement transition on top of the transition you're rejecting. The new one automatically replaces the old one.

4 Drag the edge of the transition rectangle in the Timeline, do the same thing in the Effect Controls panel's A/B timeline, or change the Duration value in the Effect Controls panel.

5 An easy way to fade audio in or out is to apply an audio crossfade transition to the beginning or end of a clip.

8 ADVANCED EDITING TECHNIQUES

Lesson overview

In this lesson, you'll learn about the following:

- Performing a four-point edit
- Changing the speed or duration of clips in your Timeline
- Replacing a clip in your Timeline with a new shot
- Permanently replacing footage in a project
- Creating a nested sequence
- Performing basic trimming on media to refine edits
- Implementing slip and slide edits to refine your clips' position or content
- Dynamically trimming media using keyboard shortcuts

 This lesson will take approximately 90 minutes.

The basic editing commands in Adobe Premiere Pro CS6 are relatively easy to master. Several advanced techniques, though, take time to learn. These techniques truly accelerate editing and provide a level of professional refinement that makes the extra effort to learn them truly worth it.

Getting started

In this lesson, you'll use several short sequences to explore advanced editing concepts in Adobe Premiere Pro CS6. The goal here is to get hands-on with the techniques you'll need for advanced editing. To do this, we'll use several short sequences to illustrate the concepts.

For this lesson, you'll use a new project file.

1   Start Adobe Premiere Pro, and open the project Lesson 08.prproj.

   The sequence 01 Four Point should already be open, but if it's not, open it now.

2   Choose Window > Workspace > Editing.

   This changes the workspace to the preset that the Adobe Premiere Pro development team created to make it easier to work with transitions and effects.

Four-point editing

▶ **Tip:** A four-point edit is often a mistake, one caused by setting too many points. The reason to use one is when you want to define which parts of a source clip should be used as well as define a different duration that you need the footage to fill in the Timeline. In this case, you will use the Change Clip Speed option (also called Fit to Fill).

In previous lessons, you used the standard technique of three-point editing. You used three In and Out points (split between the Source Monitor panel as well as the Program Monitor or Timeline panel) to describe the source, duration, and location of an edit.

But what happens when you have four points defined?

The short answer is that you have a discrepancy that must be resolved. Most likely, the duration you've set in the Program Monitor differs from the duration you've chosen in the Program Monitor or Timeline panel. At this point, Adobe Premiere Pro alerts you to the discrepancy and asks you to make an important decision.

Editing options for four-point edits

If you've defined a four-point edit, Adobe Premiere Pro opens the Fit Clip dialog to alert you to the problem. You'll need to choose from five options to resolve the conflict. You can ignore one of the four points or change the speed of the clip.

*   **Change Clip Speed (Fit to Fill):** The first choice assumes that you set four points deliberately. Adobe Premiere Pro preserves the source clip's In and Out points but adjusts its speed to match the duration you set in the Timeline or Program Monitor panel.

*   **Ignore Source In Point:** If you choose this option, the source clip's In point is ignored and dynamically determined by Adobe Premiere Pro, effectively converting your edit back to a three-point edit. The new duration matches

what's set in the Timeline or Program Monitor panel. This option is available only if the source clip is longer than the range set in the sequence.

- **Ignore Source Out Point:** When you select this option, the source clip's Out point is ignored and dynamically determined by Adobe Premiere Pro, changing to a three-point edit. The new duration matches what's set in the Timeline or Program Monitor panel. This option is also available only if the source clip is longer than the targeted duration.

- **Ignore Sequence In Point:** This choice tells Adobe Premiere Pro to ignore the In point you've set in the sequence and perform a three-point edit using only the sequence Out point. If the clip is shorter than the duration defined, you can end up with unwanted video left behind inside your original In point in the sequence from the shot you were trying to cover.

- **Ignore Sequence Out Point:** This option is similar to the previous one, in that it will ignore the Out point in the sequence you set and perform a three-point edit.

Making a four-point edit

Let's specifically make a four-point edit. The goal in this exercise is to change the duration of the clip to match the duration set in the targeted sequence.

1 If it's not loaded already, locate 01 Four Point in the Project panel and load the sequence.

This sequence contains a rough edit that we want to cut a new shot into. The clip we'll use is a different duration than what's needed for the cutaway angle.

2 Scroll through the sequence and locate the section with In and Out marks already set. You should see a highlighted range in the Timeline panel.

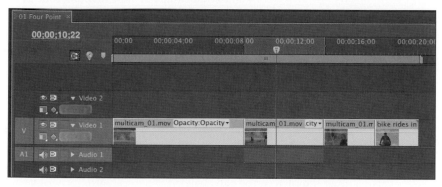

3 Locate the bin Clips to Load, and load the clip multicam_02.mov into the Source Monitor panel.

A range should already be set in the clip.

4 Click the headers of the tracks in the Timeline panel. Make sure that the video and audio are patched to track V1.

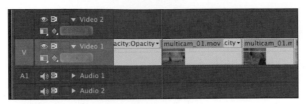

5 Click the Overwrite button to make the edit.

The Fit Clip dialog appears.

6 In the Fit Clip dialog, choose the Change Clip Speed (Fit to Fill) option. Click OK.

The edit is made in the Timeline. You'll see numbers in the edited clip that indicate the speed change.

7 Watch the sequence to see the effects of your edit and the speed change.

Retiming clips

In the previous exercise, you used one of the methods Adobe Premiere Pro offers for changing the speed of a clip. There are many reasons to change the speed of a clip, including technical necessity and artistic impact. Slow motion is one of the most often used effects in video production. It can be an effective way to add drama or to give the viewer more time to study or savor a moment. In this lesson, you will review static speed changes, the time-remapping feature, and some other tools that let you make time changes to clips.

Changing the speed/duration of a clip

Although slow motion is the most commonly used time change, speeding up clips is a useful effect as well. The Speed/Duration command can change the timing for a clip in two very different ways. You can precisely change the duration of a clip to reach a certain time. Alternately, you can change the percentage of playback (such as 50 percent to slow down a clip).

Let's explore the technique.

1   In the Project panel, load the sequence 02 Speed/Duration.

2   Right-click the Medieval_Hero_01 clip, and choose Speed/Duration from the context menu. Alternatively, you can select the clip in the Timeline panel and choose Clip > Speed/Duration.

3   You now have several options to control how the clips play back. Consider these choices:

-   Leave Duration and Speed ganged together (a chain icon between them). You can then enter a new duration or speed. Entering data in one field impacts the other.

-   Click the Gang button so that it shows a broken link. You can then enter a new speed for the clip without changing its duration (if the clip isn't long enough, empty frames are inserted).

-   Once the clips are unganged, you can also change duration without changing speed. Shortening a clip will leave a gap in the Timeline. If the clip has another immediately after it in the Timeline, making the clip longer has no effect, because the clip cannot ripple by default. In this case, select the Ripple Edit, Shift Trailing Clips option.

-   To play a clip backward, select the Reverse Speed option. You'll see a negative symbol next to the speed value in the Timeline panel.

-   If your clip has audio, consider selecting the Maintain Audio Pitch checkbox. This will attempt to maintain the clip's current pitch while the speed or duration changes. Without this option enabled, you will get a speed-up or slow-motion audio effect. It will still allow you to change the speed of the clip, but it will apply a proportionate amount of pitch correction to make the overall pitch match as closely as possible to the original source. This option is effective only for slight speed changes; dramatic resampling will produce unnatural results.

4   Change Speed to 50%, and click OK.

Play the clip in the Timeline. Render the clip by pressing Enter (Windows) or Return (Mac OS) to see smooth playback. Notice that the clip is now 12 seconds long. This is because you slowed the clip to 50 percent, making it twice its original length.

5   Choose Edit > Undo or press Control+Z (Windows) or Command+Z (Mac OS).

6   With the clip selected, press Control+R (Windows) or Command+R (Mac OS) to open the Clip Speed/Duration dialog.

Note: The Clip Speed/Duration dialog shows a Maintain Audio Pitch option if the clip has audio. Selecting this option keeps audio at the original pitch regardless of the speed at which the clip is running. This can be helpful when making small speed adjustments to clips when you want to maintain pitch in the audio or keep a character's voice at its normal pitch, even as it slows down or speeds up.

7 Click the link icon, which indicates that Speed and Duration are linked, so that the icon shows the settings unlinked (shown here). Then change Speed to 50%.

Notice that with Speed and Duration unlinked, the duration remains six seconds.

8 Click OK; then play the clip.

Notice that the clip plays at 50 percent speed, but the last six seconds have automatically been trimmed to keep the clip at its original duration.

Occasionally you will need to reverse time. You can do this in the same Clip Speed/Duration dialog.

9 Open the Clip Speed/Duration dialog.

10 Leave Speed at 50%, but this time also select the Reverse Speed option; then click OK.

11 Play the clip. Notice it plays in reverse at 50 percent slow motion.

Changing speed and duration with the Rate Stretch tool

Sometimes you'll need to find a clip that's just the right length to fill a gap in your Timeline. You might be able to find the perfect clip, one that's exactly the right length, but most times you will find a clip you want to use that is just a little too short or a little too long. This is where the Rate Stretch tool comes in handy.

▶ **Tip:** Adobe Premiere Pro has the ability to change the speed of multiple clips at the same time. Simply select multiple clips and choose Clip > Speed/Duration. When you change the speed of multiple clips, be sure to pay attention to the Ripple Edit, Shifting Trailing Clips option. This will automatically close or expand gaps to all of the selected clips after the speed change.

1 In the Project panel, load the sequence 03 Rate Stretch.

The situation in this exercise is fairly common. The Timeline is synchronized to music, and the clips contain the content you want, but the clips are just too short. You can guess and try to insert just the right Speed percentage in the Clip Speed/Duration dialog, or you can use the Rate Stretch tool to drag the clip to the needed length.

2 Select the Rate Stretch tool in the Tools panel.

3 Move the Rate Stretch tool over the right edge of the first clip, and drag it until it meets the second clip.

Notice that the speed of the first clip changes to fill the space into which you stretched it.

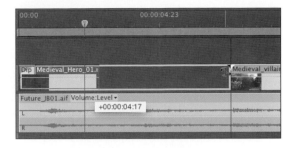

▶ **Tip:** If you change your mind about the Rate Stretch tool, you can always use it to stretch a clip back. Alternatively, you can use the Speed/Duration command and enter a Speed of **100%** to restore natural motion.

4 Move the Rate Stretch tool over the right edge of the second clip, and drag it until it meets the third clip.

5 Move the Rate Stretch tool over the right edge of the third clip, and drag it until it matches the end of the audio.

6 Play the Timeline to view the speed change made using the Rate Stretch tool.

Changing speed and duration with time remapping

Time remapping lets you vary the speed of a clip by using keyframes. This means one portion of the same clip could be in slow motion while another portion of the clip is in fast motion. In addition to giving you this flexibility, variable-speed time remapping enables you to smoothly transition from one speed to another, whether from fast to slow or from forward motion to reverse motion. Hang on—this is really fun.

1 In the Project panel, load the sequence 04 Remapping.

The sequence has a single shot that you will modify. As you add time adjustments to the clip, it will change length.

2 Adjust the height of the Video 1 track by positioning the Selection tool over the split between audio and video tracks. Drag down to make more room to see the video tracks.

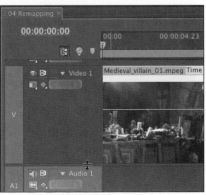

Increasing the track height makes adjusting keyframes on the clip right in the Timeline panel much easier.

3 Right-click the clip, and choose Show Clip Keyframes > Time Remapping > Speed in the clip's menu.

With this option selected, the yellow line across the clip represents the speed.

4 Drag the playhead on the Timeline to the point where the villain turns and starts walking across the room (about 00:00:01:00).

5 Press and hold the Control (Windows) or Command (Mac OS) key.

The pointer changes to a small cross.

6 Click the yellow line to create the keyframe that will be visible at the top of the clip.

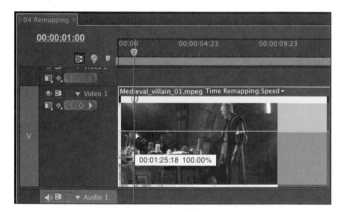

You are not yet changing the speed; you're just adding control keyframes.

7 Using the same technique, add another speed keyframe at about 00:00:06:00, just as the villain points to the wall.

Notice that by adding two speed keyframes, the clip has been divided into three "speed sections." You will now set different speeds between keyframes.

8 Leave the first section, between the beginning of the clip and the first keyframe, set as is (the Speed setting is 100%).

9 Position the Selection tool over the yellow line between the first and second keyframes, and drag it down to approximately 30%.

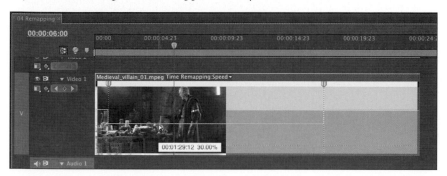

Notice the clip has stretched in length to accommodate the speed change in this section.

10 Choose Sequence > Render Effects in Work Area to render the clip for the smoothest playback.

11 Play the clip. Notice the speed changes from 100 percent to 30 percent and back to 100 percent at the end.

Setting variable speed changes on a clip can be a very dramatic effect. In the previous section, you changed from one speed to another instantly. To create a more subtle speed change, it is possible to transition from one speed to another smoothly by using speed keyframe transitions.

12 Drag the right half of the first speed keyframe to the right to create a speed transition.

Notice the yellow line now ramps down, rather than making a sudden change from 100 percent to 30 percent.

Note: If you have problems setting the speed keyframes, open the 04 Remapping Complete sequence to see the completed process.

Note: You may need to adjust the height of the Video 1 track by positioning the Selection tool over the Video 1 label and dragging the edge of the track up. This gives you more visible controls for the keyframes.

▶ Tip: You can drag the blue Bezier handles to improve the ramping to further smooth out the transition.

13 Drag the left half of the second speed keyframe to create a transition there as well.

14 Render and play the clip to see the effect.

● **Note:** To remove a time-remapping effect, you'll need to select the clip and then view the Effect Controls panel. Click the disclosure triangle next to Time Remapping effect to open it. Click the "Toggle animation" button (stopwatch) next to the word *Speed*. This sets it to the off position. A warning dialog opens. Click OK to entirely remove the effect.

Recognizing the downstream effects of changing time

You may decide to change the speed at the beginning of the Timeline after assembling many clips in your project. It's important to understand how changing the speed of a clip affects the rest of the clips "downstream."

Several issues could be caused by speed changes:

- Unwanted gaps caused by clips growing shorter because of increased playback speed
- Unwanted duration changes to the overall sequence because of the Ripple Edit option
- Potential audio problems created by changes in speed

When making speed or duration changes, always be careful to view the overall impact on the total sequence. You may want the zoom level of the Timeline panel to view the entire sequence or segment at once. Another option is to edit the clip into a new sequence and adjust it there. You can then copy and paste the clip to return it to the original sequence.

Replacing clips and footage

During the editing process, you'll frequently want to swap one clip for another. It might be a global replacement, such as replacing one version of an animated logo with a newer file. You may also want to swap out one clip in your Timeline for another in a bin. Depending on the task at hand, you can use a few methods to swap shots or media.

Dragging in a replacement clip

One method for replacing a clip is to simply drag the new shot onto the existing footage you'd like to replace. Let's start with the Replace Clip feature.

1 In the Project panel, load the sequence 05 Replace Clip.

2 Play back the Timeline.

Notice that the same clip is played twice as a picture-in-picture (PIP). The clip has some motion effects that cause it to spin onto the screen and then spin off. You will learn how to create these effects in the next lesson.

You want to replace the first PIP clip (bike low shot.mov) in the Video 2 track with a new clip called multicam_03.mov. But you don't want to have to re-create all the effects and timing. This is a great scenario for using the Replace Clip feature.

3 In the bin Clips to Load, locate the multicam_03.mov clip, and drag it on top of the first bike low shot.mov clip.

Don't drop it yet. Notice that it is longer than the clip on the Timeline.

4 Press Alt (Windows) or Option (Mac OS).

Notice that the replacement clip now becomes the exact length of the clip it is replacing. Release the mouse button to complete the Replace Clip function.

5 Play the Timeline. Notice the first PIP clip has the same effects but is using the new footage. The second PIP clip remains unchanged.

> ▶ **Tip:** If you want to adjust what portion of the clip is used for the first PIP, you could use the Slip tool to slide its contents. You'll learn how to use this tool later in the lesson.

Making a replace edit

If you'd like to have more control over how a replacement occurs, you can use the Replace Edit command. This allows you to precisely choose where to sample from the replacement clip.

1 In the Project panel, load the sequence 06 Replace Edit.

This sequence is a show bumper. One of the shots is a little boring, so you'll swap it out. However, in this case, you'll take more control over which part of the shot is used when replacing the clip. This process is called *replace edit*.

2 Place the playhead in the sequence at approximately 00;00;05;00 to provide a sync point for the edit.

3 Click the clip multicam_01.mov in the Timeline to target it for replacement.

4 From the Clips to Load bin, load the replacement clip called bike rides into frame.mov into the Source Monitor panel.

5 Drag the playhead to choose a good piece of action for the replacement.

Use some of the more active bike-riding shots at approximately 00;00;02;25.

6 Make sure the Timeline panel is active, and then choose Clip > Replace With Clip > From Source Monitor, Match Frame.

The clip is replaced.

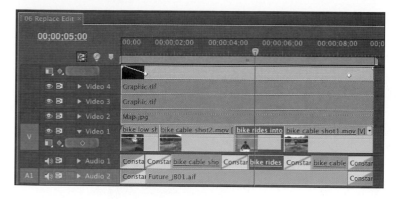

7 Watch the newly edited sequence to check the edit.

You should see that the frames positioned on the playhead in both the Source and Program Monitor panels were synchronized, determining which part of the replacement clip was used for the replace edit, while the original clip length served to set the duration.

Using the Replace Footage feature

The Replace Footage feature in Adobe Premiere Pro replaces footage in the Project panel. This can be a huge benefit when you need to replace a clip that occurs several times in a sequence or multiple sequences. When you use Replace Footage, all instances of the clip you replace are changed anywhere the original clip was used in any sequence in the project.

1 In the Project panel, load the sequence 07 Replace Footage.

2 Watch the sequence play back carefully.

In this case, let's replace a graphic that contains a date error. There is no reason to keep the previous graphic. In fact, removing it from the project can prevent accidentally using it and making an embarrassing or costly mistake.

3 In the Clips to Load bin, select the clip Graphic.tif in the Project panel.

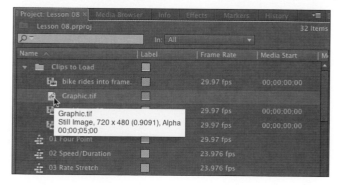

4 Choose Clip > Replace Footage.

5 Navigate to the Lesson 08 folder, choose the Graphic_Fix.tif file, and click Select (Windows) or Open (Mac OS).

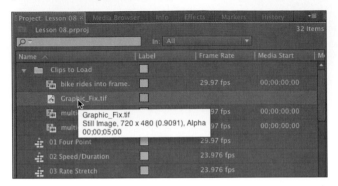

● **Note:** The Replace Footage command cannot be undone. If you want to switch back to the original clip, choose Clip > Replace Footage again to navigate and relink to the original file.

6 Play the Timeline, and notice that the incorrect graphic has been updated throughout the sequence and project.

Nesting sequences

A *nested* sequence is a sequence within another sequence. You can break up your project into more manageable chunks by creating a project segment in one sequence and dragging that sequence—with all its clips, graphics, layers, multiple audio/video tracks, and effects—into another sequence. There it will look and behave like a single audio/video clip.

Nested sequences have many potential uses:

- They simplify editing by creating complex sequences separately. This helps you avoid running into conflicts and inadvertently shifting clips on a track that is far from your current Work Area.

- They allow you to apply a motion effect to a group of clips (you'll learn more in the next lesson).

- They let you reuse sequences as a source in multiple sequences.

- They organize your work in the same way you might create subfolders in the Project panel.

- They allow you to transition to a composited group of clips as a single item.

Adding a nested sequence

One reason to use a nest is to reuse an already edited sequence. In this case, let's add an edited opening title into an already edited sequence.

1 In the Project panel, load the sequence 08 Bike Race.

This sequence contains an edited bike race that was cut using multicamera editing techniques that you'll learn in Lesson 10.

2 Set an In point at the start of the sequence.

3 Make sure that track V1 is targeted in the sequence loaded in the Timeline panel.

4 In the Project panel, locate the sequence 08A Race Open.

5 Click the sequence once to select it (do not open it).

6 Drag the sequence 08A Race Open over the Program Monitor.

A tool tip appears prompting you to choose the type of edit you want to make.

> **Tip:** A quick way to create a nested sequence is to drag a sequence from the Project panel into the appropriate track or tracks of the active sequence. You can also load a sequence as a source in the Program Monitor and use the standard Insert and Overwrite commands.

7 Hold down the Control (Windows) or Command (Mac OS) key.

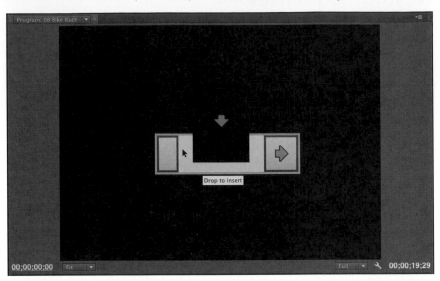

8 Release the key to perform an insert edit and add the graphic open to your sequence.

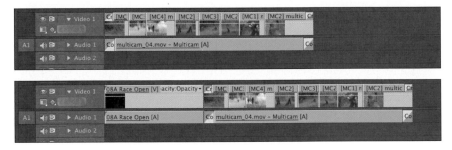

● **Note:** You cannot nest a sequence within itself. Rather, you'll be prompted to give the nested portion a new name.

9 Play back sequence 08 Bike Race.

You'll notice that the 08A Race Open sequence is added as a single clip, even though it uses multiple video tracks and audio clips within.

Nesting clips already in a sequence

In the previous exercise, you nested an entire sequence in another sequence. It's also possible to select a group of clips already in a sequence and nest them into a new sequence that takes their place in the Timeline. It does not have to be all the clips in the sequence. This can be useful for collapsing a complex set of clips into a single nested sequence.

1   In the Project panel, load the sequence 09 Collapse.

Let's create a Cube Spin transition at the edit point of the Medieval_wide_01 and Medieval_villain_02 clips. Since there are two other clips composited over the Medieval_wide_01 clip, inserting a Cube Spin transition that correctly impacts the first three clips is difficult—but not if you collapse the first segment to a single nested clip.

2   Shift+click the three clips that make up the first segment—movie_logo.psd, Title 01, and Medieval_wide_01—to select them.

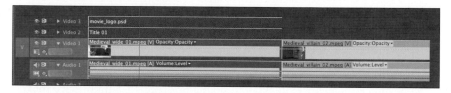

3   Right-click the selected clips, and choose Nest.

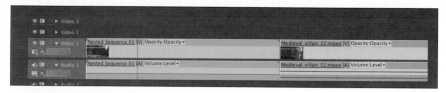

The three clips are collapsed to a single nested clip. Play the clip to see that the nest contains the three clips.

4   In the Effects panel, click the Video Transitions folder to open it. Then open the 3D Motion subfolder.

5   Drag the Cube Spin transition to the edit point between the two clips.

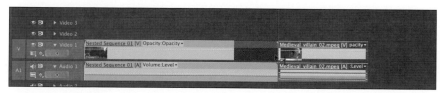

> **Tip:** If you need to make a change to a nested sequence, simply double-click a nested sequence clip to open the sequence.

6   Play back the sequence to see the impact of your work.

If necessary, render the Work Area for smoother playback.

Regular trimming

You can adjust the length of a clip in several ways. This process is generally called *trimming*. When you trim, you can make an edit either shorter or longer. Some trimming types affect only a single clip, while others adjust the relationship between two adjacent clips.

Trim in Source Monitor

The easiest way to trim a clip is to use the Source Monitor. If you take a clip that is in your sequence and load it into the Source Monitor from a sequence, you can easily adjust its In and Out points. With a clip loaded into the Source Monitor from a sequence, you can trim a clip in two basic ways:

- **Marking new In and Out points:** If you want to trim a clip, you can simply update its In or Out point. Double-click a clip in the Timeline to load it. With the clip loaded, just press the I or O key for In or Out. Alternately, you can use the Mark In and Mark Out buttons at the bottom left of the Source Monitor. If the clip has media adjacent to it in the Timeline, you can only make the selected clip shorter. You will end up with gaps on the side after making a trim.

- **Dragging In and Out points:** Instead of marking new points for a loaded clip, you can change the In and Out points by dragging. Simply place your cursor over an In or Out point in the mini Timeline in the Source Monitor. The cursor changes into a red-and-black icon indicating that a ripple edit can be performed. You can drag left or right to change the In or Out point. The same limitations apply for adjacent media in regards to gaps or extending an edit. If you hold down the Alt (Windows) or Option (Mac OS) key, you can drag the video or audio only for the clip.

Trim in a sequence

● **Note:** A regular trim is also referred to as a single-sided or overwrite trim in other editing applications.

Another way that you can trim media is directly in the Timeline panel. As you edit a sequence, you'll likely find shots that you'll want to adjust. Making a single clip shorter or longer is fairly easy (and is called a *regular trim*).

1 In the Project panel, load the sequence 10 Regular Trim.

2 Play the sequence.

The second actor's dialogue is cut off, and the shot needs to be extended.

3 Choose the Selection tool (V).

4 Place the pointer over the Out point of the last clip in the sequence.

The pointer changes into the Trim In tool (head side) or Trim Out tool (tail side) with directional arrows. Mousing over the edge of the clip changes it between trimming the Out point (open to the left) or In point (open to the right) of a clip.

5 Click and drag an edge to trim the Out point of the clip in the sequence.

A timecode tool tip appears to show you how much you've trimmed the clip. Drag an edge an additional 9:00.

● **Note:** If you make a clip shorter, it will leave a gap between the adjacent clips. You'll learn to use the Ripple Edit tool later in this lesson to automatically remove any gaps or move later clips to avoid overwriting them.

6 Release the mouse to make the edit.

Advanced trimming

The trimming methods you've learned so far have their limitations. They can leave unwanted gaps in the Timeline caused by shortening a clip. They also can prevent you from lengthening a shot if it is surrounded by an adjacent clip. Fortunately, Adobe Premiere Pro offers several more choices for trimming.

Ripple edit

A way to avoid creating gaps when trimming is to use the Ripple Edit tool. It's one of the many tools in the Tools panel. Use the Ripple Edit tool to trim a clip in the same way you used the Selection tool in Trim mode. The two differences are that the Ripple Edit tool does not leave a gap on the sequence and that the display in the Program Monitor gives a clearer representation of how the edit will work.

When you use the Ripple Edit tool to lengthen or shorten a clip, your action ripples through the sequence. That is, all clips after that edit slide to the left to fill the gap or slide to the right to accommodate a longer clip.

In this figure, the green clip is shortened by two seconds. A ripple edit changes the overall length of the project.

● **Note:** When performing a ripple edit, you can knock items on other tracks out of sync. Be sure to pay attention to the use of sync locks for any sequence where you're using a ripple edit.

1 In the Project panel, load the sequence 11 Ripple Edit.

2 Click the Ripple Edit tool (or press B on your keyboard).

3 Hover the Ripple Edit tool over the left edge of the third clip (Medieval_wide_01.mpeg) until it turns into a large, right-facing square bracket.

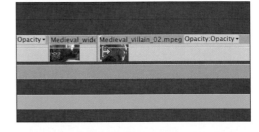

There is too much of the cutaway. Let's remove some.

4 Drag to the right until the timecode reads +00:00:02:15.

Notice that when you're using the Ripple Edit tool, the Program Monitor displays the last frame of the first clip on the left and the first frame of the second clip on the right. Watch the moving edit position on the left half of the Program Monitor.

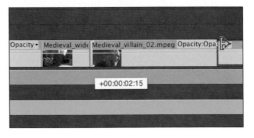

5 Release the mouse button to complete the edit.

The remaining part of the clip moves left to fill the gap, and the clips to its right slide along with it. Play that portion of the sequence to see whether the edit works smoothly. Let's continue to trim to make the clip exactly one second long.

▶ **Tip:** If you're using the standard Selection tool, just hold down the Command (Mac OS) or Control (Windows) key to temporarily switch to the Ripple Edit tool.

6 Use the Ripple Edit tool to grab the right side of the clip, and drag it to the left until the timecode removed reads -00:00:03:00.

Notice how the clips to the right (downstream) ripple to close the gap when you release the mouse button.

Rolling edit

When you used the Ripple Edit tool, it made changes to the overall length of the project. This is because one clip got longer or shorter while the rest of the sequence adjusted to close the gap (or move out of the way). There is another way, though, to change the location of an edit.

● **Note:** A ripple trim is also referred to as a *double roller trim* in other editing applications.

With a rolling edit, the overall length of the project does not change. Instead, a rolling edit takes place at an edit point between two clips, shortening one and lengthening the other proportionately. It edits two adjacent clips at the same time. A roll edit trims adjacent In and Out points and simultaneously adjusts them by the same number of frames.

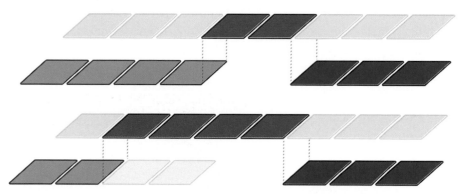

A rolling edit is applied between the first and second shots. The outgoing shot is shortened by two seconds while the incoming shot is lengthened by two seconds. No change to the overall duration of the sequence occurs.

1   In the Project panel, load the sequence 12 Trimming Edits.

   Three clips already appear on the Timeline, with enough head and tail frames to allow the edits you're about to make.

2   Select the Rolling Edit Tool (N) in the Tools panel.

3 Drag the edit point between Clip A and Clip B (the first two clips on the Timeline), using the Program Monitor split screen to find a better matching edit.

Try rolling the edit point to the right to 00;20 (20 frames). You can use the Program Monitor timecode or the pop-up timecode in the Timeline (both shown here) to find that edit.

Sliding edits

The slide edit is a special kind of trim. It is not used often but can be a timesaving edit. The Slide Edit tool works by leaving the duration of the clip you're sliding the same. What changes is that the Out point of the clip to the left and the In point of the clip to the right are modified an equal number of frames. Essentially you slide the clip forward or back in the Timeline and change the content of the shots adjacent to it. The clip's In and Out points remain unchanged. The length of the sequence does not change.

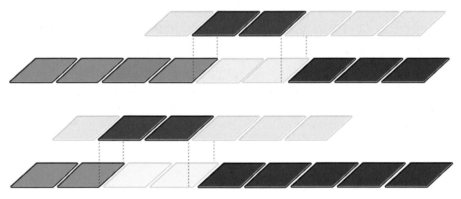

A slide edit changes the In and Out points of adjacent clips while retaining the original clip's edit points. The middle shot does not change duration or which frames are displayed, but it does move earlier or later in the sequence.

1 Continue working with the sequence 12 Trimming Edits.

2 Select the Slide Tool (U).

3 Position the Slide tool over the middle clip.

4 Drag the second clip left or right.

5 Take a look at the Program Monitor as you perform the slide edit.

The two top images are the In point and Out point of Clip B. They do not change. The two larger images are the Out point and In point of the adjacent clips—Clip A and Clip C, respectively. These edit points change as you slide the selected clip over those adjacent clips.

Clip B In point (unchanged)   Clip B Out point (unchanged)

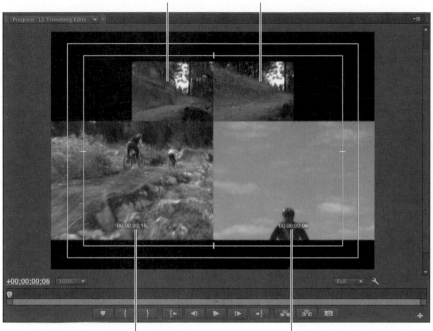

Clip A Out point   Clip C In point

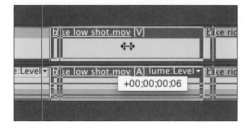

The Slide tool moves a clip over two adjacent clips.

Slip edits

The slip edit is a bit hard to grasp, but think of it this way: slipping in place. When you slip an edit, you change what portion of the shot is seen. A slip edit changes a clip's In and Out points forward or backward by the same number of frames. Using the Slip tool lets you change a clip's starting and ending frames without changing its duration or affecting adjacent clips. This changes what part of the shot is visible. The length of the sequence does not change.

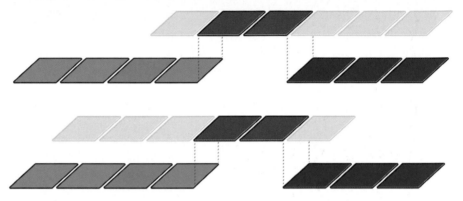

A slip edit changes the In and Out points of the selected clip while retaining the adjacent clip's edit points. The frames displayed for the clip are changed.

1 Continue working with the sequence 12 Trimming Edits.

2 Select the Slip tool (Y).

3 Drag Clip B left and right (the middle clip—bike low shot.mov).

4 Take a look at the Program Monitor as you perform the slip edit.

The two top images are the Out point and In point of Clips A and C, respectively. They do not change. The two larger images are the In point and Out point of Clip B. These edit points change as you slip Clip B *under* Clips A and C.

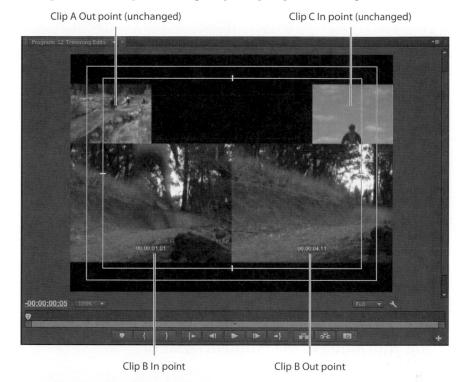

Clip A Out point (unchanged)   Clip C In point (unchanged)

Clip B In point   Clip B Out point

The Slip tool moves a clip under two adjacent clips.

Trimming in the Program Monitor panel

If you'd like to trim with a great deal of visual feedback, then you should use the Trim mode of the Program Monitor panel. This approach allows you to see both the outgoing and incoming frames of the trim you're working on.

You can perform three types of trims in the Program Monitor panel. You learned about each of these earlier in this lesson:

- **Regular trim:** This basic type of trim moves the edge of the selected clip. This type of trim trims only one side of the edit point. It moves the selected edit point either forward or backward in the Timeline, but it doesn't shift any of the other clips.

- **Roll trim:** The roll trim will move the tail of one clip and the head of the adjacent clip. It lets you shift an edit point (provided there are handles). There is no gap created, and the sequence duration doesn't change.

- **Ripple trim:** If you need to extend or shorten just one side of an edit, use a ripple trim. This will move the selected edge of the edit point either forward or backward in time. The clips that follow the edit point will shift.

● **Note:** You'll still find the Trim Monitor panel that shipped with earlier versions of Adobe Premiere Pro (Window > Trim Monitor). This is a legacy feature that doesn't utilize the ability to precisely select edits. This feature has been replaced by the new Trim mode, which is available in the Program Monitor.

Using Trim mode in the Program Monitor

When using Trim mode, the Program Monitor switches some of its buttons and controls to improve your ability for several trimming functions. To use the Trim mode, you first need to activate it. This is done by selecting an edit point between two clips. There are three ways to do this:

- With a selection or trimming tool, double-click an edit point in your Timeline.

- Press the T key to move to the closest edit point and open it in Trim mode in the Program Monitor panel.

- Using the Ripple or Roll tool, you can click and drag to create a marquee selection. Drag around one or more edit points to select them and open the Program Monitor to Trim mode.

When invoked, Trim mode shows you two video clips. The first box shows the outgoing clip (also called *A side*). The second display shows the incoming clip (also called *B side*) frames. Below the frames are five buttons and two indicators.

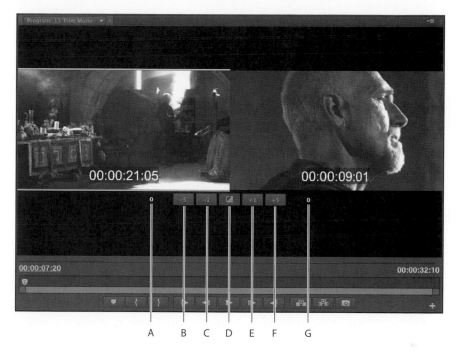

A Out Shift counter: Shows how many frames the Out point for the A side has changed.

B Trim Backward Many: When clicked, this will perform the selected trim and move it multiple frames to the left. The number moved depends on the Large Trim Offset option specified on the Trim Preferences tab of Preferences. The keyboard shortcut is Alt+Shift+left arrow (Windows) or Option+Shift+left arrow (Mac OS).

C Trim Backward: This performs the selected trim type one frame at a time and moves it to the left. The keyboard shortcut is Alt+left arrow (Windows) or Option+left arrow (Mac OS).

D Apply Default Transitions to Selection: This applies the default transition (generally a dissolve) to the video and audio tracks that have their edit points selected.

E Trim Forward: This is just like Trim Backward except it moves the selected edit point forward (to the right). The keyboard shortcut is Alt+right arrow (Windows) or Option+right arrow (Mac OS).

F Trim Forward Many: This closely matches Trim Backward Many except it moves multiple frames forward. The keyboard shortcut is Alt+Shift+right arrow (Windows) or Option+Shift+right arrow (Mac OS).

G In Shift counter: This shows how many frames the In point for the B side has changed.

Choosing a trimming method in the Program Monitor

You've already learned about the three types of trims that you can perform (regular, roll, and ripple). You also tried each in the Timeline panel. Using Trim mode makes the process easier for most because it provides richer visual feedback.

1   In the Project panel, load the sequence 13 Trim Mode.

2   With the Selection tool, double-click the edit point between clip 3 and clip 4 in the Timeline panel (there is a marker to help you find it).

3   In the Program monitor, drag the cursor slowly across the A and B clips.

    As you drag from left to right, you'll see the tool update from a Trim Out (left side), Roll (center), or Trim In (right).

● **Note:** Clicking the A or B side will switch which side is being trimmed. Clicking in the center will switch to a roll.

4   Drag in between both clips to perform a roll edit.

    The time display on the right should read 00:00:09:16.

5   Press the down-arrow key to go to the next edit.

6 Change your trimming method to a ripple edit.

The easiest way to change the trimming method is to press the shortcut Control+T (Windows) or Command+T (Mac OS) to cycle Trim modes. There are five options to cycle through. Tap the key combo once to cycle to the next shortcut. The five choices loop. You've selected a ripple edit when the Trim tool shows a yellow roller.

▶ **Tip:** You can also right-click an edit point to choose the trim type from a pop-up menu.

7 Drag four frames to the right for the incoming clip and make the edit shorter.

The time display should read 00:00:21:05. The rest of the clips ripple to close the gap. The shots are now back in sync.

● **Note:** The type of trim that's used by default may seem random, but it's not. The initial setting is chosen by the type of tool that was used to select the edit point. If you click with the Selection tool, Adobe Premiere Pro chooses a regular Trim In or Trim Out. If you click with the Ripple tool, then the Ripple In or Ripple Out tool is chosen. In both cases, cycling the roller will result in a rolling trim. Use the horizontal blue highlight to determine what type of trim is in use.

Modifier keys

There are multiple modifier keys that can be used to refine a trimming selection.

- Hold down Alt (Windows) or Option (Mac OS) when clicking to temporarily unlink audio and video. This makes it easier to select just the audio or video portion of a clip.

- Hold down the Shift key to select multiple edit points. You can trim multiple tracks or even multiple clips at the same time.

- Combine the two shortcuts to make very advanced selections for trimming.

Dynamic trimming

Because trimming often involves finding the proper rhythm for an edit, it's easier to accomplish while the sequence is playing back live. Adobe Premiere Pro lets you update a trim using keyboard shortcuts or buttons while the sequence plays back in real time.

1 Continue working with the sequence 13 Trim Mode.

2 Press the Down Arrow key twice to move to the next video edit point. Set the trim type to be a roll. You can use the shortcut Control+T (Windows) or Control+T (Mac) to cycle Trim modes.

You can stay in Trim mode while switching between edit points. Conversely, the Up Arrow key would switch you to the previous edit.

3 Press the spacebar to loop playback.

The sequence starts to play back. You'll see a few seconds loop with the shot before and after playing back. This helps you get a feel for the content of the edit.

● **Note:** To control the preroll and postroll times, open Preferences and select the Playback category. You can set the duration in seconds. Most editors find a duration of two to five seconds most useful.

4 Try adjusting the trim using the methods you've already learned.

The Trim Forward and Backward buttons at the bottom of Trim mode view work well and can adjust the edit while the clip plays back. While these work well, let's try using the keyboard for more dynamic control. The same J-K-L playback keys you use to control playback can also control trimming.

5 Press Stop to stop the playback loop.

6 Press the L key to shuttle the trim to the right.

Pressing once trims in real time. You can tap it multiple times to trim faster.

7 Press the K key to stop trimming.

Let's refine and trim back a little earlier.

8 Hold down the K key and press the J key to shuttle left in slow motion.

9 Release both keys to stop the trim.

10 To exit Trim mode, click a button in the transport control area (play/rewind buttons) of the Program Monitor or scrub in the Timeline panel.

Note: To review the shortcut, press the J key to activate Shuttle Left (moving the trim point earlier). Press the L key to activate Shuttle Right (a later point). To stop the dynamic trim, press K to activate Shuttle Stop.

Trimming with the keyboard

The following table illustrates some of the most useful keyboard shortcuts you can use when trimming.

Table 8.1 Trimming in the Timeline

MAC	WINDOWS
Trim Backward: Option+left arrow	Trim Backward: Alt+left arrow
Trim Backward Many: Option+Shift+left arrow	Trim Backward Many: Alt+Shift+left arrow
Trim Forward: Option+right arrow	Trim Forward: Alt+right arrow
Trim Forward Many: Option+Shift+right arrow	Trim Forward Many: Alt +Shift+right arrow
Slide Clip Selection Left Five Frames: Option+Shift+, (comma)	Slide Clip Selection Left Five Frames: Alt+Shift+, (comma)
Slide Clip Selection Left One Frame: Option+, (comma)	Slide Clip Selection Left One Frame: Alt+, (comma)
Slide Clip Selection Right Five Frames: Option+Shift+. (period)	Slide Clip Selection Right Five Frames: Alt+Shift+. (period)
Slide Clip Selection Right One Frame: Option+. (period)	Slide Clip Selection Right One Frame: Alt+. (period)
Slip Clip Selection Left Five Frames: Command +Option+Shift+left arrow	Slip Clip Selection Left Five Frames: Control+Alt+Shift+left arrow
Slip Clip Selection Left One Frame: Command +Option+left arrow	Slip Clip Selection Left One Frame: Control+Alt+left arrow
Slip Clip Selection Right Five Frames: Command +Option+Shift+right arrow	Slip Clip Selection Right Five Frames: Control+Alt+Shift+right arrow
Slip Clip Selection Right One Frame: Command+Option+right arrow	Slip Clip Selection Right One Frame: Control+Alt+right arrow

Review questions

1. Changing the Speed parameter of a clip to 50% has what effect on the length of the clip?

2. What tool is useful in stretching a clip in time to fill a gap?

3. Can you make time-remapping changes directly on the Timeline?

4. How do you create a smooth ramp-up from slow motion to normal speed?

5. What's the basic difference between a slide edit and a slip edit?

6. What is the difference between the Replace Clip feature and the Replace Footage feature?

Review answers

1. Reducing a clip's speed causes the clip to become longer, unless the Speed and Duration parameters have been unlinked in the Clip Speed/Duration dialog or the clip is bound by another clip.

2. The Rate Stretch tool is useful for the common situation of needing to fill a small amount of time.

3. Time remapping is best done on the Timeline; because it affects time, it is best (and most easily) used and seen within the Timeline sequence.

4. Add a speed keyframe, and split it by dragging away half of the keyframe to create a transition between speeds.

5. You slide a clip over adjacent clips, retaining the selected clip's original In and Out points. You slip a clip under adjacent clips, changing the selected clip's In and Out points.

6. Replace Clip replaces a single targeted clip on the Timeline with a new clip from the Project panel. Replace Footage replaces a clip in the Project panel with a new source clip. Any instance of the clip in any sequence in the project is replaced. In both cases, the effects of the replaced clip are maintained.

9 PUTTING CLIPS IN MOTION

Lesson overview

In this lesson, you'll learn about the following:

- Adjusting the Motion effect for clips
- Changing clip size and adding rotation
- Adjusting the anchor point to refine rotation
- Working with keyframe interpolation
- Enhancing motion with shadows and beveled edges

 This lesson will take approximately 50 minutes.

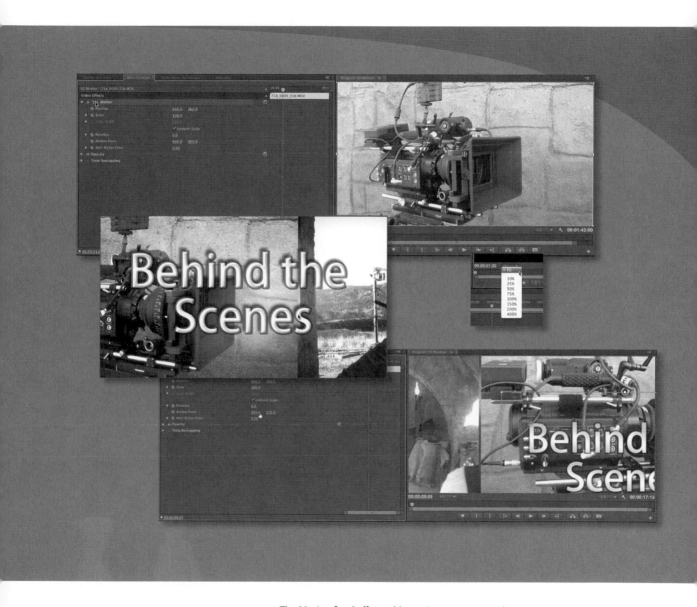

The Motion fixed effect adds motion to an entire clip. This can be useful for animating a graphic or for sizing and repositioning a video clip within the frame. You can also animate an object's position using keyframes and enhance that animation by controlling their interpolation between values.

Getting started

A common visual treatment you'll see in frequent use is to put elements into motion. Perhaps you'll see multiple video clips streaming past on-screen in floating boxes, or you'll see a video clip shrunk down and placed next to an on-camera host. You can create those effects (and more) in Adobe Premiere Pro CS6 by using the Motion fixed effect or several clip-based effects with Motion settings.

You use the Motion effect to position, rotate, or scale a clip within the video frame. You can make those adjustments directly in the Program Monitor by dragging to change its position, or you can drag or rotate its handles to change its size, shape, or orientation.

You can also adjust Motion parameters in the Effect Controls panel and animate clips by using keyframes and Bezier controls. Keyframes simply define where an object is at a particular point in time. If you use two (or more) keyframes, then it's possible to introduce animation between the frames.

Adjusting the Motion effect

Every time you add a clip into an Adobe Premiere Pro Timeline, the Motion effect is automatically applied as a fixed effect. To control the effect, you'll use the Effect Controls panel. Within you'll find the Motion effect properties (just click the triangle next to the Motion effect name).

With the Motion effect you can adjust the position, scale, or rotation of a clip. This opens up several possibilities for adjusting the frames on-screen. Let's explore how this effect has been used to reposition a clip.

1   Open Lesson-09.prproj in the Lesson 09 folder.

2   Choose Window > Workspace > Effects to switch to the Effects workspace.

3   Locate the sequence 01 Floating. It should already be loaded; if not, double-click to load the sequence.

    Let's ensure the Program Monitor is sized so you can see all of the action.

4   Open the Select Zoom Level menu in the Program Monitor, and make sure the zoom level is set to Fit.

    This helps you see and work with the Motion effect's bounding box.

5   Play the clip in the Timeline.

    This particular clip has had its Position, Scale, and Rotation properties modified. Keyframes have been used as well as interpolation.

Understanding Motion settings

While the Motion effect is automatically applied, a clip does not animate by default. Rather, it will appear at 100 percent of its original size in the center of the Program Monitor. You can choose, however, to adjust the following properties:

- **Position:** This sets where the clip is positioned along the x- and y-axes (based on its anchor point). Coordinates are calculated based on pixel position from the upper-left corner.

- **Scale (Scale Height, when Uniform Scale is deselected):** Clips are set to their full size by default (100 percent). To shrink a clip, reduce the number to 0 percent. While you can scale up to 600 percent in size, the image will become pixelated and soft.

- **Scale Width**: You must deselect Uniform Scale to make Scale Width available. Doing so lets you change the clip's width and height independently.

- **Rotation:** You can rotate an image along the z-axis. This produces a flat-spin (as if viewing a spinning turntable or carousel from above). You can input degrees or number of rotations—for example, 450° or 1 x 90. A positive number denotes clockwise rotation, and a negative number represents counterclockwise. The maximum number of rotations allowed in either direction is 90, meaning you can apply up to 180 full rotations to a clip by using the full range between the maximum negative and positive rotations.

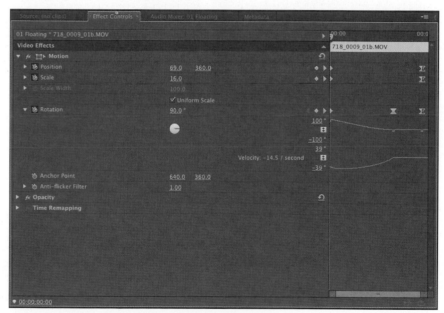

- **Anchor Point:** By default, this is the center of a clip. This can be changed, however, to define any point around which an object is set to scale or rotate.

You can set the clip to rotate around any point on the screen, including one of the clip's corners, or around a point outside the clip like a ball at the end of a rope. As you move the anchor point, you may have to reposition your clip to compensate for the offset.

- **Anti-flicker Filter**: This feature is useful for images that contain high-frequency detail, such as fine lines, hard edges, parallel lines (moiré problems), or rotation. Those characteristics can cause flickering during motion. The default setting (0.00) adds no blurring and has no effect on flicker. To add some blurring and eliminate flicker, use 1.00.

Let's look closer at the animated clip.

1 Continue using the sequence 01 Floating.

2 Click the only clip in the Timeline to make sure it is selected.

3 In the same frame with the Source Monitor, look for the tab for the Effect Controls panel and click it so it is visible.

4 Click the Motion disclosure triangle in the Effect Controls panel to display its parameters.

5 Click the Show/Hide Timeline View button to show or hide the keyframes in use.

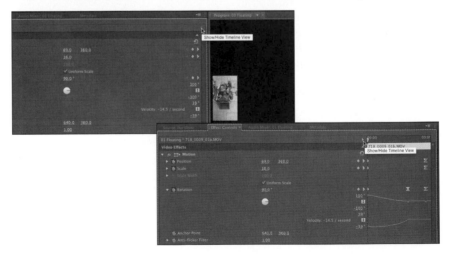

6 Click the Go to Previous Keyframe or Go to Next Keyframe arrow to jump between the existing keyframes applied to the clip.

● **Note:** It is very difficult to select a keyframe precisely with the mouse. Using the previous/next keyframe buttons helps prevent adding unwanted keyframes.

Now that you know how to view an animation, let's reset a clip. You'll animate from scratch later in this lesson.

7 Click the "Toggle animation" stopwatch button for the Position property to turn off its keyframes.

8 Click OK when prompted that all keyframes will be deleted if you apply the action.

9 Repeat steps 7 and 8 for the Scale and Rotation properties.

10 Click the Reset button (to the right of Motion in the Effect Controls panel).

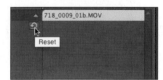

These actions return Motion to its default settings.

Examining Motion properties

The Position, Scale, and Rotation properties are spatial in nature, meaning that any changes you make are easily visible, because the object will change in size and position. These properties can be adjusted by entering numerical values, scrubbable text, or using the Transform controls.

To examine some Motion settings, follow these steps:

1 Double-click the sequence 02 Motion in the Project panel to load it.

2 Open the Select Zoom Level menu in the Program Monitor, and make sure the zoom level is set to 25% (or a zoom amount that allows you to see space around the frame).

This will make it easier to see the bounding box as you drag a clip around.

3 Drag the playhead anywhere in the clip so you can see the video in the Program Monitor.

4 Click the clip in the Timeline so it is selected and visible in the Effect Controls panel.

If necessary, click the triangle to open the Motion properties.

● **Note:** The Transform button is available in several effects and can be used for direct manipulation. Be sure to explore Corner Pin, Crop, Garbage Matte, Mirror, Transform, and Twirl.

5 Click the Transform button (next to Motion) in the Effect Controls panel.

A bounding box with a crosshair and handles appears around the clip in the Program panel.

6 Click anywhere in the clip bounding box in the Program Monitor and drag this clip around.

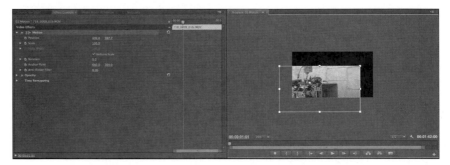

Note how the Position values in the Effect Controls panel change.

7 Drag the clip so that its center is directly over the upper-left corner of the screen, and note that the Position values in the Effect Controls panel are 0, 0 (or close to that, depending on where you placed the center of the clip).

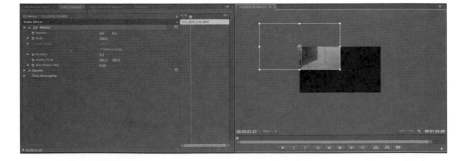

The lower-right corner of the screen is 1280, 720—the frame size of the 720p sequence setting used for this project.

8   Click the Reset button to restore the clip to its default position.

9   Click and drag the golden text for the Rotation property. Drag left or right to rotate the object.

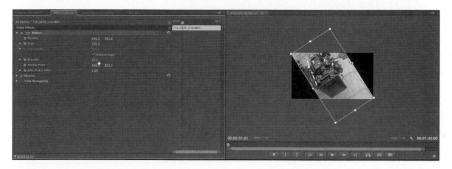

10 Click the Reset button to restore the clip to its default position.

● **Note:** Adobe Premiere Pro uses an upside-down x, y coordinate system for screen location. That coordinate system is based on a methodology used in Windows. The upper-left corner of the screen is 0, 0. All x and y values, respectively, to the left of and above that point are negative. All x and y values, respectively, to the right of and below that point are positive.

Changing clip position, size, and rotation

Simply sliding a clip around only begins to exploit the possibilities of the Motion effect. What makes the Motion effect so useful is the ability to shrink or expand the clip as well as rotate it. In this example, we're going to build a simple bumper segment for the behind-the-scenes features of a DVD.

Changing Position

Let's begin using keyframes to animate the position of a layer. For this exercise, the first thing we'll do is adjust the clip position. The picture is going to start offscreen and move across from right to left.

1   Double-click the sequence 03 Montage in the Project panel to load it.

    The sequence contains several tracks, some of which are currently disabled and will be used later in the lesson.

2   Move the playhead to the start of the sequence.

3   Open the Select Zoom Level menu in the Program Monitor, and make sure the zoom level is set to Fit.

4 Select the first video clip on track Video 3.

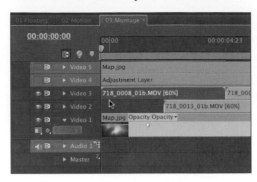

The clip's controls load into the Effect Controls panel.

5 In the Effect Controls panel, click Position's "Toggle animation" button to activate keyframing for the Position property.

6 Enter a value of **–640** into the x-axis as a starting position.

The clip moves offscreen to the left.

7 Drag the playhead to the end of the clip (00:00:4:23). You can do this in the Timeline panel or Effect Controls panel.

8 Enter a new position value for the x-axis. Use **1920** to push the clip off the right edge of the screen.

9 Play back the sequence to see the clip move.

It should float from offscreen left to offscreen right. You will see a clip on a lower track pop up suddenly. You'll animate this layer and others next.

Reusing Motion settings

Because you've applied keyframes and effects to one clip, you can save time by reusing them on other shots. It is as easy as copying and pasting to reuse effects from one clip to one or more other clips. In this example, you can apply the same left-to-right floating animation to other clips in the project.

There are several methods for reusing effects. Let's try one now.

1 In the Timeline panel, select the clip you just animated. It should be the first clip on Video 3.

2 Choose Edit > Copy.

The properties for the clip are now on your computer's clipboard.

3 With the Selection tool (V), drag from right to left to activate the five other clips located on the Video 2 and Video 3 tracks.

Note: As an alternative to selecting a clip in the Timeline, you can always select one or more effects in the Effect Controls panel. Just select the first effect you want to copy. Then hold down the Shift key and click to select multiple effects.

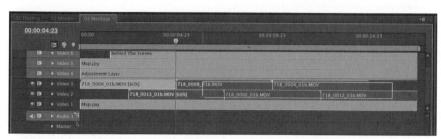

4 Choose Edit > Paste Attributes to the effect and keyframes stored on your computer's clipboard.

5 Play back your sequence to see your work so far.

Adding rotation and changing the anchor point

While moving items around the screen is useful, you can animate items even more by taking control of two different properties. The Rotation property revolves an item on the z-axis. By default it will rotate around the center of an object, its anchor point. You can, however, move this point to create new effects.

Now let's add some rotation to the clip.

1 Turn on the visibility icon for Video 6, which contains a title called *Behind the Scenes*.

2 Move the playhead to the start of the title (00:00:01:13).

3 Select the title in the Timeline.

Its controls should appear in the Effect Controls panel.

4 Click the triangle next to the Motion property if its controls aren't visible. Also click the Transform button to see the anchor point and bounding box controls.

Now, let's adjust the Rotation property only to see its effect.

5 Enter a value of **90.0°** into the Rotation field.

The title rotates in the center of the screen.

6 Choose Edit > Undo so the animation can be refined.

7 Using the scrubbable text, adjust the anchor point so the crosshair sits on top of the letter *B* in the first word.

The text will also appear to move on the screen. Values of approximately 155.0 and 170.0 should work well.

8   In the Program Monitor, click the title and drag it into the correct position to center it on-screen. You can use the bounding box as a guide to help you position the item.

Using the same values of 155.0 and 170.0 should center the object.

9   Click the stopwatch button for the Rotation property to toggle animation.

10 At the start of the clip, add a keyframe for 90.0°.

11 Move the playhead forward to 6:00 and add a second keyframe.

12 Set the rotation to 0.0°.

13 Play back the sequence to see your animation.

Changing size

You'll find a few different methods for changing the size of items in an Adobe Premiere Pro sequence. The default is that any item added to your sequence comes in at 100 percent of its original size. However, you can choose to manually adjust the size or let Adobe Premiere Pro do it for you.

Here are the three methods to choose from:

- Use the Scale property of the Motion effect in the Effect Controls panel.

- Right-click (Windows) or Control-click (Mac OS) an item and choose Scale To Frame Size (if the clip is a different frame size than your sequence).

- Scale automatically with the global preference. Choose Edit > Preferences > General (Windows) or Premiere Pro > Preferences > General (Mac OS). You can then select the Default Scale To Frame Size option and click OK.

For maximum flexibility, use only the first method so you can scale as needed without discarding quality. Let's give it a try.

1   Select the Behind The Scenes clip in the Timeline and move the playhead to the start of the clip.

2   Click the stopwatch button for the Scale property to toggle animation.

3   Enter a value of **0%** so the item starts very small.

4   Click the Go to Next Keyframe arrow for the Rotation property.

This will move the playhead accurately so you can synchronize the animation.

5 Enter a value of **100%** for the Scale property.

Adobe Premiere Pro automatically adds a new keyframe because the "Toggle animation" property is enabled.

6 Turn on the Video 4 track.

This is an adjustment layer for applying a global effect to all the footage. In this case, the Black and White effect is applied to remove the saturation from each shot. You'll learn more about adjustment layers in Lesson 13, "Adding Video Effects."

7 Turn on the Video 5 track.

This is a colored texture layer that is set to the Overlay blending mode. Blending modes let you mix the content of multiple layers together. You'll learn more about modes in Lesson 15, "Exploring Compositing Techniques."

8 Play back the sequence to see your animation.

Working with keyframe interpolation

Throughout this lesson you've been using keyframes to define your animation. The term *keyframe* originates from traditional animation where the lead artist would draw the key frames (or major poses) and then assistant animators would animate the frames in between (a process often called *tweening*). When animating in Adobe Premiere Pro, you're the master animator, and the computer does the rest of the work as it interpolates values in between the keyframes you set.

Keyframe interpolation methods

While you've already used keyframes to animate, you've only touched on their power. One of the most useful yet least utilized features of keyframes is their interpolation method. This is just a fancy way of saying how to get from point A to point B. Think of it as describing the sharp ramp-up as a runner takes off from the starting line and the gradual slowdown after she's crossed the finish line.

Temporal vs. spatial interpolation

Some properties and effects offer a choice of temporal and spatial interpolation methods for transitioning between keyframes. You'll find that all properties have temporal controls (which relate to time). Some properties also offer spatial interpolation (which refers to space or movement). Here are the essentials of each method:

- **Temporal interpolation:** Temporal interpolation deals with changes in time. It's an effective way to determine the speed at which an object moves across a motion path. For example, you can add acceleration and deceleration to a motion path with Ease or Bezier keyframes.

- **Spatial interpolation:** The spatial method commonly deals with changes in an object's shape. It's an effective way to control the shape of the motion path. For example, does an object create hard angular ricochets as it moves from keyframe to keyframe, or does the object have a more sloping movement with round corners?

Adobe Premiere Pro has five interpolation methods that control the interpolation process. Changing the method used can create a very different animation. You can easily access the available interpolation methods by right-clicking a keyframe. You can then see all five options listed (some effects offer both spatial and temporal categories).

Keyframes can be identified by their shape (from left to right): Linear, Bezier, Auto Bezier, Continuous Bezier, and Hold interpolation.

- **Linear interpolation:** The default method of keyframe interpolation is Linear. This method creates a uniform rate of change between keyframes. It often looks a bit mechanical because the software calculates in-between values or each keyframe pair while the other keyframes in use in the Timeline are ignored. When using linear keyframes, changes begin instantly at the first keyframe and continue to the next keyframe at a constant speed. At the second keyframe, the rate of change switches instantly to the rate between it and the third keyframe.

- **Bezier interpolation:** If you want the most control over keyframe interpolation, choose the Bezier interpolation method. This option provides manual controls so you can adjust the shape of the value graph or motion path segments on both sides of the keyframe. If you use Bezier interpolation for all keyframes in a layer, you'll have a smooth transition between keyframes.

- **Auto Bezier interpolation:** The Auto Bezier option attempts to create a smooth rate of change through a keyframe and will automatically update as you change values. This option works best for spatial keyframes that define position but can be used for other values as well.

- **Continuous Bezier interpolation:** This option is similar to the Auto Bezier option, but it provides some manual controls. The motion or value path will have smooth transitions, but you can adjust the shape of the Bezier curve on both sides of the keyframe with a control handle.

- **Hold interpolation:** The Hold style is an additional interpolation method that is available only for temporal (time-based) properties. This style of keyframe allows a keyframe to hold its value across time without a gradual transition. This is useful if you want to create staccato-type movements or make an object suddenly disappear. When used, the value of the first keyframe will hold until the next hold keyframe is encountered, and then the value will instantly change.

Adding Ease to Motion

A quick way to add a feeling of inertia to clip motion is to use one of the Ease presets. For example, you can create a ramp-up effect for speed. By simply right-clicking a keyframe, you can choose the Ease In or Ease Out option. Ease In is used for approaching a keyframe, while Ease Out is used when leaving a keyframe position.

1 Continue working with the previous sequence or double-click to load 04 Montage Complete in the Project panel.

2 Select the clip Behind The Scenes on track Video 6.

3 In the Effect Controls panel, locate the Rotation and Scale properties.

4 Click the disclosure triangle next to the Scale and Rotation properties to reveal the control handles and velocity graphs.

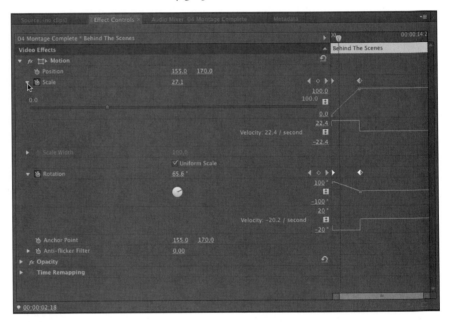

These make it easier to view the effects of keyframe interpolation. A straight line means essentially no change in speed or acceleration.

5 Right-click the first Scale keyframe and choose Ease Out since you are leaving the keyframe to begin the animation.

6 Repeat for the Rotation property's first keyframe. Use the Ease Out method.

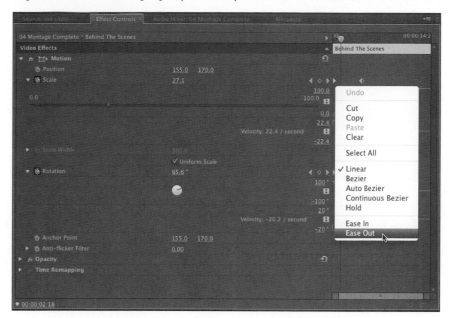

7 Look closely at the velocity graphs and see the changes in ramping.

8 For the next two keyframes, right-click and choose the Ease In method for both Scale and Rotation.

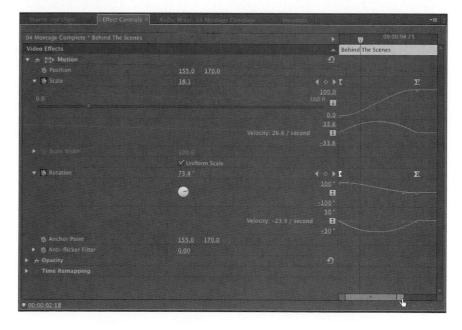

Tip: If you want to create inertia (such as a rocket lifting off), try using Ease. Right-click a keyframe, and choose Ease In or Ease Out (for approaching and leaving a keyframe, respectively).

9 Play back the sequence to see your animation.

10 Experiment by dragging the Bezier handles in the Effect Controls panel to see their effects on speed and ramping.

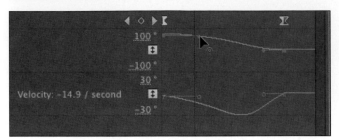

The steeper the curve you create, the sharper the animation's movement or speed increases. After experimenting, you can choose Edit > Undo if you don't like the changes.

Using other motion-related effects

Adobe Premiere Pro offers a handful of other effects for controlling motion. While the Motion effect is the most intuitive, you may find yourself wanting to enhance the effect. In this case, the use of a beveled edge or a drop shadow may come in handy. Additionally, the Transform and Basic 3D effects are useful for more control over an object (including 3D rotation).

Adding a drop shadow

A drop shadow creates perspective by adding a small shadow behind an object. This is often used to help create a sense of separation between elements. To add a drop shadow, follow these steps:

1 Continue working with the previous sequence or double-click to load 05 Enhance in the Project panel.

2 Open the Select Zoom Level menu in the Program Monitor, and change the zoom level to Fit.

3 Select the Behind The Scenes clip on track Video 6.

4   In the Effects panel, choose Video Effects > Perspective to drag a Drop Shadow effect onto the top clip.

5   Click the triangle next to the Motion effect in the Effect Controls panel to make it easier to see the Drop Shadow options.

6   Experiment with the Drop Shadow parameters in the Effect Controls panel as follows:

- Increase Distance to 15 so the shadow is further offset from the clip.
- Drag the Direction value to about 320° to see the shadow's angle change.
- Darken the shadow by changing Opacity to 85%.
- Set Softness to 25 to soften the edges of the shadow. Generally, the greater the Distance parameter, the more softness you should apply.

● **Note:** You want the shadow to fall away from any perceived light source. In this exercise, you set the light direction for bevel edges to about 320°. To make shadows fall away from a light source, add or subtract 180° from the light source direction to get the correct direction for the shadow to fall.

7   Play back the sequence to see your animation.

Adding a bevel

Another way to enhance the edges of a clip is to add a bevel. This type of effect is useful on a picture-in-picture effect or on text. Adobe Premiere Pro offers two bevels to choose from. The Bevel Edges effect is useful when the object is simply a standard video clip. The Bevel Alpha works better for text or logos, because it will detect the complex transparent areas within before applying the beveled edge.

Let's further enhance the type.

1 Continue working with the previous sequence 05 Enhance.

2 Select the Behind The Scenes clip on track Video 6.

3 Choose Video Effects > Perspective to drag a Bevel Alpha effect onto the top clip.

The edges of the text should appear slightly beveled.

● **Note:** The Bevel Edges effect produces slightly harder edges than the Bevel Alpha effect. Both effects work well on rectangular clips, but the Bevel Alpha is better suited for text or logos.

4 Increase Edge Thickness to 10 to make the edge more pronounced.

5 Increase Light Intensity to 0.8 to see a brighter edge effect.

The effect is looking pretty useful but is currently applied to both the text and the drop shadow. This is because the effect is below the drop shadow in the Effect Controls panel (stacking order matters).

6 Drag the effect above the Drop Shadow effect to change the rendering order.

7 Reduce the Edge Thickness amount to 8.

8 Examine the subtle differences in the bevel.

● **Note:** When applying multiple effects to a clip, if you're not getting the look you want, drag the order around and see whether that produces the desired result.

9 Play back the sequence to see your animation.

Transform

An alternative effect to the Motion operation is Transform. These two effects offer similar controls. There are three key differences between Transform and Motion. The Transform effect will process any changes to a clip's Anchor Point, Position, Scale, or Opacity settings before other Standard effects are rendered. This means that things like drop shadows and bevels will behave differently. The Transform effect also adds the skew and skew axis properties to create a visual angular transformation to clips. Lastly, the Transform effect is not a Mercury Engine accelerated effect, so it will take longer to process and does not offer as much real-time performance.

Let's compare the two effects by examining a prebuilt sequence.

1 In the Project panel, locate the sequence 06 Motion and Transform, and double-click to load it.

2 Play the sequence back and watch it a few times.

In both cases, a picture-in-picture is rotating twice over the background clip, while moving from left to right. Look carefully at the relationship of the shadow to each pair of clips.

- In the clips on the left, the shadow follows the bottom edge of the PIP and therefore appears on all four sides of the clip as it rotates, which obviously isn't realistic because the light source produces the shadow and it isn't moving.

- In the set on the right, the shadow stays on the lower right of the PIP, which is realistic.

3 Click the top clip of the set on the left, and view the effects applied in the Effect Controls panel: the Motion fixed effect and Drop Shadow effect.

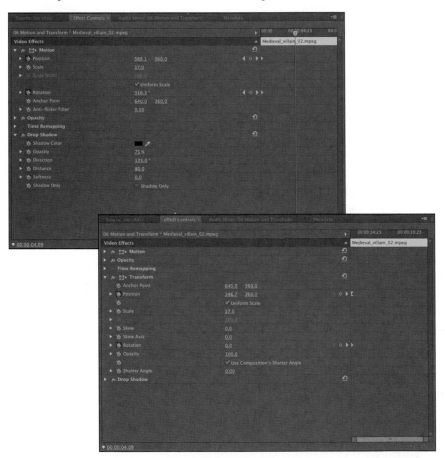

4 Now do the same for the pair on the right; you'll see that the Transform effect is producing the motion, with the Drop Shadow effect again producing the shadow.

In the screen comparison shown here, you can see that the Transform effect has many of the same capabilities as the Motion fixed effect but also adds Skew, Skew Axis, and Shutter Angle. As you just saw, the Transform effect also works more realistically with the Drop Shadow effect than the Motion fixed effects.

5 Observe the render bar above both sets of clips. If you have a Mercury Engine–compatible graphics card in your system, you'll note that the render bar is yellow on the left and red on the right.

This tells you that the Motion effect is GPU-accelerated, which makes previewing and rendering more efficient, while the Transform effect isn't.

Basic 3D

Another option for creating movement is the Basic 3D effect, which can be used to manipulate a clip in 3D space. Essentially, you can rotate the image around horizontal and vertical axes as well as move it toward or away from you. You'll also find an option to enable a *specular highlight*, which creates the appearance of light reflecting off a rotated surface.

Let's explore the effect by using a prebuilt sequence.

1 In the Project panel, locate the sequence 07 Basic 3D, and double-click to load it.

2 Drag the playhead over the sequence to quickly view the content.

The light that follows the motion, called a specular highlight, always comes from above, behind, and to the left of the viewer. Since the light comes from above, you won't see the effect until the image is tilted backward to catch the reflection. Specular highlights can be used to enhance the realism of the 3D effect.

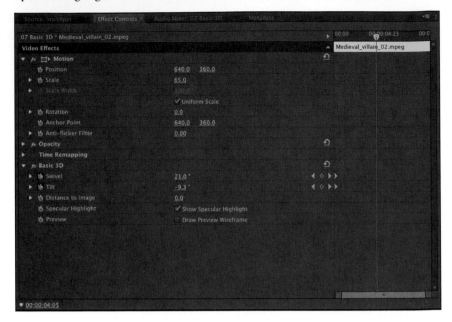

Four major properties are available to enhance the Basic 3D effect:

- **Swivel:** This controls the rotation around the vertical y-axis. If you rotate past 90°, the back side of the image is rendered, which is a mirror image of the front.

- **Tilt:** This controls the rotation around a horizontal x-axis. If you rotate beyond 90°, the back side will also be visible.

- **Distance To Image:** This moves the image along the z-axis and can simulate depth. As the distance value gets larger, the image moves further into the distance.

- **Specular Highlight:** This adds a glint of light that reflects off the surface of the rotated image, as though an overhead light were shining on the surface. This option is either on or off.

3 Experiment with the available options for the effect and modify any of the keyframes to see the impact of change.

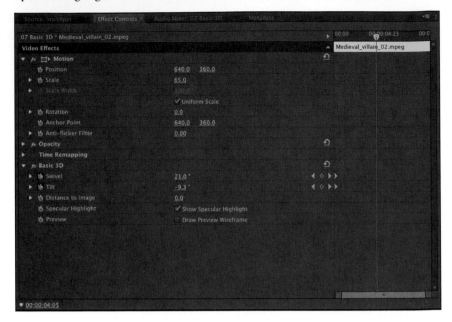
Note: Not only does Basic 3D provide GPU acceleration, but it can also swivel and tilt in both directions.

Review questions

1 Which Motion parameter will move a clip in the frame?

2 You want a clip to appear full-screen for a few seconds and then spin away. How do you make the Motion effect's Rotation feature start within a clip rather than at the beginning?

3 How can you start an object rotating gradually and have it stop rotating slowly?

4 If you want to add a drop shadow to a clip, why do you need to use some other motion-related effect besides the Motion fixed effect?

Review answers

1 The Motion parameter lets you set a new position for a clip. If keyframes are used, the effect can be animated.

2 Position the playhead where you want the rotation to begin, and click the Add/Remove Keyframe button. Then move to where you want the spinning to end, and change the Rotation parameter; another keyframe will appear.

3 Use the Ease Out and Ease In parameters to change the keyframe interpolation to be gradual rather than sudden.

4 The Motion fixed effect is the last effect applied to a clip. Motion takes whatever effects you apply before it (including Drop Shadow) and spins the entire assemblage as a single unit. To create a realistic drop shadow on a spinning object, use Transform or Basic 3D, and then place a Drop Shadow below one of those effects in the Effect Controls panel.

10 MULTICAMERA EDITING

Lesson overview

In this lesson, you'll learn about the following:

- Synchronizing clips based on sync points
- Adding clips to a sequence
- Creating a multicamera target sequence
- Switching between multiple cameras
- Recording a multicamera edit
- Finalizing a multicamera editing project

 This lesson will take approximately 45 minutes.

The process of multicamera editing begins with synchronizing multiple camera angles. You can do this using timecode or a common sync point (such as the closing of a clapboard or clapping of hands). Once your clips are synced, you can seamlessly cut between multiple angles in Adobe Premiere Pro CS6.

231

Getting started

In this lesson, you'll learn how to edit multiple angles of footage together that were shot simultaneously. Because the clips were shot at the same time, Adobe Premiere Pro CS6 makes it possible to cut seamlessly from one angle to another. The Adobe Premiere Pro multicamera editing feature is a tremendous timesaver when you're editing footage from a shoot or event captured with multiple cameras.

For this lesson, you'll use a new project that has already been started.

1   Start Adobe Premiere Pro, and open the project Lesson 10.prproj. If Adobe Premiere Pro can't locate the lesson file, refer to "Relink the lesson files" in the Getting Started section at the start of this book for two ways to search for and relink the file.

    This project has an empty sequence and four camera angles of a bike race.

2   Choose Window > Workspace > Editing.

    This changes the workspace to the preset that the Adobe Premiere Pro development team created to make it easier to edit footage.

3   Choose Window > Workspace > Reset Current Workspace to make sure the user interface is configured to the default settings. Click Yes to apply the change.

Who uses multicamera editing?

The use of multicamera editing has grown immensely in popularity as prices for high-quality cameras have continued to fall. There are many potential uses for a multicamera shoot and edit.

- **Visual and special effects:** Because of the expense associated with many special-effects shots, it is common practice to cover the shot with multiple angles. This means less cost associated with the staging of the shot and allows for greater flexibility during editing.

- **Action scenes:** For scenes that involve a lot of action, producers often use multiple cameras. Doing so can reduce the number of times that stunts or dangerous action needs to be performed.

- **Once-in-a-lifetime events:** Events such as weddings and sporting competitions rely heavily on multiple angles of coverage to ensure that the shooters capture all the critical elements of the event.

- **Musical and theatrical performances:** If you've watched a concert film, you're used to multiple camera angles being used to show the performance. The same style of editing can improve the pacing for theatrical performances as well.

- **Talk show formats:** Interview-driven segments will often cut between the interviewer and subject as well as a wide shot to show both subjects at the same time. Not only does this maintain visual interest, but it makes it easier to edit an interview to a shorter run time.

The multicamera process

The multicamera editing process has a very standardized workflow. It is essential that you follow the steps in order because of the complicated nature of the process. Once you have your footage loaded into Adobe Premiere Pro, there are really only six stages to complete.

1 **Load your footage:** To edit your footage, you need to load it into Adobe Premiere Pro. Ideally, the cameras will be closely matched in frame rate and frame size, but you can mix and match if needed.

2 **Determine your sync points:** The goal is to keep the multiple angles running in sync with each other so you can seamlessly switch between them. You will need to identify a point in time that exists in all angles to synchronize or use matching timecode.

3 **Create a multicamera source sequence:** The angles must be added to a specialized sequence type called a *multicamera source sequence*. This is essentially a specialized clip that contains multiple video angles.

4 **Create the multicamera target sequence:** The multicamera source sequence is added to a new sequence for editing. This new sequence is the *multicamera target sequence*.

5 **Record the multicamera edits:** A special panel, the Multi-Camera Monitor lets you switch between camera angles.

6 **Adjust and refine edits:** Once the edit is roughed out, you can refine the sequence with standard editing and trim commands.

Creating a multicamera sequence

● **Note:** For this lesson, we'll stick with four camera angles because of the limited space available on the book's DVD-ROM and downloadable files.

While Adobe Premiere Pro has supported multicamera editing for years, the feature got some big improvements in CS6. Previously, editors could use only four camera angles; Adobe has removed this limitation in Adobe Premiere Pro CS6. It is now possible to use many more angles; the only limiting factor is the computing power required to play back your selected clips. If your computer and hard drives are fast enough, then you should be able to play back several streams in real time.

Determining the sync points

To synchronize multiple angles of footage, you'll need to determine how you want to build the multicamera sequence. You can select from four methods to use for the sync references. The method you choose is a matter of personal choice as well as how the footage was shot.

- **Timecode:** Many professional cameras allow the timecode to be synchronized across multiple cameras. This can be performed by connecting multiple cameras to a common sync source or by carefully configuring the cameras and syncing the recording process. In many cases, the Hours number is offset to identify the camera number. For example, camera 1 would start at 1:00:00:00, and camera 2 would start at 2:00:00:00. You can choose to ignore the Hours number when syncing with timecode.

- **In points:** If you have a common starting point, you can set an In point on all clips you want to use. This method is effective as long as all cameras are rolling before the critical action starts.

- **Out points:** This method is similar to syncing with an In point but instead uses a common Out point. Out-point syncing is ideal when all cameras capture the ending of critical action (such as crossing the finish line) but the cameras were started at different times.

- **Clip markers:** In and Out points can be accidentally removed from a clip. If you'd like to mark a clip in a more robust fashion, you can use a marker to identify a common sync point. Markers are more difficult to accidentally remove from a clip.

Say you have four clips that recorded the same bike race from four different camera angles, but the four cameras started recording at different times. Your first task is to find the same point in time for all four clips so they will be in sync.

1. In the Project panel, click the triangle next to the bin Multicam Media to open it.

2. Double-click the clip MULTICAM_01.mov to load it into the Source Monitor panel.

3 Move the Source Monitor playhead to where the first woman claps her hands together (about 00:00:01:03).

These clips do not have audio, so use the visual clap as a reference.

4 Right-click in the Source Monitor, and choose Add Marker.

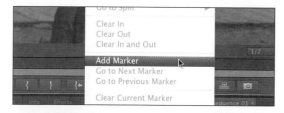

This adds a little small marker at the Source Monitor playhead.

5 Repeat the process and add a marker for the remaining three clips in a similar manner.

You can also press the M key to add a marker or click the Add Marker button.

● **Note:** All four multicamera clips were recorded at the same time, so using the hand clap near the start of the clips is a good way to sync them all up. Because they are at four different angles, you might have to look closely at some clips to see the exact frame where the hands touch.

Add clips to a multicamera source sequence

Once you have identified the clips you want to use as well as their common sync points, you can create a multicamera source sequence. This is a specialized type of sequence that is designed for multicamera editing. If you've used earlier versions of Premiere Pro, the process has changed a great deal and is much easier to create.

1 Select all of the master clips in the Multicam Media bin.

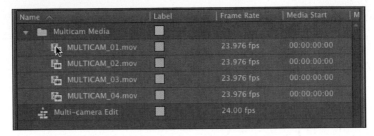

> ▶ **Tip:** The clip you click first in the bin when selecting angles will become the audio track that is used for the multicamera source sequence (even when changing angles). Another approach is to just place a dedicated audio recording on another track and sync it. A third option, Audio Follows Video, can be chosen from the Multi-Camera Monitor submenu (upper-right corner of panel) to sync the audio changes to the video.

2 Right-click one of the clips to open the context menu and choose "Create multi-camera source sequence."

You can also choose Clip > Create multi-camera source sequence. A new dialog opens asking how you want to create the multicamera source sequence.

3 Choose the Clip Marker method.

Since there is only one marker in each clip, you can use the default choice, which is Unnamed Marker 1.

4 Name the sequence *Synced Clips for Race*.

5 Click OK.

Adobe Premiere Pro adds a new multicamera source sequence to the bin.

6 Double-click the multicamera source sequence to load it into the Source Monitor panel.

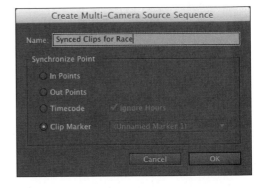

7 Drag the playhead through the clip to view the multiple angles.

● **Note:** Adobe Premiere Pro automatically adjusts the multicamera grid to accommodate the number of angles in use. For example, if you have up to 4 clips, you would see a 2x2 grid. If you used between 5 and 9 clips, you'd see a 3x3 grid; if you used 16 angles, the grid will be 4x4; and so on.

Some angles start in black because the cameras began recording at different times. The clips are displayed in a grid to show you all of the angles at once.

Create the multicamera target sequence

Once you've made the multicamera source sequence, you'll need to place it into another sequence. Essentially it will behave like a clip in your sequence. However, this clip has multiple angles of footage to choose from as you edit.

There are two ways to create a sequence that is ready to edit. The first method is to right-click the multicamera source sequence and choose New Sequence from Clip. The second method is to autoconform an existing sequence.

1 Locate the sequence Multi-camera Edit.

It should already be open. If not, double-click to open it in the Timeline panel.

2 Drag the newly created multicamera source sequence onto the Timeline.

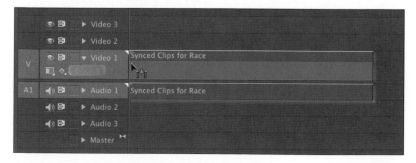

A new dialog opens to warn you about the clip mismatching the sequence settings. This dialog opens by default when you drag the first clip into a new sequence and the two do not have a matching frame size or rate.

3 Click the "Change sequence settings" button to make the two items match.

You now have a ready-to-use multicamera target sequence.

Using track targeting

When dragging clips from the Source Monitor to the Timeline, you target the track by dragging the clip to it. If you're adding clips to the Timeline by using the Source Monitor's Insert or Overlay button, you need to target your selected tracks or tell Adobe Premiere Pro which track or tracks you want the clip to go to.

You must do two things to target the track or tracks you want to be the destination. First, highlight (by selecting) the track or tracks you want to be the destination; then, target the track by dragging the source track indicator to the desired track. This may sound like a lot to do to target a single video or audio track, but this combination of tools can be very useful, such as when you have clips with multiple audio tracks attached.

Switching multiple cameras

Once you've properly built the multicamera source sequence and added it to a multicamera target sequence, you're ready to edit. This task is handled in real time using the Multi-Camera Monitor. You can switch between the different angles by clicking or by using a keyboard shortcut.

Enable recording

The editing of multiple camera angles is actually referred to as *recording*. In the Multi-Camera Monitor, your footage plays back in real time. As you choose the desired edits, the results are captured into your computer's memory. When you stop playback, the edits are applied to the open sequence.

1 Choose Window > Multi-Camera Monitor to open the Multi-Camera Monitor.

2 Make the window easier to see by maximizing its size. You can drag a corner of the panel to resize it or click the maximize button along the top edge.

3 Play back the footage once to get familiar with it. Press the spacebar to see all four angles play in real time.

4 When finished, press the up-arrow key to go to the start of the clip.

5 Familiarize yourself with the available keyboard shortcuts.

Press the 1 key to select Camera 1, press the 2 key to select Camera 2, and so on. The first nine angles are assigned to the keys 1–9 by default.

6 When you're ready to record, click the red Record button to start recording. You can also press the 0 key as a shortcut.

7 Press the spacebar to start the clip playing back.

8 Switch between the multiple camera angles based on your personal preference. Use the keyboard shortcuts 1–4 that correspond to the camera angle you want to switch to while recording.

9 When you reach the end of the recording, the light will turn off automatically.

Alternatively, you can click Stop at any time and then press 0 (zero) to toggle recording off. When you stop, the recorded edits are applied to the multicamera target sequence. The sequence now has multiple cut edits. Each clip's label starts with *[MC#]*. The number represents the video track used for that edit.

10 Click the Maximize button to return the Trim Monitor panel to normal size.

● **Note:** After making your edits, you can always change them in the Multi-Camera Monitor or on the Timeline.

Move it so you can see your Timeline.

11 Play back the sequence and review your edit.

Re-record multicamera edits

The first time you record a multicamera edit, you'll likely miss a few edits. Perhaps you cut too late (or too early) to an angle. You also may decide that you like one angle better than another.

1   Move the playhead to the start of the Timeline panel.

2. Press the Play button in the Multi-Camera Monitor to start playback.

    The angles in the Multi-Camera Monitor switch to match the existing edits in your Timeline.

3   When the playhead reaches the spot you want to change, switch the active camera.

You can press one of the keyboard shortcut keys (in this case 1–4) or click the desired camera's preview in the Multi-Camera Monitor.

4   When you're done editing, stop playback by pressing the spacebar.

    The Multi-Camera Monitor automatically stops recording.

Finalizing multicamera editing

Once you've performed a multicamera edit in the Multi-Camera Monitor, you can refine it and then finalize. The resulting sequence is like any other sequence you've built, so you can use any of the editing or trimming techniques you've learned so far. There are a few other specialized options available, however.

Switching an angle in the Multi-Camera Monitor

If you're happy with the timing of an edit but not the angle chosen, you can always swap the angle for another. One way to do this is to change an edit in the Multi-Camera Monitor.

1   If closed, open the Multi-Camera Monitor by choosing Window > Multi-Camera Monitor.

2   Click the Go To Previous (or Next) Edit Point button or use the Page Up or Page Down key to navigate between edit points.

The playhead will not move in the Timeline panel.

3   Click a different camera to change the corresponding edit.

4   When finished, close the Multi-Camera Monitor.

Changing an angle in the Timeline

If you're familiar with your camera angles, you can switch between them without ever opening the Multi-Camera Monitor. To change a multicamera edit in the Timeline, follow these steps:

1   Move the playhead over the clip you want to change to view it.

2   Right-click the clip in the Timeline panel that you want to change.

3   Choose Multi-Camera from the context menu, and choose the camera angle you want to use.

Additional multicamera editing tips

The skills of editing multicamera sources take time to build. You may find that this is a complex style of editing (especially as the number of angles increases). Here are a few additional helpful tips on multicamera editing in Adobe Premiere Pro:

- You can use any of the Timeline editing tools to change the edit points of a multicam sequence.

- You can replay the multicam sequence with the Multi-Camera Monitor from any point to reedit the project.

- If you don't have a good visual clue in the video to sync multiple clips, look for a clap or loud noise in the audio track. It's often easier to sync video by looking for a common spike in the audio waveform.

- Audio is taken by multicamera angle 1 by default. This is the first clip that you select in the bin; you can then Control+click (Windows) or Command-click (Mac OS) to select additional angles. You can change this by going to the Multi-camera submenu (in the upper-right corner of the panel) and choosing Audio Follows Video. Now the audio will change with each camera angle chosen.

Working with Multiple Audio Tracks

If you need audio to switch with each camera angle, follow these steps:

1 Double-click the multicamera source sequence in the Project panel to open it.

2 Click the visibility icon next to all of the audio tracks that you want active.

3 Close the multicamera source sequence.

4 Edit the multicamera source sequence into a sequence or select one that's already in use.

5 Select just the audio track by Alt-clicking (Windows) or Option-clicking (Mac) in the Timeline panel.

6 Choose Clip > Multi-Camera > Enable.

7 Open the Multi-Camera Monitor panel.

8 Click the submenu button in the upper-right corner of the Multi-Camera Monitor panel and choose the Audio Follows Video option.

9 Edit using the techniques you've learned in this chapter.

Review questions

1 Describe four ways to set sync points for multicamera clips.

2 Identify two ways to have the multicamera source and multicamera target sequences match settings.

3 Name two ways to switch between angles in the Multi-Camera Monitor.

4 How can you modify an angle after closing the Multi-Camera Monitor?

Review answers

1 The four ways are In points, Out points, timecode, and markers.

2 You can either right-click the multicamera source sequence and choose New Sequence from Clip or drag the multicamera source sequence into an empty sequence and let it auto-conform the settings.

3 To switch angles, you can either click the preview angle in the monitor or use the corresponding shortcut key (1–9) for each angle.

4 You can use any of the standard trimming tools in the Timeline to adjust the edit points for an angle. If you want to swap the angle, right-click it in the Timeline, choose Multi-Camera from the context menu, and choose the camera angle you want to use.

11 EDITING AND MIXING AUDIO

Lesson overview

In this lesson, you'll learn about the following:

- Working in the Audio workspace

- Understanding audio characteristics

- Adjusting clip audio volume

- Adjusting audio levels in a sequence

- Using the Audio Mixer

 This lesson will take approximately 50 minutes.

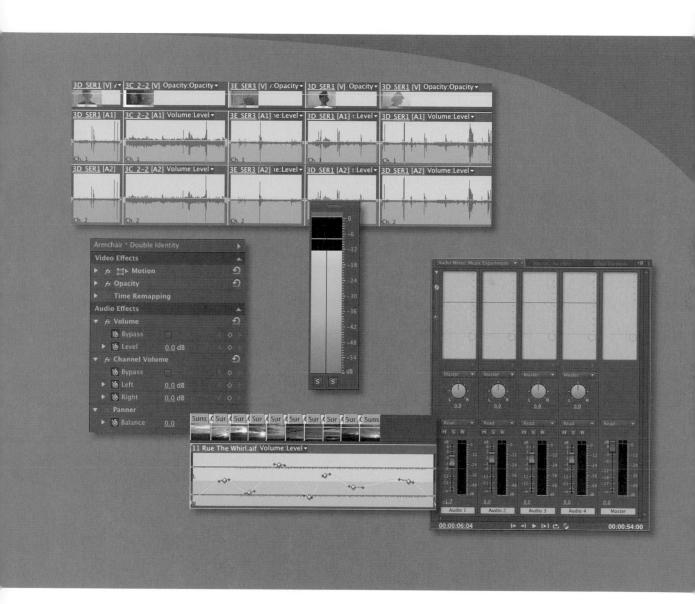

Until now, our focus has been primarily on working with visuals. No doubt about it, the pictures count, but professional editors generally agree that sound is at least as important as the images on the screen— sometimes more important!

In this lesson, you'll learn some audio mixing fundamentals, using the powerful tools provided by Adobe Premiere Pro CS6. Believe it or not, good sound can sometimes make the pictures look better.

Getting started

It's rare to have audio recorded on-camera that is perfect for your final output. There are several things you might want to do with sound in Adobe Premiere Pro:

- Tell Adobe Premiere Pro how to interpret recorded audio channels differently from the way they were recorded in-camera. For example, audio recorded as stereo can be interpreted as separate mono tracks.
- Clean up background sound. Whether it is system hum or the sound of an air-conditioning unit, there are tools for adjusting and tuning your audio.
- Adjust the volume of different audio frequencies in your clips (different tones) using EQ effects.
- Adjust the volume level on clips in the bin and on segments in your sequence. The adjustments you make on the Timeline can vary over time, creating a complete sound mix.
- Add music.
- Add spot effects, such as explosions, door slams, or atmospheric environmental sound.

Consider the difference it makes if you turn the sound off when watching a horror movie. Scenes that were scary a moment ago can look like comedy without an ominous soundtrack.

Music works around many of our intellectual critical faculties and directly influences our emotions. In fact, your body reacts to sound whether you want it to or not. For example, it's normal for your heart rate to be influenced by the beat of the music. Fast music will tend to raise your heart rate, and slow music will tend to lower your heart rate. Powerful stuff!

In this lesson, you'll begin by learning how to use the audio tools in Adobe Premiere Pro and then make adjustments to clips and a sequence. You'll also use the Audio Mixer to make changes to your sequence track volumes "on the fly," while your sequence plays.

Setting up the interface to work with audio

Adobe Premiere Pro gives access to most aspects of the interface via the Window menu. You could open each of the tools used for working with audio one by one by going to the menu and selecting them. But there's a quicker way.

1 Open Lesson 11.prproj. If Adobe Premiere Pro can't locate the lesson file, refer to "Relink the lesson files" in the Getting Started section at the start of this book for two ways to search for and relink the file.

2 Choose Window > Workspace > Audio.

3 Choose Window > Workspace > Reset Current Workspace.

4 Click Yes in the Reset Workspace dialog.

The Audio workspace

You'll recognize most of the components of the Audio workspace. One obvious difference is that the Audio Mixer is displayed in place of the Source Monitor. The Source Monitor is still in the frame; it's just hidden, grouped in the frame with the Audio Mixer.

You'll notice the audio meters have gone too. This is because the Audio Mixer has its own audio meter.

The Audio Mixer is a special part of the Adobe Premiere Pro interface. While the effects and controls you have used so far relate to clip segments in a sequence, the Audio Mixer makes changes to whole tracks. You can combine adjustments made using the Effect Controls panel and the Audio Mixer.

The other difference in the Audio workspace is simply a repositioning of the existing panels to allow you to focus on your sound.

Master track output

When you create a sequence, you define the number of audio channels it produces by choosing an audio Master setting. If your sequence were a media file, this is how many audio channels it would have:

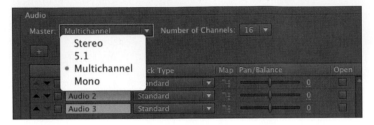

- **Stereo:** Outputs two audio channels: Left and Right.
- **5.1:** Outputs six audio channels: Middle, Front-Left, Front-Right, Rear-Left, Rear-Right, and Low Frequency Effects (LFE).
- **Multichannel:** Outputs between 1 channel and 16 audio channels—you can choose.
- **Mono:** Outputs one audio channel.

Once you have created a sequence, you cannot change the audio Master setting. This means, with the exception of multichannel sequences, you cannot change the number of channels your sequence will output.

You can add or remove audio tracks at any time, but the audio Master setting is fixed. If you need to change your audio Master setting, you can easily copy and paste clips from a sequence with one setting to a new sequence with a different setting.

What is an audio channel?

You could be forgiven for thinking that Left and Right audio channels were in some way identifiably different. In fact, they are both simply mono audio channels designated as Left or Right. When recording sound, it is the standard configuration to have Audio Channel 1 Left and Audio Channel 2 Right.

We know Audio Channel 1 is Left because of the following:

- It is recorded from a microphone pointing left.
- It is interpreted as Left in Adobe Premiere Pro.
- It is output to a speaker positioned on the left.

None of these factors changes the fact that it is still a single mono channel.

If you do the same for audio recorded from a microphone pointing right (but with Audio Channel 2), then you have stereo audio. It's really just two mono audio channels.

Audio meters

To use audio meters, do the following:

1 Choose Window > Audio Meters.

In the default Audio workspace, the audio meters are quite small. You'll need to make them bigger so you can work with them.

2 Drag the left edge of the panel a little to make them wider so you can see the buttons at the bottom of the panel. You'll keep them on-screen while going through this lesson.

The primary function of the audio meters is to give you an overall mix output volume for your sequence. As your sequence plays, you'll see the level meter dynamically change to reflect the volume.

About audio level

The scale on the audio meters is decibels, denoted by dB. The decibel scale is a little unusual in that the highest volume is designated as 0. Lower volumes become larger and larger negative numbers until they reach negative infinity.

If a recorded sound is too quiet, it might get lost in the background noise. Background noise might be environmental, such as an air-conditioning system making a hum. It also might be system noise, such as the quiet hiss you hear from your speakers when no sound is playing.

When you increase the overall volume of your audio in Adobe Premiere Pro, background noise gets louder too. When you decrease the overall volume, background noise gets quieter. This means it is often better to record audio at a higher level than you need and then reduce the volume later to remove (or almost remove) the background noise.

Depending on your audio hardware, you may have a different signal-to-noise ratio, that is, a bigger or smaller difference between the sound you want to hear (the signal) and the sound you don't want to hear (the system noise). Signal-to-noise ratio is often shown as SNR, measured in dB.

If you right-click the audio meters, you can choose a different display scale. The default is a range from 0dB to −60dB.

You can also choose between static and dynamic peaks: When you get a loud "spike" in audio levels that makes you glance at the meters, the sound is gone by the time you look. With static peaks, the highest peak is marked and maintained in the meters so you can see what the loudest level was in that playback segment up to that point. You can click the audio meters to reset the peak. With dynamic peaks, the peak level will continually update.

Smoothing volume between keyframes

Those adjustments are pretty dramatic. You might want to smooth the adjustments over time, and this is easy to do.

Right-click any of your keyframes.

You'll see a range of standard options, including Ease In, Ease Out, and Delete. If you use the Pen tool, you can lasso multiple keyframes and then right-click any one of them to apply a change to them all.

> ✓ Linear
> Bezier
> Auto Bezier
> Continuous Bezier
> Hold
>
> Ease In
> Ease Out
>
> Delete

The best way to learn about the different kinds of keyframe is to select each kind, make some adjustments, and see the results. In the following example, all of the keyframes have been set to Continuous Bezier, which maintains the same curved line into the keyframe and out.

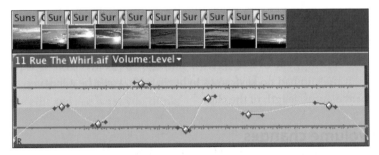

Track vs. clip keyframes

Until now, all of your adjustments have been made to clip segments. Adobe Premiere Pro has similar controls available for whole tracks. The track-based keyframes work in the same way as the clip-based ones. Of course, the difference is that they don't move with the clips.

● **Note:** Adjustments you make to your clips are applied before adjustments you make to your tracks.

This means you can set up keyframes for your audio level using track controls and then try different music tracks. Each time you put new music into your sequence, you'll hear it through the adjustments you have made to your track.

To switch to working with track keyframes rather than clip keyframes, do the following:

1 Select the Sunset Montage sequence in the Sequences bin, right-click it, and choose Duplicate. It's a good idea to try new things on a copy of your sequence, rather than risking making unwanted changes to the original.

2 Rename the copy to Music Experiment.

3 Open the new sequence, Music Experiment.

4 With the Selection tool, select the music clip 11 Rue The Whirl.aif, and delete it.

5 Use the Audio 1 Show Keyframes button menu to choose Show Track Volume. You don't need Show Track Keyframes, because you're working with just volume (rather than lots of effects).

6 Lower the overall volume for the track by dragging the track rubber band down, and then add a series of keyframes so you can hear the results when you add some music. In practice, you would set keyframes so that the music dips under voice-over or live-action speech.

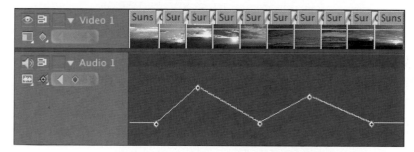

7 Drag the 11 Rue The Whirl.aif clip straight from the Music bin to the Audio 1 track. Position the clip at the start of the sequence. Play your sequence. You'll hear the results of the music, combined with the track keyframes.

8 Undo to remove the music, and add the clip 06 Departure From Cairo.aif from the Cairo Music bin instead. Play the sequence, and once again, you can hear the results of your keyframes.

This powerful approach to using keyframes on the Timeline might take a little planning to make the most of it, but it's worth the effort! It allows you to try lots of different music tracks before you settle on the one you want.

▶ **Tip:** Be sure to switch back to clip keyframes to continue working on your sequence. While viewing track keyframes, you can't select your clips.

Working with the Audio Mixer

While the Effect Controls panel gives you control over clip segments in sequences, the Audio Mixer provides control over tracks. The keyframes you have just added to your Music Experiment sequence are the kind the Audio Mixer adds and can respond to.

Overview of the Audio Mixer

The Audio Mixer is broadly divided into three parts.

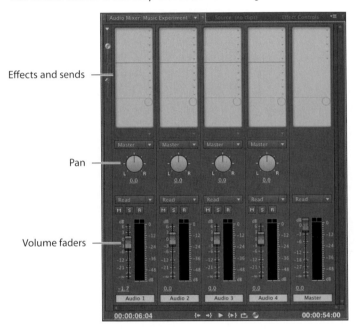

- **Effects and sends:** You can use drop-down menus here to add special effects to a whole track or send the audio from the track to a submix.

- **Pan:** This is just like the Pan control in the Effect Controls panel. However, the adjustments you make here apply to the whole track.

- **Volume faders:** These are industry-standard controls, based on real-world audio mixing desks. You move the fader up to increase the volume and move it down to decrease the volume. You can also use the volume faders to add keyframes to your track audio rubber band while you play the sequence (see "Understanding automation modes" later in this chapter).

What is a submix?

Submixes act as conduits for audio tracks. Audio tracks usually send their audio to the Master output directly.

You can, instead, configure multiple audio tracks to send their audio to a submix. This allows you to use one set of controls (the submix) to adjust things like volume and pan, or to apply one special effect, for multiple tracks.

The submix sends its audio to the Master output, just as a regular track does. The main difference is that you can't put any audio clips into a submix track; they exist only to combine the outputs from multiple tracks.

For example, imagine you have recorded audio for five people in a darkened room, and you want it to sound like a cavern, with a strong reverb. Each original audio source is on its own track in the sequence.

One option would be to put the reverb special effect on each track. This would work, but it would be a lot of work for your system to play back, and it would require a lot of clicks if you wanted to change the effect—you'd have to make each adjustment five times.

If, instead, you send the output from each of the five tracks to a single submix, you can apply the reverb effect to that submix. You'll hear the five tracks via the submix, so you need to adjust only one effect, and your system will need to calculate only one effect, instead of five.

Understanding automation modes

Using the Audio Mixer, you can add new keyframes to your audio tracks while your sequence plays. This way, you can create an audio mix "live." Simply play your sequence and adjust the volumes for tracks using the Audio Mixer.

Adobe Premiere Pro needs to know how you would like the Audio Mixer fader control to interact with existing keyframes. You just need to choose the right automation mode before you begin.

Here's what each mode means:

```
  Off
  Read
  Latch
• Touch
  Write
```

- **Off:** In this mode, the fader will ignore any keyframes and remain exactly where it is. You can make any changes you like to the fader, and it will affect the playback volume for the whole track.

- **Read:** In this mode, the fader follows existing keyframes, dynamically changing the playback volume for the track. You cannot add keyframes using the fader in this mode.

- **Latch:** In this mode, the fader will follow existing keyframes, but if you grab the fader and make adjustments, new keyframes will be applied to the track, replacing existing ones. When you release the fader, it stays where you put it, so if the sequence keeps playing, a new "flat" level adjustment is made to the track, continuing to replace existing keyframes until you stop playback.

- **Touch:** In this mode, the fader will follow existing keyframes, but if you grab the fade and make adjustments, new keyframes will be applied to the track, replacing existing ones. When you release the fader, it returns to following existing keyframes.

- **Write:** In this mode, the fader does not follow existing keyframes at all. As you play the sequence, new keyframes are created based on the position of the fader, replacing existing ones. When you release the fader, as in Latch mode, it will stay where you leave it, adding a flat level adjustment until you stop playback.

Try this for yourself:

1 Use the Music Experiment sequence you created earlier. Make sure the Audio 1 track is set to display track keyframes or track volume. Either is fine because the default keyframe type is Audio volume.

2 Position the Timeline playhead at the beginning of the sequence.

3 Using the Audio Mixer, set the automation mode for the Audio 1 to Touch.

● **Note:** You will not see new keyframes until you stop playback.

4 Play the sequence and, while it plays, make some adjustments to the Audio 1 fader. When you stop playback, you'll see the new keyframes that you added.

5 Try each of the other automation modes to compare the results.

You can adjust keyframes you create this way just as you would adjust keyframes created using the Selection tool or the Pen tool.

▶ **Tip:** You can adjust Pan in the same way as you would adjust volume using the Audio Mixer. Simply play your sequence and make adjustments using the Audio Mixer's Pan control.

Producing a 5.1 mix with Adobe Audition

The advanced audio features in Adobe Premiere Pro include support for 5.1 audio. You can even work with 5.1 audio clips and master to 5.1 audio. However, Adobe Audition has a dedicated surround sound mixer that makes 5.1 mixes amazingly fast and easy.

If you plan to use surround sound in your sequence, consider completing your video edit in Adobe Premiere Pro and switching to Adobe Audition for your mix.

Review questions

1 How can you solo an individual audio channel while playing a clip in the Source Monitor to hear only that channel?

2 What is the difference between mono and stereo audio?

3 How can you view the waveforms for any clip that has audio in the Source Monitor?

4 What is the difference between normalization and gain?

5 What is the difference between a J-cut and an L-cut?

6 Does the Audio Mixer add keyframes to clip segments or tracks?

Review answers

1 Use the Solo buttons at the bottom of the audio meters to selectively hear an audio channel for clips in the Source Monitor.

2 Stereo audio has two audio channels, and mono audio has one. It is the universal standard to record audio from a Left microphone as channel 1 and audio from a Right microphone as channel 2 when recording stereo sound.

3 Use the Settings button menu on the Source Monitor to choose Audio Waveform. You can do the same with the Program Monitor, but you probably won't need to; clips can display waveforms on the Timeline.

4 Normalization automatically adjusts the gain setting for a clip based on the original volume. You can use the Gain setting to make manual adjustments.

5 The sound for the next clip begins before the visuals when using a J-cut. With L-cuts, the sound from the previous clip remains until after the visuals begin.

6 The Audio Mixer works exclusively with tracks, never clips. When you add keyframes using the Audio Mixer, you will not be able to see them (though they will still have an effect) unless you set your audio track to Show Track Keyframes.

12 SWEETENING SOUND

Lesson overview

In this lesson, you'll learn about the following:

- Sweetening sound with audio effects
- Adjusting equalization (EQ)
- Applying effects in the Audio Mixer
- Cleaning up noisy audio

 This lesson will take approximately 60 minutes.

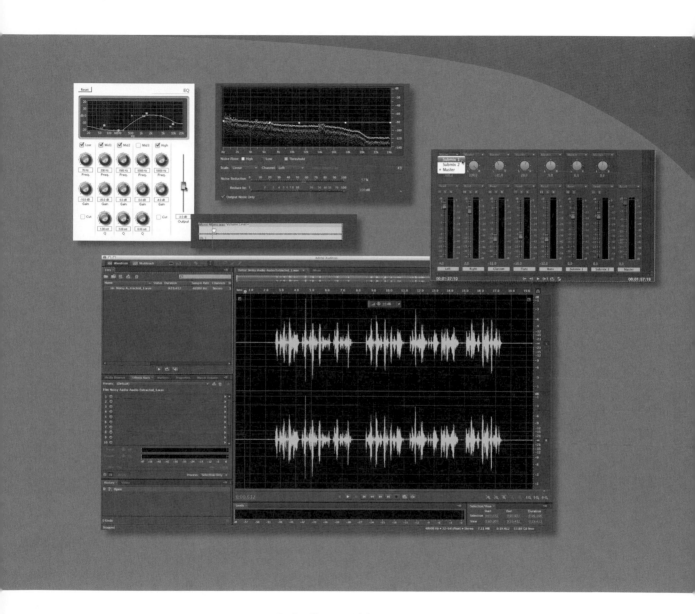

Audio effects in Adobe Premiere Pro CS6 can dramatically change the feel of your project. To take your sound to a higher level, leverage the integration and power of Adobe Audition CS6.

Getting started

You'll find more than 30 audio effects in Adobe Premiere Pro CS6. These effects can be used to change pitch, create echoes, add reverb, and remove tape hiss. All of the effects can have keyframes set as well as have their parameters adjusted over time.

Additionally, you can use the Audio Mixer to blend and adjust the sounds from all the audio tracks in your project. You can also combine multiple audio tracks into a single submix and apply effects, panning, or volume changes to those groups as well as to individual tracks.

For this lesson, you'll use a new project file.

1 Start Adobe Premiere Pro, and open the project Lesson 12.prproj.

The sequence 01 Effects should already be open.

2 Choose Window > Workspace > Audio.

This changes the workspace to the preset that the Adobe Premiere Pro development team created to make it easier to work with audio editing.

3 Choose Window > Workspace > Reset Current Workspace, and click Yes in the dialog that opens.

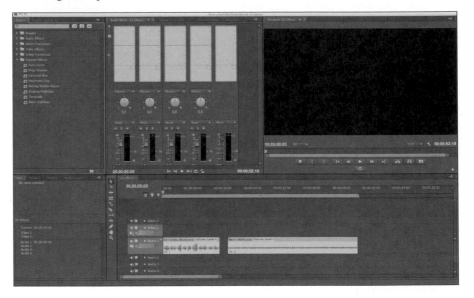

Sweetening sound with audio effects

Ideally, your audio will come in perfectly. Unfortunately, video production is rarely a process filled with ideals. At some point, you'll need to turn to audio effects to fix problems. In this lesson, you'll try a few of the most useful effects in Adobe Premiere Pro.

These can be used for a variety of tasks including the following:

- **DeNoiser**: This audio effect can detect and remove hiss or noise automatically.

- **Reverb**: This can increase the "presence" in the recording with reverb. Use it to simulate the sound of a larger room.

- **Delay**: This effect can add a slight (or pronounced) echo to your audio track.

- **Bass**: This effect can increase the low-end frequencies of an audio clip. It works well on narration clips, particularly for male voices.

- **Treble**: This adjusts the higher-range frequencies in an audio clip.

● **Note:** Be sure to expand your knowledge about audio effects in Adobe Premiere Pro. You are wise to experiment with different effects, because they are nondestructive. This means they do not change the original audio clip. You can add any number of effects to a single clip, change parameters, and then delete those effects and start over.

Adjusting bass

Adjusting the amplitude of the lower frequencies can improve the overall sound for a male voice. In this example, let's modify an announcer's voice.

1 Play back the first clip in the 01 Effects sequence to get familiar with its sound.

2 Click the Effects panel to make it active.

3 Open the Audio Effects folder in the Effects panel.

4 Drag the Bass effect to the Ad Cliches Mono.wav clip.

5 Open the Effect Controls panel.

6 Increase the Boost property to add more bass.

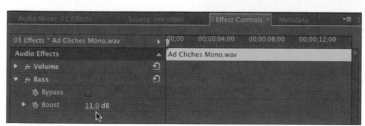

Experiment using different values to increase or decrease the presence of bass until you hear a sound you like. Be sure to pay attention to your overall audio levels because adjustments can change the volume of the clip. You may need to use the Audio Mixer panel to maintain proper levels.

Adding a delay

The use of a delay is a stylized effect. It can be used on an announcer's voice to add drama or used to create a feeling of space using stylized echoes.

1   In the Audio Effects folder in the Effects panel, locate the Delay effect.

2   Drag the Delay effect onto the Ad Cliches Mono.wav clip.

3   Play the clip back to hear the Delay effect. Currently, there is an echo that is offset by one second.

4   Experiment by adjusting these three parameters:

    • **Delay**: This refers to the time before the echo plays (zero to two seconds).

    • **Feedback**: This is the percentage of echo added back to audio to create echoes of echoes.

    • **Mix**: This is the relative loudness of echo.

5   Play the clip to hear the impact of each adjustment.

6   Enter the following values to get a classic stadium announcer effect.

    • **Delay**: .250 seconds

    • **Feedback**: 20%

    • **Mix**: 10%

7   Play the clip, and move the sliders to experiment with the effect.

    Lower values are more palatable, even with this over-the-top audio clip. Remember that less is more. Generally speaking, a subtle effect is more pleasant to the listener.

Adjusting pitch

Another adjustment you can make is pitch. This is a useful way to change the overall degree of a tone for a sound produced by the voice. By modifying pitch, you can change the energy level, apparent age, or even species of a speaker.

1   In the Audio Effects folder in the Effects panel, locate the PitchShifter effect.

2   Drag the PitchShifter effect onto the Ad Cliches Mono.wav clip.

3   In the Effect Controls panel, click the disclosure triangle for the Custom Setup properties to show the parameters for the effect.

This panel includes three items: knobs, presets, and a Reset button. You can tell an audio effect has presets by the tiny triangle next to what would normally be the Reset button and the addition of a rectangular Reset button (as shown here).

4 Try some of the presets, and note their values below the knobs in the Effect Controls panel.

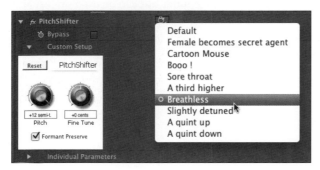

5 Use the Individual Parameters sliders to tweak the sound. Experiment by using wildly different pitch settings from −12 to +12 semitone steps, and switching Formant Preserve on and off.

Adjusting treble

Earlier you applied and adjusted the Bass effect to modify the lower frequencies of an audio track. If you'd like to modify the opposite range, use the Treble effect. Treble is not simply the Bass effect in reverse. Treble increases or decreases higher frequencies (4,000 Hz and greater), while the Bass effect changes low frequencies (200 Hz and less). The human-audible frequency range is roughly 20 Hz to 20,000 Hz.

1 Drag the playhead so it is over the second clip in the Timeline panel (Music Mono).

2 Play the second clip to get familiar with its sound.

3 In the Audio Effects folder in the Effects panel, locate the Treble effect.

4   Drag the Treble effect onto the Music Mono clip.

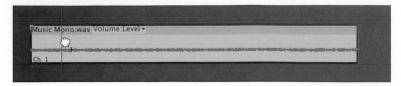

5   Increase the Boost property to add more treble.

Experiment using different values to increase or decrease the presence of treble until you hear a sound you like.

Adding reverb

Reverb is similar to the Delay effect but is better suited to musical tracks, and it can simulate how a sound would be perceived in different types of rooms. It works particularly well for pieces that feature strong guitar but can be used on just about any clip that you like. It is a powerful effect that can give some real life to audio recorded in an acoustically flat room—a room such as a recording studio with minimal reflective surfaces.

1   In the Audio Effects folder in the Effects panel, locate the Reverb effect.

2   Drag the Reverb effect onto the Music Mono clip.

3   In the Effect Controls panel, open Reverb's Custom Setup.

4   If necessary, click the Show/Hide Timeline View button to make more room for the graphic interface.

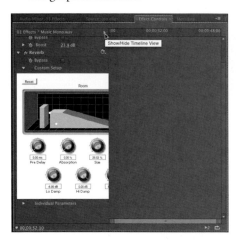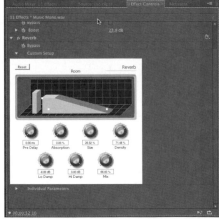

5 Click the Presets button, and try some of the presets.

Note their values below the knobs in the Effect Controls panel.

6 Experiment with the seven control knobs.

- **Pre Delay**: This is the apparent distance the sound travels to the reflecting walls and back.

- **Absorption**: This assesses how much of the sound is absorbed (not reflected).

- **Size**: This refers to the apparent relative size of the room.

- **Density**: This is the density of the reverb "tail." The greater the Size value, the greater the Density range (from 0% to 100%).

- **Lo Damp**: This dampens low frequencies to prevent the reverb from rumbling or sounding muddy.

- **Hi Damp**: This dampens high frequencies. A lesser Hi Damp setting makes the reverb sound softer.

- **Mix**: This is the amount of reverb.

▶ **Tip:** The Reverb effect is a Virtual Studio Technology (VST) plug-in. These are custom-designed audio effects that adhere to a standard set by Steinberg audio. Invariably, those who create VST audio effect plug-ins want them to have a unique look and offer some very specialized audio effects. Many VST plug-ins are available on the Internet.

Adjusting EQ

If you have a good amplifier or car stereo, it probably features a graphic equalizer. The EQ controls go beyond simple Bass and Treble knobs and add multiple sliders (often called *bands*) for greater control over the sound. There are two kinds of equalization effects in Adobe Premiere Pro: an EQ effect (with five bands) and the Parametric EQ effect, which offers a single band (but can be combined multiple times).

Standard EQ

● **Note:** In the next exercise, use the suggested numbers for guidance. Feel free to experiment with values, however, because your taste and speakers may vary.

The EQ effect in Adobe Premiere Pro is similar to a traditional three-way EQ (which controls lows, mids, and highs). This effect, however, offers three midfrequency controls for even greater accuracy. This is a useful effect to smooth out a sound and emphasize (or deemphasize) part of a track.

1 In the Project panel, locate the sequence 02 EQ and open it.

   This sequence contains one musical track.

2 Locate the EQ effect in the Effects panel (try using the search field at the top of the window), and drag it onto the clip.

3 In the Effect Controls panel, click the triangle next to the Custom Setup section of the EQ effect.

   You may need to adjust the size of the window or scroll to see all the controls at once.

4 Play the clip to get familiar with its sound.

5 Select the check box to activate the Low frequency filter.

6 Set the Low frequency to 70 Hz to change the affected area, and lower the gain to –10.0 dB. This decreases the intensity of the Bass area.

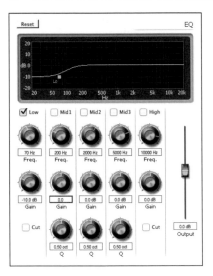

7 Play the sequence to hear the changes.

   Let's refine the vocals.

8 Select the check box to activate the Mid1 frequency filter.

9 Set its gain to −20.0 dB and adjust the Q factor to 1.0 for more transition on the EQ adjustment.

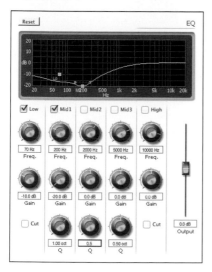

10 Play back the sequence to hear the changes.

11 Select the check box to activate the Mid2 frequency filter.

12 Set its frequency to 1500 Hz and its gain to 6.0 dB. Adjust the Q factor to 3.0 for more transition on the EQ adjustment.

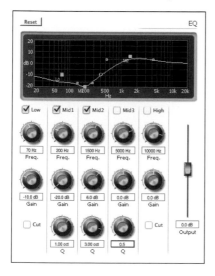

13 Play back the sequence to hear the changes.

14 Select the check box to activate the High frequency filter, and set its gain to −8.0 dB to lower the highest frequencies.

The overall volume is too high, and the audio meters show that the level for your file is too loud.

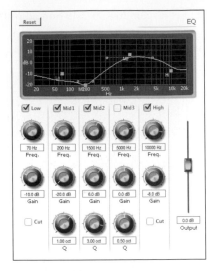

● **Note:** Avoid setting the volume too high (the VU meter line will turn red). That leads to distortion.

15 Lower the Output slider for the effect to approximately −3.0 dB.

16 Play the sequence to hear the changes.

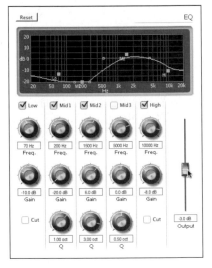

Parametric EQ

▶ **Tip:** Another way to use the Parametric EQ effect is to target a specific frequency and either boost it or cut it. You can use this effect to cut a particular frequency, like a high-frequency noise or a low hum.

If you want the ability to go beyond five frequency ranges, then the Parametric EQ may meet your needs. Although you can select only one frequency range with the Parametric EQ, you can use it multiple times and select multiple frequencies. This lets you build as complex an equalizer as you need within the Effect Controls panel.

1 In the Project panel, locate the sequence 03 Parametric EQ and open it.

This sequence contains one musical track and already has the Parametric EQ effect applied seven times. Each effect is currently disabled by the use of the Bypass check box.

2 Play the clip to get familiar with its sound.

There are seven effects applied that affect the audio. They are arranged from low frequencies (top of list) to high frequencies (bottom of list).

3 Deselect the first Bypass check box.

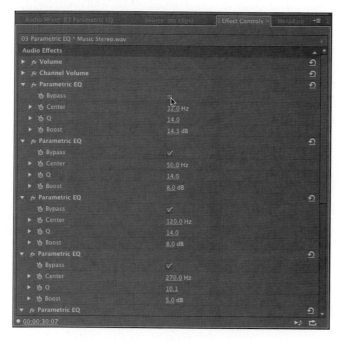

4 Play the sequence to hear the changes.

5 Continue deselecting the Bypass check boxes one at a time, and listen to the change in the audio track after each deselection.

Applying effects in the Audio Mixer

When you work with audio tracks, you may become overwhelmed. Every clip on every track will play together at the same time. In the previous lesson, you learned how to use the Audio Mixer panel to start mixing the volume of your tracks so they played in a unified and intelligible manner. You also may recall learning about submixes.

● **Note:** Listing all the attributes of all the audio effects is beyond the scope of this book. To learn more about audio effect parameters, search Adobe Premiere Pro Help.

Creating an initial mix

A submix essentially lets you control the volume and other characteristics for multiple audio tracks at once. While you can adjust volume levels by using each clip's volume graph in the Timeline or Volume effect in the Effect Controls panel, it's much easier to use the Audio Mixer to adjust volume levels and other characteristics for your initial mix.

Using a panel that looks a lot like a production studio's mixing hardware, you move track sliders to change volume, turn knobs to set left/right panning, add effects to entire tracks, and create submixes. Submixes let you direct multiple audio tracks to a single track so you can apply the same effects, volume, and panning to a group of tracks without having to change each of the tracks individually.

In this exercise, you will mix a song recorded by a choir in a studio:

1 Double-click Music Sonoma Stereo Mix (in the Media Bin), and play it in the Source Monitor. This is how your final mix should sound.

2 In the Project panel, locate the sequence 04 Submixes, and double-click to load it.

3 Play the 04 Submixes sequence, and note that the instruments are way too loud compared to the choir.

4 Select and adjust the Audio Mixer panel so you can see all five tracks plus the master track. You'll want to leave extra room for two more tracks. You can resize a panel by dragging on the bar in between the panels or the corner handle.

5 Change the track names along the bottom row of the Audio Mixer by selecting each one in turn and typing a new name: *Left, Right, Clarinet, Flute,* and *Bass* (as shown here).

Those name changes also appear in the audio track headers in the sequence.

6 Play the sequence, and adjust the sliders in the Audio Mixer to create a mix that you think works well.

A good place to start is setting Left to +4, setting Right to +2, and dropping the Clarinet, Flute, and Bass to –12, –10, and –12, respectively.

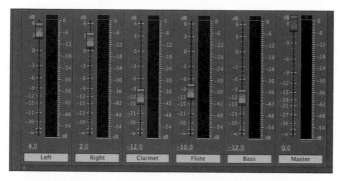

7 Watch the master track VU (volume unit) meter as you make your adjustments.

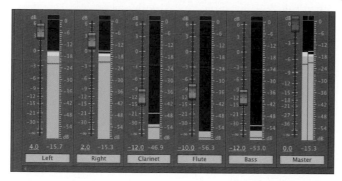

Little hash marks that float above the volume meters indicate the loudest passages. When you've set the audio meters to Dynamic Peaks (the default setting), they remain for a couple of seconds and then move as the music volume changes. These hash marks provide a good way to see how balanced your left and right channels are. You want them to approximately line up most of the time. If you want to change to Static Peaks, right-click the audio meters and choose this option. Now peaks will hold for the entire duration of playback.

8 Adjust each channel's Left/Right Pan by using the knobs at the top of each track (when completed, your parameters should match those shown here):

- **Left**: All the way left (−100)

- **Right**: All the way right (+100)

- **Clarinet**: Left-center (−20)

- **Flute**: Right-center (+20)

- **Bass**: Centered (0)

Creating a submix

As you place your audio clips into audio tracks on the Timeline, you can choose to apply effects and set volume and panning on a clip-by-clip basis. As you did earlier, you can also use the Audio Mixer to apply volume, panning, and effects to entire tracks. In either case, by default Adobe Premiere Pro sends audio from those clips and tracks to the master track.

But sometimes you might want to route tracks to submix tracks before sending them onto the master track. The purpose of submix tracks is to save you steps and ensure some consistency in how you apply effects, volume, and panning. In the case of the Sonoma recording, you can apply Reverb with one set of parameters to the two choir tracks, and you can apply Reverb with different parameters to the three instruments. The submix can then send the processed signal to the master track, or it can route the signal to another submix.

1 Continue working with the sequence 04 Submixes from the previous exercise.

2 Right-click an audio track header in the Timeline, and using the figure shown here as a guide, choose Add Tracks.

3 Set the Add values for Video Tracks and Audio Tracks to 0, set the Add value for Audio Submix Tracks to 2, and set Track Type for Audio Submix Tracks to Stereo; then click OK.

That adds two submix tracks to the Timeline and two tracks to the Audio Mixer (they have a darker hue), and it adds those submix track names (Submix 1 and Submix 2) to the pop-up menus at the bottom of the Audio Mixer.

4 Adjust the size of the Audio Mixer panel (if needed) to see all of its controls.

5 Click the Left track's Track Output Assignment pop-up menu (at the bottom of the Audio Mixer), and select Submix 1.

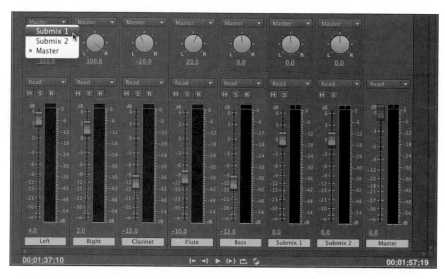

6 Do the same for the Right track.

Now both the Left and Right tracks have been sent to Submix 1. Their individual characteristics—panning and volume—will not change.

7 Send the three instrument tracks to Submix 2.

Applying effects to a submix

Now that the tracks are properly patched, you can adjust them using the two sub-mixes. Let's use the Reverb effect you explored earlier in this lesson.

1 If necessary, click the Show/Hide Effects and Sends disclosure triangle at the top of the Audio Mixer panel.

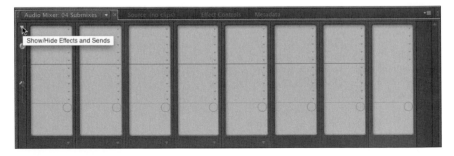

2 Click the Solo button for the Submix 1 Track.

3 Click the Effect Selection button for the Submix 1 track (the little drop-down list to the right of the panel), and choose Reverb from the pop-up menu.

4 Adjust the Reverb parameters to make it sound like the choir is singing in a large auditorium. Click the menu at the bottom (currently labeled PreDelay). Switch to Size, and set it to about 60. This is a good place to start.

5 Apply Reverb to the Submix 2 track.

6 Click the Solo Track button for Submix 2, and disable the Solo switch for Submix 1.

7 Apply a Reverb effect to Submix 2, and adjust to your personal taste. Try to set its parameters to create a sound a bit less dramatic than the voices.

8 Click the Solo button on Submix 2 to disable it.

9 Play the track, and listen to these two submixes as a single mix to hear how they sound.

10 Feel free to tweak the Volume and Reverb settings.

11 Play your sequence to review your overall mix.

▶ **Tip:** After working in the Audio Mixer for a while and then returning to the Timeline, you might not hear anything. Audio Mixer Mute and Solo settings do not show up in the Timeline but are still in effect when you play a clip in the Timeline, even if the Audio Mixer is closed. So, check those Mute and Solo settings before shutting down the Audio Mixer.

Cleaning up noisy audio

Of course, it's always best to record perfect audio at the source. However, some-times you cannot control the origin of the audio and it's impossible to re-record it, so you are stuck needing to repair a bad audio clip. You'll find versatile tools in Adobe Premiere Pro for fixing common audio problems.

Highpass and Lowpass effects

The Highpass and Lowpass effects often work to improve a clip, used together or independently. The Highpass effect is used to remove all frequencies that fall below a certain frequency (think of it as letting all things higher than the threshold pass through). The Lowpass filter is the direct opposite. It eliminates all frequencies above the specified Cutoff frequency. The Highpass and Lowpass effects are avail-able for 5.1, stereo, or mono clips.

1   In the Project panel, locate the sequence 05 Noisy Reduction, and double-click to load it.

2   Play back the sequence to get familiar with the sound quality.

3   In the Effects panel, locate the Highpass effect, and drag it onto the clip.

4   Play your sequence.

It probably sounds overly processed because the threshold is set too high.

5   In the Effect Controls panel, adjust the Cutoff slider to a lower value.

You can play back the clip and make adjustments at the same time to hear the adjustment being applied in real time. Adjust the value to minimize some of the lower-frequency noise in the background. A value near 200.0 Hz works well.

6   In the Effects panel, locate the Lowpass effect, and drag it onto the clip.

7   Adjust the Cutoff slider for the Lowpass effect.

Experiment with different values to familiarize yourself with how the two effects interplay. It is possible to remove all noise by setting the two effects to overlapping values. Pull down some of the higher frequencies that are making the recording sound "tinny."

Notch effect

The Notch effect is useful for removing all frequencies that are near a specified value. The effect essentially targets a frequency range and then eliminates those sounds. The effect works well for removing power-line hum and other electrical interference. In this clip, you can hear the sounds of fluorescent light bulbs buzzing overhead.

Note: A 60 Hz or 50 Hz hum can be caused by many electrical problems, cable problems, or equipment noise. The frequency varies because of the different electrical systems used around the world.

1 Continue working with the sequence 05 Noisy Reduction.

2 Click the Bypass option for both the Highpass and Lowpass effects to temporarily disable them.

3 Play back the sequence and listen for the electrical hum. You may need to turn up your speakers.

4 In the Effects panel, locate the Notch Effect and apply it to your clip. Drag the filter to the top of the stack so it is applied first.

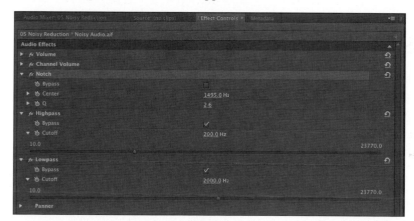

5 Adjust the Center slider to target the frequency to be removed.

Power-line hum tends to be either 50 Hz or 60 Hz.

6 Adjust the Q slider to affect the range being processed by the effect.

A low setting creates a narrow band; a high setting creates a wide band.

While this is helping a bit, let's take a more aggressive approach to the repair.

Dynamics

Another audio effect that is easy to use is the Dynamics effect. It provides a robust set of controls for multiple properties that can be combined or used independently to adjust audio. You will likely find that the graphical controls in the Custom Setup view are easiest to use, but you can adjust values in the Individual Parameters view.

You can use the following properties to adjust audio with the Dynamics effect:

- **AutoGate**: This cuts off a signal when its level falls below the specified threshold. This is a very useful way to remove unwanted sounds (such as background noise behind an interview or narrator).

- **Compressor**: This option is used to balance the dynamic range and create a consistent audio level throughout the duration of the clip.

- **Expander**: This option is used to reduce all signals below the specified threshold. It is similar to using the AutoGate controls but can be more subtle in its adjustments. Be sure to adjust both the threshold and the ratio while playing back the clip to find the right settings that sound natural while still removing the unwanted noise.

- **Limiter**: Use the Limiter option to reduce clipping in audio clips that peak too high. You can set a threshold between –60 dB and 0 dB. Adobe Premiere Pro reduces all signals that exceed the threshold to the same level as the threshold.

1 Continue working with the sequence 05 Noisy Reduction.

2 Remove all other effects from the Effect Controls panel for the selected clip.

3 In the Effects panel, locate the Dynamics effect, and apply it to your clip.

4 In the Effect Controls panel, expand the Custom Setup controls for the effect, and scroll the window to view all controls.

5 Enable the AutoGate option only, and listen to the clip.

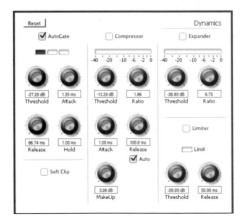

The background noise should be dramatically reduced. Adjust the Threshold dial to taste.

6   Make sure the Compressor option is active, and adjust its settings to taste to make the sound a bit fuller. Play back the clip, and adjust as needed.

7   Disable the AutoGate option and enable the Expander to try to remove the background noise in a different manner.

8   Play the clip, and adjust the Threshold and Ratio for the Expander option to taste.

9   Enable the Limiter option, and set it to –12.00 dB, which is a level commonly used in audio mastering.

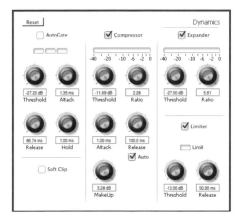

10 Play the clip, and look at the audio meters (if not visible, you can enable them under the Window menu).

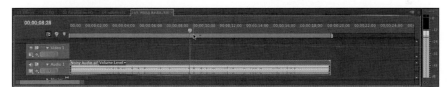

Removing background noise with Adobe Audition

Adobe Audition is a companion application to Adobe Premiere Pro found in both the Creative Suite and Creative Cloud families that feature Adobe Premiere Pro. This dedicated audio application does a great job offering advanced mixing and effects to improve your overall sound. If you have Adobe Audition installed, you can try the following:

1 In Adobe Premiere Pro, open the sequence 06 Send to Audition from the Project panel.

2 Select the clip Noisy Audio.aif in the Timeline.

3 Right-click the clip and choose Edit Clip in Adobe Audition. A new version of the audio clip is extracted and added to your project.

Adobe Audition opens, along with the new clip.

4 Switch to Adobe Audition.

5 The stereo track should be visible in the Editor panel.

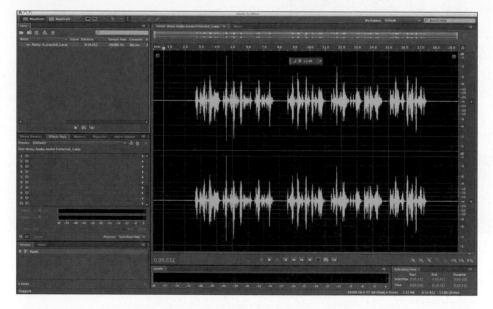

Adobe Audition presents you with a large waveform for the clip. You now need to select the part of the clip that's just the noise to define it; then you can reduce that noise through the whole clip.

6 Play back the clip again. Notice that the beginning contains several seconds of just noise.

Removing background noise
with Adobe Audition (continued)

7 Using the Time Selection tool (the I bar tool in the toolbar), click and drag to highlight the section of noise you just identified.

8 With the selection active, choose Effects > Noise Reduction/Restoration > Capture Noise Print. You can also press Shift+P.

If a dialog appears informing you that the noise print will be captured, click OK to acknowledge the message.

9 Choose Edit > Select > Select All to select the entire clip.

10 Choose Effects > Noise Reduction/Restoration > Noise Reduction (process). You can also press Shift+Control+P (Windows) or Shift+Command+P (Mac OS). A new dialog opens so you can process the noise.

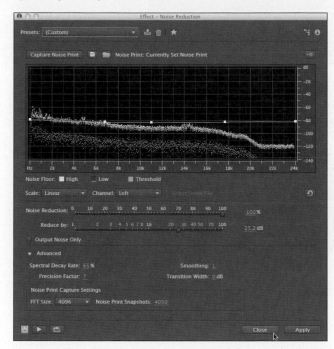

(continued on next page)

Removing background noise
with Adobe Audition (continued)

11 Select the Output Noise Only check box. This option allows you to hear only the noise you're removing, which is helpful so you don't accidentally remove too much of the audio you want to keep.

12 Click the Play button at the bottom of the window, and adjust the Noise Reduction and Reduce By sliders to remove noise from the clip. Try not to pull down much or any of the voice.

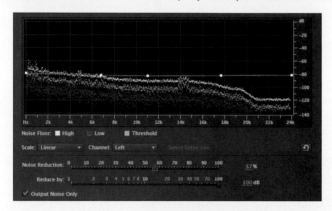

13 Deselect the Output Noise Only check box, and listen to your cleaned-up audio.

14 In the Advanced section, you can further refine the noise reduction. Be sure to try the Spectral Decay Rate option if your audio sounds too much like you're listening to a phone call from under the ocean.

15 When you're satisfied, click the Apply button to apply the cleanup.

16 Choose File > Close, and save your changes.

17 Switch back to Adobe Premiere Pro where you can listen to the cleaned-up audio track.

Review questions

1   To change the apparent speed of an audio clip without changing its duration, which effect would you use?

2   What's the difference between the Delay and Reverb effects?

3   How do you apply the same audio effect with the same parameters to three audio tracks?

4   Name three ways to remove background noise from a clip.

Review answers

1   The PitchShifter effect can modify the apparent pitch or energy level for a clip while still maintaining sync with a video clip.

2   Delay creates a distinct, single echo that can repeat and gradually fade. Reverb creates a mix of echoes to simulate a room. It has multiple parameters that take the hard edge off the echo you hear in the Delay effect.

3   The easiest way to create a submix track is to assign those three tracks to that submix track and apply the effect to the submix.

4   You can use a Notch or Dynamics effect within Adobe Premiere Pro or send the clip to Adobe Audition to use its advanced noise reduction controls.

13 ADDING VIDEO EFFECTS

Lesson overview

In this lesson, you'll learn about the following:

- Working with fixed effects
- Browsing effects with the Effects Browser
- Applying and removing effects
- Using effects presets
- Using keyframing effects
- Exploring frequently used effects

 This lesson will take approximately 75 minutes.

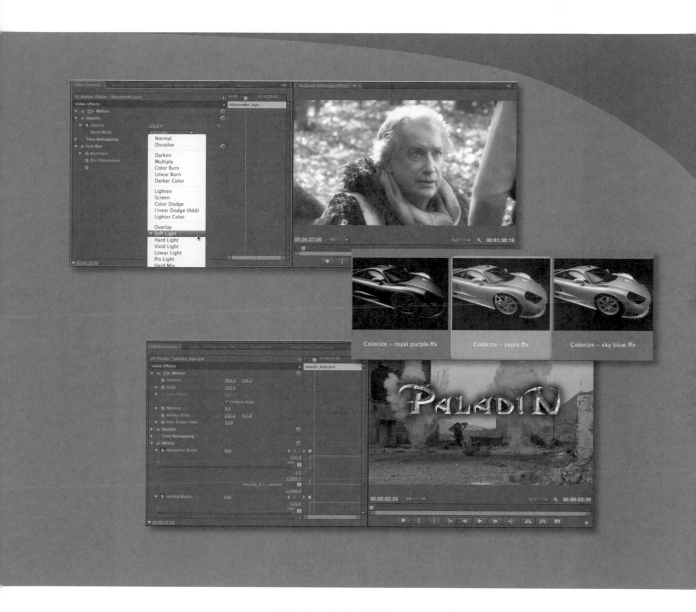

Adobe Premiere Pro CS6 features more than 100 video effects. Most effects come with an array of parameters, all of which you can *animate*—have them change over time—by using precise keyframe controls.

Getting started

Video effects can be used for many reasons. They can solve problems with image quality (such as exposure or color balance). They can create complex images through compositing using techniques such as chromakeying. They can also be used to solve a variety of production problems such as camera vibration and rolling shutter. Effects can also be used for stylistic purposes. You can alter the color or distort footage. You can animate the size and position of a clip within the frame.

Working with effects

Adobe Premiere Pro makes working with effects easy. You can drag an effect to a clip, or you can select the clip and double-click the effect in the Effects Browser. You can combine as many effects as you want on a single clip, which can produce surprising results. Moreover, you can use an adjustment layer to add the same effects to a collection of clips.

When it comes to choosing which video effects to use, the choices in Adobe Premiere Pro can be a bit overwhelming. The application has more than 100 built-in effects. Several effects are also available from third-party manufacturers for sale or free download. It's important to understand how effects are treated in Adobe Premiere Pro.

Fixed effects

Once you add a clip to a sequence, it will automatically have a few effects applied. These effects are called *fixed* effects, and they can be thought of as controls for the standard geometric, opacity, and audio properties that every clip should have. All fixed effects can be modified using the Effect Controls panel.

1   Start Adobe Premiere Pro, and open Lesson 13.prproj.

2   Double-click to open the sequence 01 Fixed Effects.

3   Click to select the first clip in the Timeline.

4   Switch to the Effects workspace by choosing Window > Workspace > Effects.

If your workspace doesn't look similar to what you see here, choose Window > Workspace > Reset Current Workspace.

5   Select the Effect Controls panel (it should be docked with the Source Monitor).

6   Examine the fixed effects applied.

By default, fixed effects are automatically applied to every clip in a sequence, but they do not change the clip until they are manipulated.

7 Click the disclosure triangle next to each to show their properties.

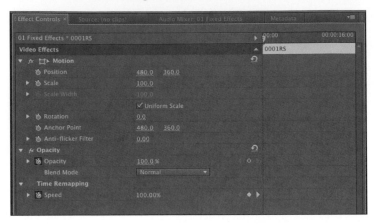

- **Motion:** The Motion effect allows you to animate, rotate, and scale a clip. You can also use advanced antiflicker controls to decrease shimmering edges for an animated object. This comes in handy when you scale a high-resolution source and Adobe Premiere Pro must resample the digital image.

- **Opacity:** The Opacity effect lets you control how opaque or transparent a clip is. Additionally, you can access multipurpose blending modes to create special effects and real-time composites. You'll explore this more in Lesson 15, "Exploring Compositing Techniques."

- **Time Remapping:** This property lets you slow down, speed up, or reverse playback, or even freeze a frame. We explored its uses in Lesson 8, "Advanced Editing Techniques."

- **Volume:** If an edited clip has audio, the Volume effect is automatically applied. You can use the effect to control the volume for the individual clip.

8 Click to select the second clip in the Timeline. Look closely at the Effect Controls panel.

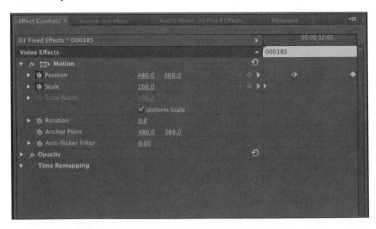

These effects have keyframes, meaning that their values have been changed over time. In this case, a small scale and pan were applied to the clip to create a digital zoom and recompose the shot. We'll explore keyframes more later in this chapter.

9 Press Play to watch the current sequence back a few times and compare the two shots.

The Effects Browser

Besides the fixed effects you've already explored, Adobe Premiere Pro has standard effects. You'll use standard effects to affect a clip's image quality and appearance. Because you'll have more than 100 effects to choose from, Adobe Premiere Pro attempts to simplify the process by organizing them. You'll find 16 standard categories (third-party effects may add more choices). These categories group effects into logical tasks such as Distort, Keying, and Time. This makes it easier to choose the correct effect that you want to apply.

1 Click the Project panel.

2 Double-click to open the sequence 02 Browse.

3 Click to select the clip in the Timeline.

4 Click the Effects tab to select the Effects Browser. You can press the shortcut key Shift+7 to select it.

5 Double-click the Video Effects folder to open it.

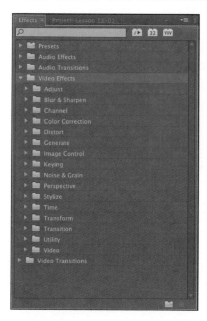

6 Click the New Custom Bin icon at the bottom of the panel.

The New Custom bin/folder appears in the Effects panel below Video Transitions. Let's rename the bin.

7 Click once to select the bin.

8 Click once more directly on the bin's name (Custom Bin 01) to highlight it and change it.

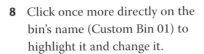

9 Change its name to something like *Favorite Effects*.

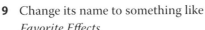

● **Note:** The effects remain in their original folder and also appear in yours. You can use custom folders to build effect categories that match your work style.

10 Open any Video Effects folders, and drag a few effects into your custom bin. For now, just choose ones that sound interesting to you. You can add or remove effects from the Favorite Effects bin at any time.

● **Note:** With so many Video Effects subfolders, it's sometimes tricky to locate the effect you want. If you know part or all of an effect's name, start typing it in the search box at the top of the Effects tab. Adobe Premiere Pro immediately displays all effects and transitions that contain that letter combination, narrowing the search as you type.

As you browse the many effects, you'll notice several icons next to many of the effects names. Knowing what these icons represent may influence which effects you choose to use in a project.

Accelerated effects   32-bit color   YUV effects

Accelerated effects

The first icon (which has an accelerated playback triangle) indicates that the effect is accelerated by your graphics processing unit (GPU). Remember that the GPU (typically called a *video card*) can greatly enhance the performance of Adobe Premiere Pro. If at all possible, try to use a card that is supported by the Mercury Playback Engine; with a supported card installed, these effects often offer accelerated or even real-time performance and need rendering only on final export. You'll find a list of supported cards on the Adobe Premiere Pro product page.

GPU acceleration offers the following benefits:

- You can stack multiple effects onto multiple video layers and play them back without rendering, often in real time.

- The 32-bit floating-point pipeline supports all the 32-bit effects available in Adobe Premiere Pro.

32-bit color (high-bit-depth) effects

You'll find that some effects have an icon next to them with the number 32. This indicates that the effects support processing in a 32-bits-per-channel mode, which is also called *high bit depth* or *float processing*.

You should use high-bit-depth effects when either of the following is true:

- You're working with video shot with 10- or 12-bits-per-channel codecs (such as RED or ARRI).

- You want to maintain greater image fidelity when multiple effects are applied to any footage.

Additionally, 16-bit photos or Adobe After Effects files rendered in 16- or 32-bits-per-channel color space can take advantage of high-bit-depth effects.

To take advantage of high-bit-depth effects, make sure your sequence has the Maximum Bit Depth video-rendering option selected. You'll find this choice in the New Sequence or Sequence Settings dialog.

Note: When using any 32-bit effects, try to use only 32-bit effects in the chain for maximum quality. If you mix and match effects, the effects will have to switch back to 8-bit space to process, which will reduce the overall precision and accuracy of the image.

YUV effects

If you need to use effects that process the color in an image, it's likely that they have been optimized to work in YUV. Effects without the YUV label in Adobe Premiere Pro process in the computer's native RGB space, which can make adjusting exposure and color less accurate.

The YUV effects break down the video into a Y channel (or luminance channel) and two channels for color info (without brightness). This is how most video footage is structured natively. These filters make it easy to adjust contrast and exposure without shifting color.

Note: You'll see many Video Effects categories. Some effects are difficult to categorize and could reside in multiple categories or in categories by themselves, but this taxonomy works reasonably well.

Applying effects

● **Note:** You can reorder standard effects by dragging them up or down in the list, but you can't reorder fixed effects. This can cause problems because effects might be scaled after another effect is applied.

Virtually all the video effect parameters are accessible within the Effect Controls panel, making it easy to set the behaviors and the intensity of those effects. You can add keyframes independently to every attribute listed in the Effect Controls panel to make those behaviors change over time. In addition, you can use Bezier curves to adjust the velocity and acceleration of those changes.

1 Continue working with the sequence 02 Browse.

2 If necessary, click the Effects tab next to the Project panel to make it visible.

3 Type **black** into the Effects Browser search field to narrow the results. Locate the Black & White video effect.

4 Drag the Black & White video effect on the clip Cowboy in the Timeline.

Applying this effect immediately converts your full-color footage to black and white—or, more accurately, *grayscale*. It also puts that effect in the Effect Controls panel.

5 Make sure the clip Cowboy is selected in the Timeline panel.

6 If necessary, click the Effect Controls tab to open it.

7 Toggle the Black & White effect off and on by clicking the "fx" button next to the effect name in the Effect Controls panel. Be sure the current-time indicator is on this footage clip to view the effect.

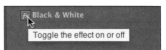

Toggling an effect on and off is a good way to see how it works with other effects. This toggle switch is the only parameter available with the Black & White effect. The effect is either on or off.

8 Check that the clip is selected so that its parameters are displayed in the Effect Controls panel, click Black & White to select it, and then press the Delete key.

9 Type **direction** into the Effects Browser search field to narrow the results. Locate the Directional Blur video effect.

10 In the Effects Browser, double-click the effect to apply it.

11 In the Effect Controls panel, expand the Directional Blur effect's filter, and note that there are options the Black & White effect did not have: Direction, Blur Length, and a stopwatch next to each option (the stopwatch icon is to activate keyframing, which we will cover later in this lesson).

12 Set Direction to 90.0 degrees and Blur Length to 4 to simulate the scene being filmed with a slow shutter speed.

13 Expand the Blur Length option, and move the slider in the Effect Controls panel.

As you change that setting, it shows up in real time in the Program Monitor.

14 Open the Effect Controls panel menu, and choose Remove Effects.

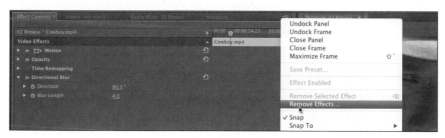

15 Click OK in the dialog that pops up asking which effects you want to remove. You want to remove them all.

This is an easy way to start fresh.

▶ **Tip:** Fixed effects in Adobe Premiere Pro have to process in a specific order, which can lead to unwanted scaling or resizing. While you can't reorder fixed effects, you can bypass them and use other effects, which are similar. For example, you can use the Transform effect instead of the Motion effect or the Alpha Adjust effect instead of the Opacity effect. Although these effects are not identical, they are a very close match and behave similarly. You may choose to use them when you need to reorder effects that perform these actions.

Other ways to apply effects

To make working with effects more flexible, there are three ways to reuse an effect.

- You can select an effect from the Effect Controls panel, choose Edit > Copy, select the Effects Controls panel of a destination clip, and choose Edit > Paste.

- To copy all the effects from one clip so you can paste them to another clip, select the clip in the Timeline and choose Edit > Copy, select the destination clip, and choose Edit > Paste Attributes.

- You can create an effects preset to store a particular effect with settings for reuse later. We'll cover this technique later in this lesson.

Using adjustment layers

Sometimes you'll want to apply an effect to multiple clips. Adobe Premiere Pro CS6 offers an easy way to do this called an *adjustment layer*. The concept is simple: Create a new layer that can hold effects and sit above other video tracks. Everything beneath the adjustment layer will be processed by the effect. You can adjust the trim handles and opacity of the adjustment layer to further control the effect. It also makes it much easier to adjust a single effect, rather than multiple instances applied to several clips.

Let's create a global effect for a sequence that's already been edited.

1 Click the Project panel.

● **Note:** This sequence has been simplified to reduce space on the disk. This sequence originally used multiple audio tracks.

2 Double-click to open the sequence 03 Multiple Effects.

3 At the bottom of the Project panel, click the New Item button and choose Adjustment Layer. Click OK to create the adjustment layer to match the dimensions of the current sequence.

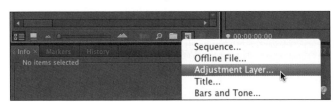

A new adjustment layer is added to the Project panel.

4 Drag the adjustment layer to track Video 2 in the current Timeline.

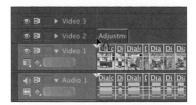

5 Drag the right edge of the adjustment layer so it extends to the end of the sequence.

The adjustment layer should look like this.

Let's create a film-look effect by using filters and modifying the opacity of the adjustment layer.

6 In the Effects Browser, search for and locate the Fast Blur effect.

7 Drag the effect onto the adjustment layer.

8 Move the playhead position to 27:00 to have a good close-up shot to use when designing the effect.

9 In the Effect Controls panel, set Blurriness to a heavy value like 25.0 pixels. Be sure to select the Repeat Edge Pixels checkbox to apply the effect evenly.

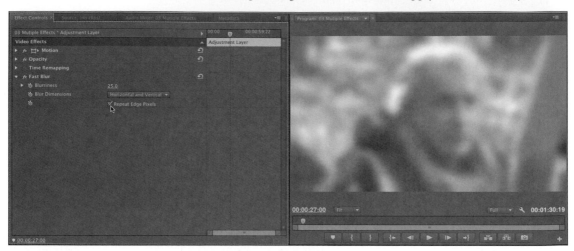

Let's blend the effect using a blending mode to create the film look. Blending modes let you mix two layers together based on their brightness and color values. You'll learn more about them in Lesson 15.

10 Click the disclosure triangle next to the Opacity property in the Effect Controls panel.

11 Change the blending mode to Soft Light to create a gentle blend.

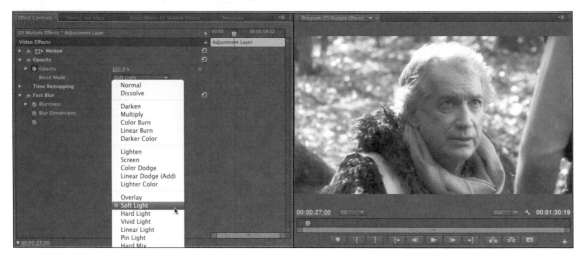

12 Set Opacity to 75% to fade the effect.

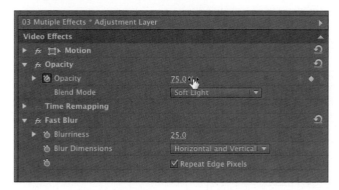

You can click the visibility icon of the adjustment layer (the eyeball next to Video 2) in the Timeline panel to see the before and after states of the effect.

Before the adjustment layer is applied

With the adjustment layer and blending modes

Sending a clip to Adobe After Effects

If you're working with a computer that also has Adobe After Effects installed, you can easily send clips back and forth between Adobe Premiere Pro and After Effects. Thanks to the close relationship between Adobe Premiere Pro and After Effects, you can seamlessly integrate the two tools much more easily than any other editing platform. This is a useful way to significantly extend the effects capabilities of your editing workflow.

The process you'll use to move clips is called Dynamic Link. Dynamic Link is revolutionary and will totally change how you approach working with media throughout the post-production process. With Dynamic Link you can seamlessly exchange clips with no unnecessary rendering.

1 In an open sequence, select the clips you want in an After Effects composition. For this exercise, you can use the sequence 04 Dynamic Link.

2 Right-click any of the selected clips.

3 Choose Replace With After Effects Composition.

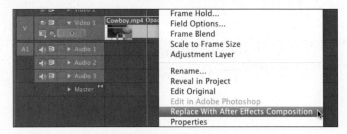

4 If it's not running already, After Effects launches. If the After Effects Save As dialog appears, enter a name and location for the After Effects project, and click Save. Name the project *Lesson 13-01.aep* and save it to the Lessons folder. A new composition is created and inherits the sequence settings from Adobe Premiere Pro. The new composition is named based on the Adobe Premiere Pro project name, followed by "Linked Comp."

5 In the After Effects project panel, double-click to load the Lesson 13-01 Linked Comp 02.

There are lots of ways to apply effects with After Effects. To keep things simple, let's work with animation presets. For more on effects workflow, see the *Adobe After Effects CS6 Classroom in a Book*.

6 Locate the Effects & Presets panel, click its submenu in the upper-right corner, and choose Browse Presets.

Sending a clip to Adobe After Effects (continued)

7 Adobe Bridge launches to let you visually browse the presets.

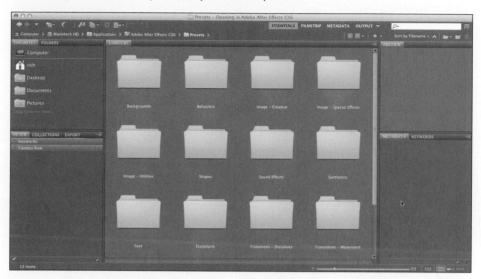

You can navigate through folders to see icons for each preset. Click an icon to see a preview of the effect.

8 Double-click the Image-Creative folder to browse presets.

9 You can single-click a preset to see an animated preview.

10 Double-click the Colorize - sepia.ffx preset; when you switch back to After Effects, the preset will be applied to the selected layer.

11 Switch back to After Effects to see the applied effect.

12 Select the clip in the Timeline, and press the E key to see the applied effects.

(continues on next page)

Sending a clip to Adobe After Effects (continued)

13 Twirl down the disclosure next to the Tint and Fill effects to see their controls.

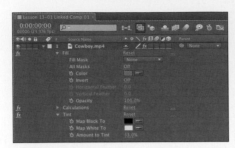 

14 Click the swatches for each color to adjust which colors are used for the Tint effect. Move the sepia tone into slightly cooler tones.

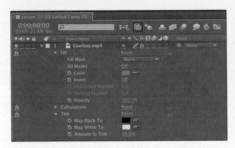 

15 Click the RAM Preview button to preview the effect. After the frames are cached, the file will play back in real time.

16 Choose File > Save to capture your changes.

17 Switch back to Adobe Premiere Pro. The frames will process in the background and be handed off from Adobe After Effects to Adobe Premiere Pro. You can also select the clip in the Timeline and choose Sequence > Render Effects in Work Area.

You can browse and download several presets from the Adobe website by visiting *www.adobe.com/go/learn_ae_cs3additionalanimationpresets*. Most of the posted presets are free. This is also an excellent way to explore the larger After Effects community.

Keyframing effects

The concept of keyframes dates back to traditional animation. The lead animator would draw the keyframes (or major poses), and then assistant animators would animate the frames in between (a process often called *tweening*). These days, you're the master who sets the major keyframes, and the computer does the rest of the work as it interpolates values in between the keyframes you set.

Adding keyframes

You can change almost all parameters for all video effects over time through the use of keyframes. For example, you can have an effect gradually change out of focus, change color, or lengthen its shadow.

1 Click the Project panel.

2 Double-click to open the sequence 05 Keyframes.

3 Watch the clip back a few times to get familiar with the footage.

4 In the Effects Browser, locate the Lens Flare effect. Apply it to the video layer.

5 Twirl down the disclosure triangle next to the Lens Flare effect, and adjust the Lens Flare effect so it is positioned like the following figure.

● **Note:** If you don't move the playhead to the clip you're applying an effect to, you won't see that clip or its effect in the Program Monitor. Selecting a clip does not move the playhead to that clip.

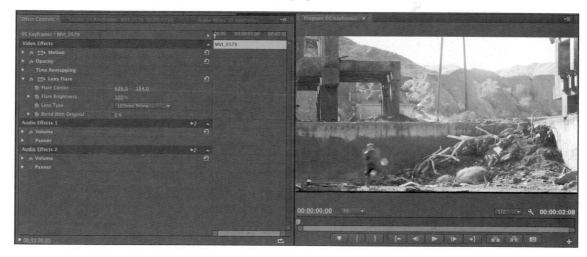

6 Expand the display of the Effect Controls panel until its view is wide enough. You can drag in between panels to resize them. If needed, click the Show/Hide Timeline View button.

7 Put the playhead at the start of the sequence.

8 Click the stopwatch icons to toggle animation for the Flare Center and Flare Brightness properties.

9 Move the playhead to the end of the clip.

You can drag the playhead directly in the Effect Controls panel. Make sure you see the last frame of video and not black.

10 Adjust Flare Center and Flare Brightness so the flare drifts across the sky with the camera pan and gets brighter. Use the following figure for guidance.

11 Play back the sequence to watch the effect animate over time.

▶ **Tip:** Be sure to use the Next and Previous Keyframe buttons to move between keyframes efficiently. This will discourage Adobe Premiere Pro from adding unwanted keyframes.

Adding keyframe interpolation and velocity

Keyframe interpolation changes the behavior of an effect parameter as it moves toward or away from a keyframe. The default behavior you've seen so far is linear; in other words, you have a constant velocity between keyframes. What generally works better is something that mirrors your experience or exaggerates it, such as a gradual acceleration or deceleration.

Adobe Premiere Pro offers a way to control those changes: keyframe interpolation and the Velocity graph. Keyframe interpolation is the easiest (basically two clicks), while tweaking the Velocity graph can become challenging. Getting a handle on this feature will take some time and practice on your part.

For this lesson, you can use the previous sequence or open 06 Interpolation.

1   Make sure you can see the Effect Controls panel's Timeline (click the Show/Hide Timeline View button near the top of the panel if needed).

2   Position the current-time indicator at the beginning of the clip.

    The Lens Flare effect is currently animated before the camera movement, so it can be tweaked for more natural movement.

3   Right-click (Windows) or Control-click (Mac OS) the first keyframe for the Flare Center property.

4   Choose the Temporal Interpolation > Ease Out method to create a gentle transition into the move from the keyframe.

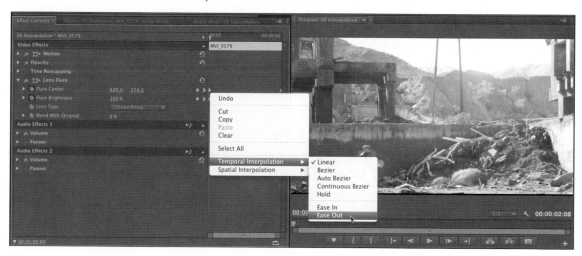

● **Note:** When working with position-related parameters, the context menu for a keyframe will offer two types of interpolation options: spatial interpolation (related to location) and temporal interpolation (related to time). You can make spatial adjustments in the Program Monitor as well as in the Effect Controls panel. You can make temporal adjustments on the clip in the Timeline and in the Effect Controls panel. These motion-related topics are covered in Lesson 9.

5 Right-click the second keyframe for the Flare Center property. Choose the Temporal Interpolation > Ease In method to create a gentle transition from the stationary position of the last keyframe.

Let's modify the Flare Brightness property.

6 Click the first keyframe for Flare Brightness and then hold down the Shift key and click the second keyframe so both are active.

7 Right-click either Flare Brightness keyframe and choose Auto Bezier to create a gentle animation between the two properties.

8 Play back the animation to watch the changes you've made.

Let's further refine the keyframes with the Velocity graph.

9 Place the mouse cursor over the Effect Controls panel and then press the ` (grave) key to maximize the panel full-screen. This will let you better see the keyframe controls.

10 Twirl down the disclosure triangles next to the Flare Center and Flare Brightness properties.

The Velocity graph shows the velocity between keyframes. The sudden drops or jumps represent sudden changes in acceleration—*jerks*, in physics parlance. The farther the point or line is from the center, the greater the velocity.

11 Try adjusting the handles of the keyframes to change how steep or gentle the velocity curve is.

12 Press the ` key to restore the default window arrangement.

13 Play back your sequence to see the impact of your changes. Continue to experiment until you have the hang of keyframes and interpolation.

Understanding interpolation methods

Here's a rundown of the keyframe interpolation methods of Adobe Premiere Pro.

- **Linear:** This method is the default behavior, which creates a uniform rate of change between keyframes.
- **Bezier:** This method lets you manually adjust the shape of the graph on either side of a keyframe. Beziers allow for sudden acceleration changes into or out of a keyframe.
- **Continuous Bezier:** This method creates a smooth rate of change through a keyframe. Unlike with Bezier, if you adjust one handle, the handle on the other side of the keyframe moves in a complementary fashion to ensure a smooth transition through the keyframe.
- **Auto Bezier:** This method creates a smooth rate of change through a keyframe even if you change the keyframe parameter value. If you choose to manually adjust the keyframe's handles, it changes to a Continuous Bezier point, retaining the smooth transition through the keyframe. The Auto Bezier option can occasionally produce unwanted motion, so try one of the other options first.
- **Hold:** This method changes a property value without a gradual transition (sudden effect change). The graph following a keyframe with the Hold interpolation applied appears as a horizontal straight line.
- **Ease In:** This method slows down the value changes entering a keyframe.
- **Ease Out:** This method gradually accelerates the value changes leaving a keyframe.

Effects presets

To save time on repeated tasks, Adobe Premiere Pro supports effect presets. You'll find that there are several presets included for specific tasks already, but the true power lies in creating your own presets to solve repetitive tasks. When you create an effect preset, it can even store keyframes for animation.

● **Note:** Effects are great ways to animate or move a graphic or some text over a video clip.

Using built-in presets

You can use one of the effects presets included with Adobe Premiere Pro. These are useful for tasks such as beveling, picture-in-picture effects, and stylized transitions.

1 Click the Project panel.

2 Double-click to open the sequence 07 Presets.

This sequence has two clips, a video shot and a logo superimposed. Let's animate a reveal of the logo using an animation preset.

3 In the Effects panel, expand the Presets bin and expand the Mosaics bin. If you don't see it, clear the search field.

4 Drag the Mosaic In preset onto the paladin-logo.psd clip on Video 2.

5 Play back the sequence to watch the logo animate onto the screen.

6 Click the paladin-logo.psd clip on Video 2, and view its controls in the Effect Controls panel.

7 Experiment with adjusting the position of the keyframes in the Effect Controls panel to customize the effect.

Saving effects presets

Although there are several effect presets to choose from, creating your own is a really good idea. This process is easy and creates a preset file that you can easily move between computers. The process comes down to selecting exactly what you want.

1 Click the Project panel.

2 Double-click to open the sequence 08 Creating Presets.

This Timeline has two clips and two instances of a show logo.

3 Play back the sequence to watch the initial animation.

4 Select the first instance of paladin_logo.psd.

5 Select the Effect Controls panel, and choose Edit > Select All to choose all of the effects applied to the clip.

You can also select individual properties if you want only part of the effects stored. Control+click (Windows) or Command+click (Mac OS) multiple effects in the Effect Controls panel. In this case, however, use all.

6 In the Effect Controls panel, click the submenu and choose Save Preset.

7 In the Save Preset dialog, name the effect *Logo Animation.*

8 Choose one of the following preset types to specify how Adobe Premiere Pro should handle keyframes in a preset:

- **Scale:** Proportionally scales the source keyframes to the length of the target clip. Any existing keyframes on the original clip are deleted.

- **Anchor to In Point:** Preserves the position of the first keyframe as well as the relationship of other keyframes in a clip. Other keyframes are added to the clip relative to its In point. Use this option for this exercise.

- **Anchor to Out Point:** Preserves the position of the last keyframe as well as the relationship of other keyframes in a clip. Other keyframes are added to the clip relative to its Out point.

9 Click OK to store the affected clip and keyframes as a new preset.

10 In the Effects panel, locate the Presets folder.

11 Locate the newly created Logo Animation preset.

12 Drag the Logo Animation preset onto the second instance of the paladin_logo.psd file in the Timeline.

13 Watch the sequence play back to see the newly applied title animation.

Frequently used effects

Throughout this lesson you've explored several effects. Although it's beyond the scope of this book to explore all of the effects, we'll cover three additional effects that are very useful in many editing situations. By looking at the possibilities, you'll have a better appreciation for the options that lie ahead.

Image stabilization and rolling shutter reduction

The Warp Stabilizer effect is a new addition to Adobe Premiere Pro CS6. It can remove jitter caused by camera movement (which is more and more common with today's lighter-weight cameras). The effect is useful because it can remove unstable parallax-type movements (where images appear to shift on planes). Additionally, the effect can repair a visual artifact that is common with CMOS-type sensors (such as those on DSLR cameras) and has the ability to compensate for rolling shutter. This makes the images appear to have an optical bending of material that has strong vertical lines.

Let's explore the effect.

1 Click the Project panel.

2 Double-click to open the sequence 09 Warp Stabilizer.

3 Play back the sequence to evaluate the wobbly shot.

4 Select the clip in the Timeline panel.

5 In the Effects Browser, locate the Warp Stabilizer effect. Double-click it to apply it to the selected shot.

The Warp Stabilizer effect is applied to the layer. The footage is immediately analyzed between its In and Out points.

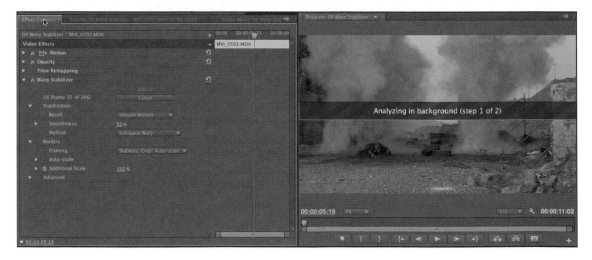

The analysis process takes two steps, and you'll see a banner across the footage as it's being analyzed. You can also see a progress update in the Effect Controls panel. While the analysis is in progress, you can keep working in the sequence.

6 You can enhance the effect with several useful Stabilization method options, including these three:

- **Result:** You can choose Smooth Motion to retain the general camera movement (albeit stabilized), or you can choose No Motion to attempt to remove all camera movement. For this exercise, choose Smooth Motion.

- **Smoothness:** This option specifies how much of the original camera movement should be retained for Smooth Motion. Use a higher value to smooth out the shot the most. Experiment with this shot until you're happy with its stability.

- **Method:** You can use the four methods available. The two most powerful, because they warp and process the image more heavily, are Perspective and Subspace Warp. If either method creates too much distortion, you can try switching to Position, Scale, and Rotation, or just Position.

7 Play back the sequence.

▶ **Tip:** If you notice that some of the details in the shot appear to wobble, you may be able to improve the overall effect. In the Advanced section, choose the Detailed Analysis option. This makes the Analysis phase do extra work to find elements to track. You can also use the Enhanced Reduction option from the Rolling Shutter Ripple option under the Advanced category. These options are much slower but produce superior results.

Timecode burn-in

If you need to send a review copy of a sequence to a client or colleague, the Timecode effect is very useful. You can apply the effect to an adjustment layer and have it generate a visible timecode for the entire sequence. This is helpful because it allows others to make specific feedback based on a unique point in time. You can control the display of Position, Size, Opacity, the timecode display, and its format and source.

1 Click the Project panel.

2 Double-click to open the sequence 10 Timecode Burn-In.

3 In the Project panel, click the New Item list, and choose Adjustment Layer. Click OK.

A new adjustment layer is added to the Project panel.

4 Drag the adjustment layer to track Video 2 in the current Timeline.

5 Drag the right edge of the adjustment layer so it extends to the end of the sequence.

6 In the Effects Browser, locate the Timecode effect. Drag it onto the adjustment layer to apply it.

7 Set Time Display to 24 to match the frame rate of the sequence.

8 Choose a timecode source. In this case, use the Generate option and set the Starting Timecode option to 01;00;00;00 to match the sequence.

9 Adjust the Position and Size options for the effect.

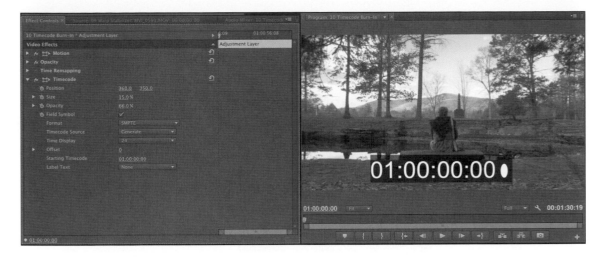

It's a good idea to move the timecode window so it's not blocking critical action in the scene or obscuring any graphics. If you plan to post the video to the Web for review, be sure to size the timecode burn-in so it's easy to read.

● **Note:** If you want to show the timecode for the original clip, you'll need to apply the timecode effect directly to every clip in the sequence.

Lighting effects

Lighting is one of the most intense effects in Adobe Premiere Pro. You can add up to five virtual lights to creatively adjust the effect. You can modify a light effect's property including the lighting type, direction, intensity, color, lighting center, and lighting spread. This exercise combines hands-on, step-by-step tasks with experimentation. The purpose is to introduce you to a couple more advanced lighting effects and to encourage you to explore further.

1 Choose Help > Adobe Premiere Pro Help.

2 Search Adobe Premiere Pro Help for *Lighting effects*.

  This gives you an explanation of each parameter—25 in all—in the Lighting effects. Every Adobe Premiere Pro video and audio effect has such a listing in Adobe Premiere Pro Help. This also illustrates how complete and useful Adobe Premiere Pro Help is. Quickly read the article to familiarize yourself with the effect.

3 Quit Help to return to Adobe Premiere Pro.

4 Load the sequence 11 Lighting Effects.

5 Choose Video Effects > Adjust, select Lighting Effects, and drag it to the clip in the Video 1 track.

6 Expand Lighting Effects and Light 1. You will leave off Lights 2 through 4.

The effect creates a single virtual light that is added to the image. Let's adjust the light so it's more realistic in this scene.

7 In the Program Monitor, set the Zoom level to 25%.

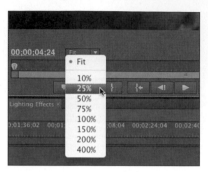

8 In the Effect Controls panel, click the Lighting Effects name to highlight it.

A virtual outline showing the shape of the light appears.

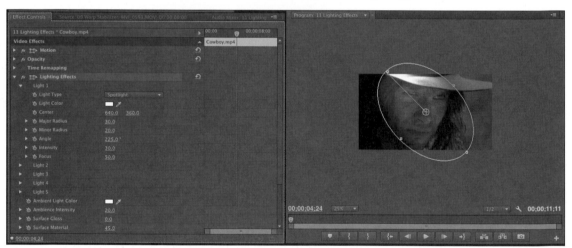

9 Adjust the angle of the effect so the light appears to be coming from the lower-left corner.

10 Adjust the Intensity and Ambience Intensity options to taste.

11 Using the handles in the Program Monitor, adjust the shape and position of the light.

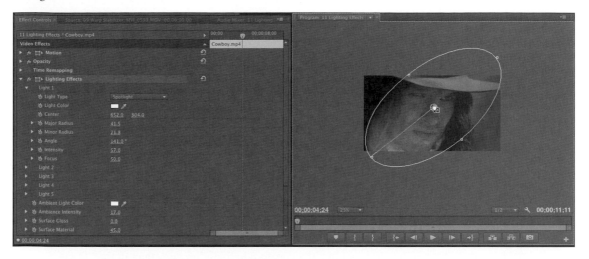

12 In the Program Monitor, set the Zoom level to Fit.

13 Toggle the effect on and off in the Effect Controls panel to evaluate how it looks.

Lighting effects off

Lighting effects on

Review questions

1 What are two ways to apply an effect to a clip?

2 List three ways to add a keyframe.

3 Dragging an effect to a clip turns on its parameters in the Effect Controls panel, but you don't see the effect in the Program Monitor. Why not?

4 Describe how you can apply one effect to multiple clips.

5 Describe how to save multiple effects to a custom preset.

Review answers

1 Drag the effect to the clip, or select the clip and double-click the effect in the Effects panel.

2 Move the current-time indicator in the Effect Controls panel to where you want a keyframe, and activate keyframing by clicking the "Toggle animation" button; move the current-time indicator, and click the Add/Remove Keyframe button; and with keyframing activated, move the current-time indicator to a position, and change a parameter.

3 You need to move the Timeline current-time indicator to the selected clip to see it in the Program Monitor. Simply selecting a clip does not move the current-time indicator to that clip.

4 Add an adjustment layer above the clips you want to affect. You can then apply an effect that will modify all the clips below the layer.

5 You can click the Effect Controls panel and choose Edit > Select All. You can also Control+click (Windows) or Command+click (Mac OS) multiple effects in the Effect Controls panel. Once selected, choose the Save Preset command from the menu that appears.

14 COLOR CORRECTION AND GRADING

Lesson overview

In this lesson, you'll learn about the following:

- Working in the Color Correction workspace

- Using vectorscopes and waveforms

- Using color correction effects

- Fixing exposure and color balance problems

- Working with special effects

- Creating a look

 This lesson will take approximately 60 minutes.

In this lesson, you'll learn some key techniques for improving the look of your clips. Industry professionals use these techniques every day to give television programs and films the "pop" and atmosphere that set them apart.

Editing your clips together is just the first part of the creative process. Now it's time to work with color.

Getting started

It's time to switch gears again. Until now you've been organizing your clips, building sequences, and applying special effects. All of these skills come together when working with color correction.

To get the most from the Adobe Premiere Pro CS6 color correction tools, you'll need to think in terms of color composition: Consider the way your eyes register color and light; the way cameras record it; and the way your computer screen, a television screen, a video projector, or a cinema screen displays it.

Adobe Premiere Pro has multiple color correction tools and makes it easy to create your own presets. In this lesson, you'll begin by learning some fundamental color correction skills and then meet some of the most popular color correction special effects, before using them to deal with some common color correction challenges.

1 Open Lesson 14.prproj in the Lesson 14 folder. If Adobe Premiere Pro can't locate the lesson file, refer to "Relink the lesson files" in the Getting Started section at the start of this book for two ways to search for and relink the file.

2 Choose Window > Workspace > Color Correction to switch to the Color Correction workspace.

3 Choose Window > Workspace > Reset Current Workspace.

4 Click Yes in the Reset Workspace dialog.

Color-oriented workflow

Now that you've switched to a new workspace, it's a good time to switch to a different brain—or at least, a different kind of thinking. With your clips in place, it's time to look at them less in terms of the action and more in terms of whether they fit together—whether they look like they were shot at the same time, in the same place, and with the same camera.

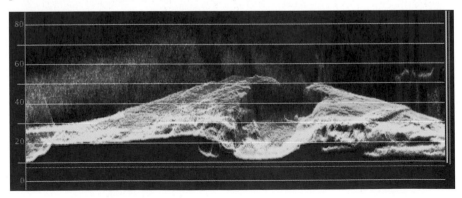

There are two main phases to working with color:

1 Make sure your clips have matching colors, brightness, and contrast.

2 Give everything a look—a particular tonality or color tint.

You'll use the same tools to achieve both of these goals, but it's common to approach them in this order, separately. If two clips from the same scene don't have matching colors, it creates a jarring continuity problem.

The Color Correction workspace

Like the other specialized workspaces, the Color Correction workspace mainly just repositions and resizes multiple panels to make a convenient layout for the task at hand.

There are a couple of noteworthy changes:

• There's a new Reference Monitor (covered shortly).

• The Effect Controls panel takes a large part of the screen.

You'll notice the Timeline panel shrinks to accommodate the new Reference Monitor and the larger Effect Controls panel. This is fine because, by the time you get to working on color correction, you won't be editing your clips and should not need to see lots of clips at once.

Video scope essentials

You might have wondered why the Adobe Premiere Pro interface is so gray. There's a very good reason: Vision is highly subjective. In fact, it's also highly relative. If you see two colors next to each other, the way you see one is changed by the presence of the other. To prevent the Adobe Premiere Pro interface from influencing the way you perceive colors in your sequence, Adobe has made the interface almost entirely gray. If you've ever seen a professional color grading suite—where artists provide the finishing touches films and television programs—you've probably noticed the entire room is gray! Grading artists sometimes have a large gray piece of card, or a section of a wall, that they can look at for a few moments to "reset" their vision before checking a shot.

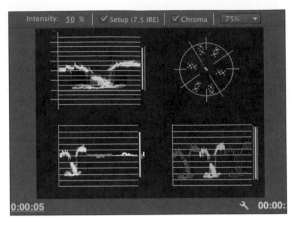

The combination of your subjective vision and the variation that can occur in the way computer monitors and television monitors display color and brightness create a need for an objective measurement.

Video scopes provide just that. And they're used throughout the media industry; learn them once, and you'll be able to use them everywhere.

1   If it's not open already, open the Double Identity sequence from the sequences bin.

2   Position the Timeline playhead so that it is over the first clip in the sequence, 3D_SER1.

You should see the lady walking in the street, in your Program Monitor, along with a second display of the same clip in the Reference Monitor.

The Reference Monitor

The Reference Monitor looks and behaves very much like the Source and Program Monitors. It displays the contents of the current sequence in much the same way that the Program Monitor does. The main difference is that there are no editing controls.

You can't add an In point or an Out point, for example. Instead, there are Timeline navigation controls and a Gang to Program Monitor button.

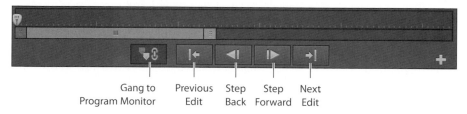

Gang to Program Monitor / Previous Edit / Step Back / Step Forward / Next Edit

When the Gang to Program Monitor button is selected, the Reference Monitor moves in sync with the Timeline and Program Monitor. When the button is off, you can move the Reference Monitor playhead independently.

The Gang to Program Monitor option is very useful, because the Reference Monitor can display the vectorscope or various waveforms in the same way that the Source and Program Monitors can. When you group the Reference Monitor and use one of the scopes, you get dynamically updated objective information about the clips in your sequence at the same time as watching regular playback in the Program Monitor.

Because you can turn off ganging, you can also use the Reference Monitor to compare shots in a sequence, and you can always use the Source Monitor to compare with shots in the bin, of course.

YC waveform

To work with color in Adobe Premiere Pro, you'll also need to get familiar with the YC waveform. Click the Settings button menu in the Reference Monitor and set it to YC Waveform.

As you play your sequence or scrub the time ruler by clicking and dragging with the mouse, the YC waveform updates to show analysis of the current frame.

If you're new to waveforms, they can look a little strange, but they're actually very simple. They show you the brightness and color intensity of your images.

Every pixel in the current frame is displayed in the waveform. The brighter the pixel, the higher it appears. The pixels have their correct horizontal position—that is, a pixel halfway across the screen will be displayed halfway across the waveform—but the vertical position is not based on the image.

Instead, the vertical position indicates brightness or color intensity; both the brightness and color intensity waveforms are displayed together, using different colors.

- 0, at the bottom of the scale, represents no luminance at all and/or no color intensity.

- 100, at the top of the scale, represents a pixel that is fully bright. On the RGB (red, green, and blue) scale, this value would be 255.

- If you're working on an NTSC sequence, the waveform will automatically use the IRE scale. If you're working on a PAL sequence, the waveform will automatically use the Millivolts scale, where 0 is actually 0.3 volts.

This all might sound rather technical, but in practice it's pretty straightforward. There's a visible baseline that represents "no brightness" and a top level that represents "fully bright." The numbers on the edge of the graph might change, but the use is essentially the same.

YC stands for luminance (brightness) and chrominance (color).

The letter C, for chrominance, makes simple sense, but the letter y, for luminance, might take a little explaining. It comes from a way of measuring color information that uses an x-, y-, and z-axis, where y represents the luminance. The idea was originally to create a simple system for recording color, and the use of y to represent brightness, or luminance, stuck.

It's not too important which letter you use, as long as you know what it is for!

Intensity: 50 % ☑ Setup (7.5 IRE) ☑ Chroma

The controls along the top of the YC waveform display give you some easy choices:

- **Intensity:** This simply changes the brightness of the display in the waveform.

- **Setup (7.5 IRE):** This applies only to some cases of analog, standard-definition (SD) video, where the 0 point is actually 7.5, instead of 0. Selecting this checkbox has no significant effect on the way the waveform display works. It simply moves the 0 point up to 7.5.

- **Chroma:** This control turns off and on the display of color information in the waveform display.

We're not working with analog SD video, so turn off the Setup (7.5 IRE) option. We're also just going to work with the luminance for now, so turn off the Chroma option too.

Now you should see a simpler display that looks like the one shown here.

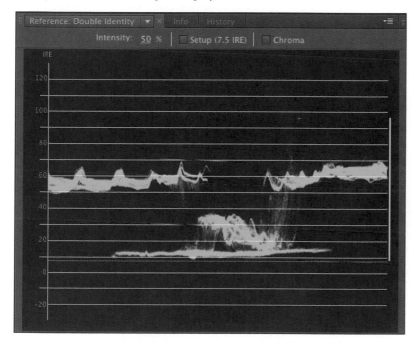

Tip: It can sometimes seem as if the waveform display is showing an image. Remember, the vertical position of the pixels in your images is not used in a waveform display.

You should be able to see the parts of the picture where the smoky background of the image is displayed, toward the left and right (with some ridges where there is a pattern in the background). You should also be able to see a darker section, in the middle, where the lady is. If you play the sequence, you'll see the waveform display update.

The waveform display is extremely useful for showing how much contrast you have in your images and for checking whether you are working on video that has "legal" levels—that is, the minimum and a maximum brightness or color saturation permitted by a broadcaster. Broadcasters adopt their own standards for legal levels, so you will need to find out for each case where your work will be broadcast.

You can see right away that we do not have great contrast in this shot. There are some strong shadows but very few *highlights*—pixels in the upper part of the waveform display.

Vectorscope

While the YC waveform display shows luminance in terms of the vertical position of pixels displayed, with brighter pixels displayed at the top and darker pixels displayed at the bottom, the vectorscope shows only color.

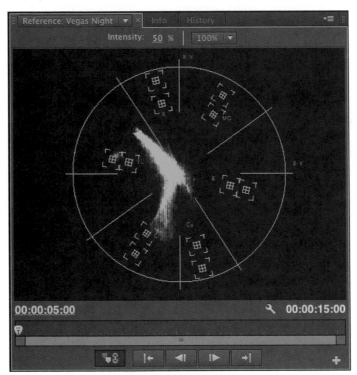

Click the Reference Monitor Settings button menu, and choose Vectorscope. Open the sequence Vegas Night in the Sequences bin. There's just one clip in this sequence.

Pixels in the image are displayed in the vectorscope. If a pixel appears in the center of the circle, it has no color saturation. The closer to the edge of the circle, the more color a pixel has.

If you look closely at the vectorscope, you'll see a series of markings indicating primary and secondary colors.

- R = Red
- G = Green
- B = Blue
- YL = Yellow
- CY = Cyan
- MG = Magenta

About primary and secondary colors

Red, green, and blue are primary colors. It is common for display systems, including television screens and your computer monitor, to combine these three colors in varying relative amounts to produce all of the colors you see.

There is a beautiful symmetry to the way a standard color wheel works, and a color wheel is essentially what the vectorscope displays.

Any two primary colors will combine to produce a secondary color. Secondary colors are the opposite of the remaining primary color.

For example, red and green combine to produce yellow, which is the opposite of blue.

The closer a pixel is to one of these colors, the more of that color it has. While the waveform display gives an indication of where a pixel is in the picture, thanks to the horizontal position, there is no position information in the vectorscope.

It's clear enough to see by eye what is happening in this shot of Las Vegas. There's a lot of yellowy red and some vivid green. Notice there is also some cyan at the top left of the image. This is indicated by the streak of peaks reaching out toward the CY marking.

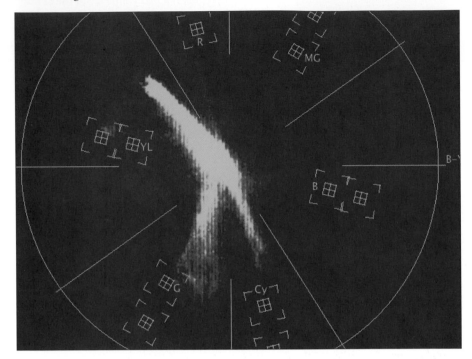

The vectorscope is helpful because it gives you objective information about the colors in your sequence. If there is a color cast, perhaps because the camera was not calibrated properly, it's often obvious in the vectorscope display. You can simply use one of the Adobe Premiere Pro color correction effects to reduce the amount of the unwanted color or add more of the opposite color.

Some of the controls for color correction special effects, such as Fast Color Corrector, have the same color wheel design as the vectorscope, so it's easy to see what you need to do.

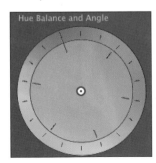

Additive and subtractive color

Computer screens and televisions use *additive color*, which means the colors are created by generating light in different colors and combining them to produce a precise mix. You produce white by combining equal amounts of red, green, and blue.

When you draw with color on paper, it is usually white paper, so it begins with a full spectrum of colors. You subtract from the white of the paper by adding pigment. The pigment prevents parts of the light reflecting on the paper. This is called *subtractive color*.

When using additive color, primary colors are used. When using subtractive color, secondary colors are used. In a sense, they are flip sides of the same color theory.

RGB Parade

Use the Reference Monitor's Settings button menu to switch to the RGB parade.

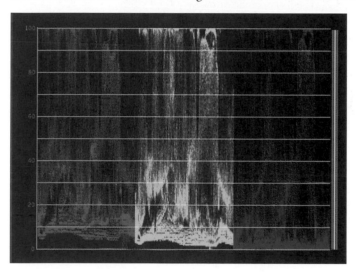

The RGB parade provides a waveform-style display, the same as the YC waveform. The difference is that the red, green, and blue levels are displayed separately. To fit all three colors in, each image is squeezed horizontally to one third of the width of the display.

You'll notice the three parts of the RGB parade have similar patterns in them, particularly where there are white or gray pixels, because these parts will have equal amounts of red, green, and blue. The RGB parade is one of the most frequently used tools in color correction because it clearly shows the relationship between the primary color channels.

Y'CbCr Parade

Use the Reference Monitor's Settings button menu to switch to the Y'CbCr parade.

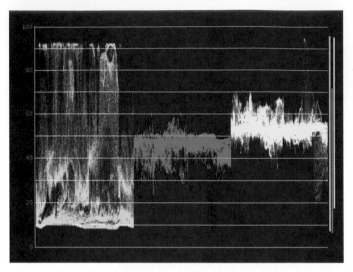

Though computer monitors use a "color additive" system, using RGB to indicate color levels, most cameras actually record using a "color difference" system, often expressed as Y'CbCr (for digital signals), signifying the following:

- **Y':** Luminance
- **Cb:** Chroma-blue
- **Cr:** Chroma-red

The Y' information forms a stand-alone black-and-white image, with Cb and Cr determining the hue and saturation color information for each pixel. The hue and saturation are defined by values along two lines—referred to as *vectors*—across the standard color wheel, which you'll find marked on your vectorscope.

The vertical vector is labeled as "R-Y" (the analog version of the digital Cr), and the horizontal vector is labeled "B-Y" (the analog equivalent to Cb).

Every color available can be expressed by using these two vectors. You can see how coordinates can be generated through this sort of "longitude and latitude."

Though the challenges associated with transmitting video have changed with the advent of digital video, the color difference system persists, partly because it is a more efficient way to compress, store, and transmit video signals.

The Y'CbCr parade displays three types of information, in much the way that the RGB parade does, by compressing the images horizontally to show all three at once. In this case, the first waveform is the luminance (the same as the regular waveform display), the second waveform corresponds to the vectorscope's B-Y axis; and the third waveform corresponds to the vectorscope's R-Y axis.

Combination views

There are also two combination views that give you several of the display modes at once. These are particularly useful if you have plenty of space on your computer screen to enlarge the Reference Monitor.

They allow you to see lots of views at once.

- **Vect/YC Wave/YCbCr Parade:** Shows a combination view of the vectorscope, YC waveform, and YCbCr parade

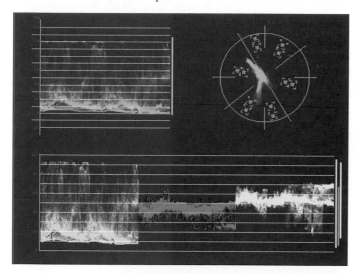

- **Vect/YC Wave/RGB Parade:** Shows a combination view of the vectorscope, YC waveform, and RGB parade

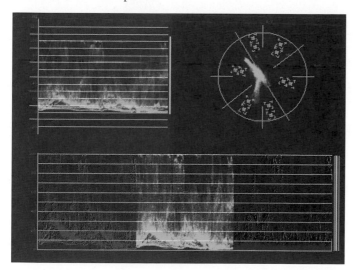

An overview of color-oriented effects

▶ **Tip:** You can always find an effect using the search box at the top of the Effects panel. Often, the best way to learn how to use an effect is to apply it to a clip with a good range of colors, highlights, and shadows and then to adjust all the settings and watch the result.

The color correction special effects are added, modified, and removed in the same way as all of the other effects in Adobe Premiere Pro. Just as with the other effects, you can use keyframes to modify the color correction effect settings over time.

There are many ways to work with color and light in Adobe Premiere Pro. Here are a few effects you may want to try first.

Coloring effects

There are several effects to adjust existing colors. The following two are for creating a black-and-white image and applying a tint and for simply turning a color clip into a black-and-white one.

Tint

Use the eyedroppers or color pickers to reduce any image to just two colors. Whatever you map to black-and-white replaces any other colors in the image.

Black-and-White

Convert any image to simple black-and-white. This is useful when combined with other effects that can add color.

Color removal or replacement

These effects allow you to make changes to colors selectively, rather than modifying the entire image.

Leave Color

Use the eyedropper or color pickers to select a color you would like to keep. Adjust the Amount to Decolor setting to turn the saturation down on every other color.

Use the Tolerance and Edge Software controls to produce a more subtle effect.

Change to Color

Use the eyedroppers or color pickers to select a color you want to change and the color you'd like it to become.

Use the Change menu to select the method you'd like the effect to use to apply the adjustment.

Change Color

Similar to the Change to Color effect, this effect gives subtle controls to adjust one color to another. Rather than matching another color, you change the hue and finesse the selection using the Tolerance and Softness controls.

Color Correction

These effects include a range of controls to adjust the overall look of your video or to make precise selections to adjust individual colors or color ranges.

Fast Color Corrector

As the name suggests, Fast Color Corrector is a quick and easy-to-use effect for adjusting the colors and luminance levels in your clips. You'll be using this effect to adjust the white balance for a shot later in this lesson.

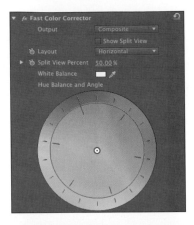

Three-Way Color Corrector

Very similar to Fast Color Corrector, this effect has separate controls for adjusting color for the shadows, midtones, and highlights of your clips. This effect also has powerful secondary color correction controls that allow you to selectively color-correct pixels that have a specific color, brightness, or amount of color saturation.

You'll use this effect to work on a clip later in this lesson.

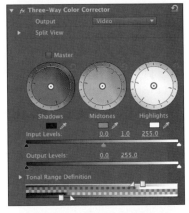

RGB Curves

The RGB Curves effect is a simple graph control that gives natural-looking, subtle results. The horizontal axis of each graph represents the original clip, with shadows on the left and highlights on the right. The vertical axis represents the output from the effect, with shadows at the bottom and highlights at the top.

A straight line from the bottom-left corner to the top-right corner means no change. Drag the line to reshape it, changing the relationship between the original clip levels and the resulting output levels.

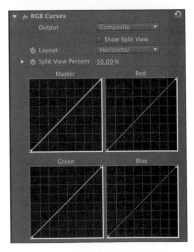

We'll be using another form of curve effect to work on exposure problems with clips later.

RGB Color Corrector

This color correction effect provides precise controls for adjusting an image. You can make changes to the overall image or make selective adjustments to the red, green, and blue parts of the image.

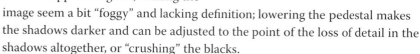

- **Gamma:** Adjusts the midtones.

- **Pedestal:** Adjusts the black point. Raising the pedestal makes the shadows appear brighter, making the image seem a bit "foggy" and lacking definition; lowering the pedestal makes the shadows darker and can be adjusted to the point of the loss of detail in the shadows altogether, or "crushing" the blacks.

- **Gain:** Adjusts the highlights, or white point.

You can achieve interesting results by lowering the pedestal and increasing the gain, giving you strong shadows and bright highlights, and thus increasing the contrast.

Technical color effects

As well as creative effects, the color correction repertoire in Adobe Premiere Pro includes effects used for professional video production.

Video Limiter

Video Limiter gives you precise control over the maximum and minimum levels for your video. It is designed to give natural results. For example, rather than simply chopping off parts of the image that are too bright, the image is compressed to bring it into the legal range. Be sure to examine the parameters of the Video Limiter effect and determine which combination of settings work with any given shot.

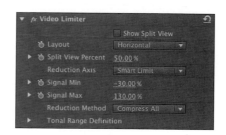

Broadcast Colors

The Broadcast Colors effect gives you a simpler interface for ensuring your levels are legal. Once you know your accepted maximum signal, do the following:

1   Choose between NTSC and PAL video.

2   Choose whether you'd like the effect to reduce luminance or reduce saturation for pixels that go beyond the limit you set.

3   Specify a maximum signal amplitude, using the IRE scale.

The Broadcast Colors effect will adjust all pixels that fall outside the maximum you set. You can use the Key Out Safe and Key Out Unsafe options to display which pixels will be affected by the Broadcast Colors effect.

Fixing exposure problems

Let's look at three clips that have exposure issues and use some of the Color Correction effects to address them.

1   Open the sequence Exposure in the Sequences bin. This sequence has three clips.

2   Set the Reference Monitor to show the YC waveform. Make sure Chroma and Setup (7.5 IRE) are deselected.

The first clip is the lady walking. The environment is smoky. If you position the Timeline playhead over the first clip, and look at the waveform, you can see there's not much contrast in the shot.

100 IRE means fully exposed, and 0 IRE means not exposed at all. None of the image comes close to these levels. Your eye quickly adjusts to the image, and it'll soon look fine. Let's see whether we can bring it to life a little.

3   Add the Luma Curve effect to the clip.

▶ **Tip:** If you increase the size of Effect Controls panel, the Luma Waveform control will get bigger, making it easier to apply subtle adjustments.

4   Click the Luma Waveform control in the Effect Controls panel to create a control point and reshape the line to make a subtle *S* shape. Use the following example as a guide. You'll get the best perceived results if you have a frame from a later part of the clip on-screen. Around 00:00:06:20 there's a section of sharp focus.

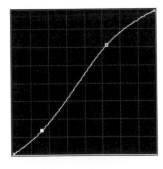

5 Your eye is likely to adjust very quickly to the new image. Try toggling the Luma Curve effect off and on to compare the image before and after.

The subtle adjustment you made adds more depth to the image, giving it stronger highlights and shadows. As you toggle the effect off and on, you'll see the waveform monitor changing. We still don't have bright highlights in the image, but that's fine because its natural colors are mainly midtones.

Underexposed images

Move the Timeline playhead to the second clip in the sequence, Cowboy Dark. When you first look at this clip, it might look OK. There's a shadowy area to the left, but there's a reasonable amount of detail in the lighter area to the right.

Now take a look at the waveform. The bottom of the waveform is crushed to 0. Any pixels below 0 are effectively lost. There is no detail or texture in that area because all the pixels are completely black.

The problem with crushed blacks like this is that increasing the brightness will simply change the strong shadows into gray, and no detail will emerge.

1 Add the Brightness & Contrast effect to the clip.

2 Use the Brightness control in the Effect Controls panel to increase the brightness. Rather than clicking the number and typing a new number, click and drag to the right so you can see the change happening incrementally.

As you drag, notice that the whole waveform moves up. This is fine for bringing out the highlights in the image, but the shadows remain a flat line. You're simply changing the black shadows to gray. If you drag the Brightness control all the way to 100, you'll see just how flat the image still is.

3 Remove the Brightness & Contrast effect.

4 Try to make an adjustment using the Luma Curve effect or the RGB Curves effect. Here's an example of a Luma Curve effect that would improve the image.

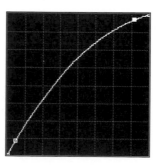

▶ **Tip:** You can remove a control point from the curve control by dragging it completely out of the graph.

Overexposed images

Move the Timeline playhead to the third clip in the sequence. This is the same shot, but this time it is overexposed. Notice, later in the shot, the rim of the hat is burned out. Just as with the crushed blacks in the previous example, there is no detail in burned-out whites. This means lowering the brightness will simply change the rim of the hat from white to gray, and no detail will emerge.

Notice the shadows don't reach 0 in this shot. The lack of properly dark shadows has a flattening effect on the image.

Try using one of the curves effects to improve the contrast range. Here's an example that might work.

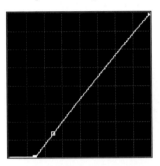

When is color correction right?

Making adjustments to images is a highly subjective approach. Though there are precise standards for image formats and broadcast technologies, whether an image should be light, dark, blue tinted, or green is ultimately a subjective choice. The reference tools, such as the waveform display, are a helpful guide, but only you can decide when the picture looks right.

If you're producing video for display on televisions, it is vital that you have a television screen connected to your Adobe Premiere Pro editing system to view your content. Television screens display color in dramatically different ways to computer monitors.

The difference is quite similar to the difference between looking at colors in photos on your computer monitor and then seeing the colors as they are produced by your printer.

Fixing color balance

Your eyes adjust to compensate for changes in the color of light around you automatically. It's an extraordinary ability that allows you to see white as white, even if objectively it's orange, for example, because it's lit by tungsten light.

Camera operators can automatically adjust their white balance to compensate for different lighting in the way that your eyes do. With the right calibration, white objects look white, whether you are recording indoors, under more orange tungsten light, or outdoors in more blue daylight.

Sometimes automatic white balance is a little bit hit or miss, so professional shooters often prefer to manually set the white balance. If the white balance is set wrong, you can end up with some interesting results. The most common reason for a color balance problem in a clip is that the camera was not calibrated properly.

Basic white balance (Fast Color Corrector)

Open the sequence Color in the Sequences bin. If you set the Timeline playhead over the first shot in this sequence, you can see

someone using a clever technique to find out what was written on a pad of paper. Something is not quite right, though—that paper isn't white, and it should be.

Apply the Fast Color Corrector effect to the clip. This effect shares many controls with another effect, Three-Way Color Corrector. We'll look over the controls for that effect next. In the meantime, let's find out why this effect is described as Fast.

1   Make sure the paper clip is selected in the sequence so the Effect Controls panel will display the Fast Color Corrector effect controls.

2   Select the White Balance eyedropper in the Effect Controls panel.

3   Click a part of the paper pad that should be white. Be careful to avoid the gray area with the pencil marks or the colored lines.

The White Balance control tells the Fast Color Corrector effect what should be white. By default, you'll notice the color swatch is pure white. When you select a different color with the eyedropper, the Fast Color Corrector effect adjusts all colors in the image by the difference between pure white and the color you selected.

In this example, you selected a creamy orange color—the result of the lighting on the scene. The Fast Color Corrector adjusts all colors in the scene toward blue.

You can see exactly what the effect is doing by looking at the color wheel, located just below the White Balance control. Like the vectorscope, the color wheel represents colors with increasing intensity toward the edge of the circle. Rather than measuring color, the color wheel in the Fast Color Corrector applies an adjustment. The more the small circle at the center of the wheel is moved toward the edge, the more adjustment is applied.

▶ **Tip:** The difference made with color correction can be quite subtle. Toggle the effect off and on in the Effect Controls panel to see a before-and-after comparison.

You can see, in this example, that Adobe Premiere Pro has applied a small adjustment toward cyan blue. In this way, using the White Balance control and the color wheel can help you to learn about color correction and the adjustments needed to balance whites.

Primary color correction

The words *primary* and *secondary* have more than one meaning. Historically, the place where "color timing" was applied was during the film transfer process at the telecine. A *primary correction* involved adjusting the relationship between the primary colors (red, green, and blue) in the printer lights. A *secondary correction* involved focusing on certain color ranges within an image, often through adding adjustments of secondary colors. So, while *primary* and *secondary* define types of colors on a color wheel, you can also use these terms to describe stages in the color correction workflow.

Broadly speaking, primary color correction still involves overall color correction adjustments to the whole image. These days, you can also employ adjustments through secondary colors and still consider it "primary" because the entire image is affected, *and* it's typically most effective to make these adjustments first.

Because secondary color correction (so designated because it is typically done after primary adjustments) usually involves more subtle fine-tuning, the name has come to mean applying adjustments to selected pixels within an image.

Let's look at primary color correction first. The Three-Way Color Corrector effect works in a very similar way to the Fast Color Corrector effect, but with more advanced controls. The effect was updated for Adobe Premiere Pro CS6. It is a very powerful color correction tool that, combined with the Reference Monitor and the new Adjustment Layer feature, helps you achieve professional color correction results.

Before we start working on a clip, let's run through the main controls:

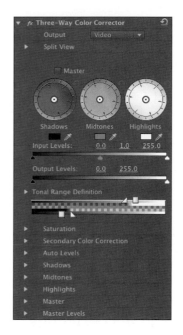

- **Output:** Use this menu to view your clip in color or black-and-white. Viewing in black-and-white is useful for identifying contrast.

- **Show Split View:** Turn on Show Split View to see a "before" and "after" version of your clip, with one half changed by the effect and the other half unaffected. You can choose a horizontal or vertical layout and change the percentage of the split.

- **Shadows Balance, Midtones Balance, Highlights Balance:** Each color wheel allows you to make subtle adjustments to the colors in your clip. If you select the Master checkbox, adjustments you make will apply to the whole clip, not just the shadows, midtones, or highlights. Note that the adjustments you make with the Master mode on are independent of adjustments you make to the individual parts of the clip.

- **Input Levels:** Use the slider controls to change the Shadow, Midtone, and Highlight levels for this clip.

- **Output Levels:** Use the slider controls to adjust the minimum brightness and maximum brightness for the clip. The Input Levels relate directly to this control, so, for example, if you set your Input Shadow level to 20, and your Output Shadow level to 0, anything in your clip that has a pixel brightness of 20 or less will be lowered to 0.

About levels

Eight-bit video—which describes all SD broadcast video—is measured on a brightness scale from 0 to 255. When you adjust Input Levels or Output Levels, you change the relationship between the displayed levels and the original clip levels.

For example, if you set the Output white to 255, Adobe Premiere Pro will use the maximum brightness range for the video. If you set the Input white to 200, Adobe Premiere Pro will stretch the original clip brightness so that 200 becomes 255. The result is that your highlights will get brighter, and pixel values originally greater than 200 will *clip*, or become flat white, losing any detail.

The Input levels have three controls: Shadows, Midtones, and Highlights. By changing these levels, you change the relationship between the original clip levels and the way those levels are displayed during playback.

- **Tonal Range Definition:** Use the sliders to define the range of pixels affected by the Shadows, Midtones, and Highlights controls. For example, if you drag the highlight slider left, you'll increase the amount of pixels adjusted when using Highlights controls. The triangle-shaped slider allows you to define the extent of a softening between the levels you are adjusting. Click the Tonal Range Definition disclosure triangle to get access to individual controls and the Show Tonal Range checkbox. If you check the box, Adobe Premiere Pro displays your image in just three gray tones, so you can identify which parts of your picture will be affected when you make adjustments. Black pixels are shadows, gray pixels are midtones, and white pixels are highlights.

- **Saturation:** Use this to adjust the amount of color in the clip. You have a Master control that will adjust the overall clip and separate controls for the Shadows, Midtones, and Highlights.

- **Secondary Color Correction:** This advanced color correction feature allows you to define specific pixels you would like to adjust, based on their color or brightness. The Show Mask option shows you which pixels you have selected to apply the color correction adjustment to. Using this feature, you could, for example, selectively adjust pixels with a particular shade of green.

- **Auto Levels:** Use this feature to automatically adjust the Input levels. You can click the Auto buttons or use eyedroppers. To use the eyedroppers, select one (Black, Gray, or White), and then click a reciprocal part of the picture. For example, select the White Level eyedropper, and then click the brightest part of the picture. Adobe Premiere Pro updates the Levels controls based on the selections you make.

- **Shadows, Midtones, Highlights, Master:** These controls allow you to make the same adjustments as the Shadows, Midtones, Highlights, and Master color balance controls, but with more precision. When you change one, the other updates automatically.

- **Master Levels:** These controls allow you to make the same adjustments as the Input Levels and Output Levels controls, but with more precision. When you change one, the other updates automatically.

The second clip in the Color sequence shows a scene in an office. This clip has a range of shadows, midtones, and highlights. It also has a range of colors. It looks pretty flat and seems to have a color cast. Taking a look in the vectorscope confirms it: There's a blue tint.

1 To begin, apply the Three-Way Color Corrector effect to the clip and switch to the Effect Controls panel.

Now let's fix the shot.

2 Expand the Auto Levels controls.

3 Click the Auto Black Level, Auto Contrast, and Auto White Level buttons in turn. Notice the Input Levels controls adjust to reflect the new levels.

Adobe Premiere Pro has identified the darkest pixels for the Black level and the brightest pixels for the White Level and has balanced them for the Gray level.

4 Use the eyedropper controls for the Shadows, Midtones, and Highlights Color Balance controls to select black, gray, and white items in the shot. This will correct the color cast.

▶ **Tip:** If you'd like to try using the eyedropper controls instead, you might find it helpful to change the zoom setting for the Program Monitor to 100%, making it easier to click the pixels you want.

5 Take a look at the vectorscope. If it looks like the shot still has an overall color cast, switch on the Master mode for the Color Balance controls, and drag any of the wheels away from the color cast shown in the vectorscope.

Once you have applied Color Balance adjustments, you make want to tweak the Input levels to fine-tune the result.

The Three-Way Color Corrector effect gives you very precise control over your clips. If you prefer to make broader adjustments, you can always use the Fast Color Corrector.

Secondary color correction

As described earlier, secondary color correction involves applying color correction adjustments to selected pixels, rather than the whole image. The adjustments you make are the same as those you might make with the Fast Color Corrector effect or Three-Way Color Corrector effect; the only difference is the limited selection.

Let's try this with the office shot. In the background, there's a window showing a green neon sign outside. Let's warm up that part of the shot.

1 Continue to work with the second shot in the Color sequence. Apply another instance of the Three-Way Color Corrector effect to the clip.

2 It can get fairly confusing working with the same effect twice. Click the disclosure triangle () for the first instance of the Three-Way Color Corrector effect in the Effect Controls panel to collapse the settings and hide them from view.

3 Expand the Secondary Color Correction controls for the new instance of the Three-Way Color Corrector effect. Click the first of the three center eyedroppers to select it.

4 Use the eyedropper to select the green in the window.

5 Turn on the Show Mask option. In this view, Adobe Premiere Pro shows selected pixels in white and unselected pixels in black. Clearly, we need to pick a broader selection.

6 Use the second center eyedropper to select another part of the window. This eyedropper adds to the selection, while the third eyedropper removes from the selection. As soon as you select an eyedropper, the image returns to its original state for you to make your selection.

7 Continue using the eyedroppers to make selections until the Mask view gives a pretty clean white area where the window is in the picture.

8 While clicking with the eyedroppers, you've been applying Hue, Saturation, and Luma selections. Expand these controls now. You can see manual controls to set these levels, including Start and End Softness, which blend between the selected and unselected pixels. Try adjusting these a little to smooth the edges of the mark. When you're happy with the result, turn off the Show Mask option.

9 You have now selected only a portion of the image to be adjusted. At the top of the Three-Way Color Corrector controls, turn on the Master option. Now use the outer edge of the Color Balance wheels as a hue control. Drag any of the wheel edges around to transform the green color. See whether you can turn it into a warmer color.

▶ **Tip:** It is quite likely that your selection includes part of the desk lamp, because the colors are the same as the portion of the image you're fixing. This is something that you can avoid by using a second copy of the clip and a Garbage Matte effect. For more information about garbage mattes, see Lesson 15, "Exploring Compositing Techniques."

Using secondary color correction, only the green colors found in the window are changed.

Special color effects

Several special effects give you great creative control over the colors in your clips. Others have important functional controls to make sure your content meets the stringent requirements for broadcast television.

Here are a few effects of note.

The Leave Color effect

Use this effect to select one color you would like to remain in color, while every other color is removed.

Use the Color to Leave eyedropper to choose the color you want to leave unaffected. Use the Amount to Decolor control to specify how much color to remove. The Tolerance and Edge Softness controls finesse your selection, while the Match

Colors menu lets you choose to select the color based on the Hue setting or the RGB levels.

The Change to Color effect

Use this effect to select one color you would like to change and a second color you would like it to match.

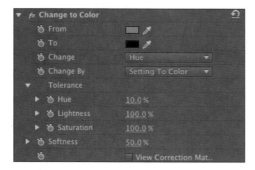

Use the From eyedropper to select a color you would like to change in the scene; then use either the To eyedropper or the To color picker to select the color you would like it to become.

Here is a before-and-after example of this effect.

Before   After

Broadcast legalization

When video is broadcast, there are specific limits that are permitted for maximum luminance, minimum luminance, and color saturation. Although it's possible to confine your video levels to the limits permitted using manual controls, it's easy to mix parts of your sequence that need adjustment.

The Video Limiter effect automatically limits the levels of clips to ensure they meet the standards you set.

You'll need to check the limits applied by your broadcaster before setting the Signal Min and Signal Max controls with this effect. Then it's simply a question of choosing the Reduction Axis option—do you want to just limit the luminance, chrominance, or both, or set an overall "smart" limit?

The Reduction Method menu allows you to choose the parts of your video signal you would like to adjust. You'll usually choose Compress All.

▶ **Tip:** While it is common to apply the Video Limiter effect to individual clips, you might also choose to apply it to the whole sequence by nesting it in another sequence. For more information about nesting sequences, see Lesson 8, "Advanced Editing Techniques."

Creating a look

Once you've spent a little time with the color correction effects available in Adobe Premiere Pro, you should get a feel for the kinds of changes you can make and the impact those changes have on the overall look and feel of your footage.

You can use regular effect presets to create a look for your clips. You can also apply an effect to an adjustment layer to give your sequence an overall look.

In the most common color correction scenario, you would do the following:

• Adjust each shot so that it matches the other shots in the same scene. This way, there is color continuity.

• Next, apply an overall look to your production.

You can try this now with the Double Identity sequence.

1   Open the Double Identity sequence in the Sequences bin.

2   In the Project panel, click the New Item button menu and choose Adjustment Layer. The settings should automatically match the sequence, so just click OK.

3   Drag and drop the new adjustment layer onto the Video 3 track in the sequence.

    The default duration for adjustment layers is the same as the duration of still images. It's too short for this sequence.

4 Trim the adjustment layer until it stretches from the beginning to the end of the sequence.

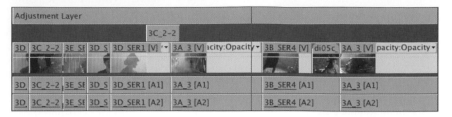

5 Apply any color correction effect to the adjustment layer, and make any changes you would like. Your changes will apply to every clip in the sequence.

● **Note:** If you use adjustment layers in this way on a sequence that has graphics and titles, you may want to ensure the adjustment layer is on a track between the graphics/titles and the video. Otherwise, you will adjust the appearance of your titles too.

Sending clips to Adobe SpeedGrade

Adobe SpeedGrade is a powerful color correction application included with Creative Suite 6 Production Premium and Creative Suite 6 Master Collection.

Adobe Premiere Pro has powerful color correction tools but is primarily an editing system. Adobe SpeedGrade is completely devoted to the task of color correction, and it provides superior tools for the purpose.

You can share your Adobe Premiere Pro sequence with Adobe SpeedGrade in one of two ways.

- Export your sequence as an EDL that you can import into Adobe SpeedGrade by choosing File > Export > EDL.

- Choose File > Send To Adobe SpeedGrade. Adobe Premiere Pro will create an .irpc file, readable by Adobe SpeedGrade, and export your sequence in the high-quality DPX format to go with it.

Review questions

1 Why is the Reference Monitor ganged to the Program Monitor?

2 How do you change a monitor display to show the YC waveform?

3 How do you turn off the display of chroma information in the YC waveform?

4 Why use monitors like the vectorscope rather than depending on your eyes?

5 How can you apply a look to a sequence?

6 Why might you need to limit your luminance or color levels?

Review answers

1 The Reference Monitor shows the contents of the current sequence, just as the Program Monitor does. By ganging them together, you can be sure the Reference Monitor is displaying the same content, even when you are looking at the vectorscope or waveform display.

2 Click the Settings button menu and choose the display type you would like.

3 Uncheck the Chroma box at the top of the YC waveform display.

4 The way we perceive color is highly subjective *and* relative. Depending on the colors you have just seen, you will see new colors differently. The vectorscope display gives you an objective reference.

5 You can use effect presets to apply the same color correction adjustments to multiple clips or add an adjustment layer and apply the adjustment to that. Any clips on lower tracks covered by the adjustment layer will be affected.

6 If your sequence is intended for broadcast television, you will need to ensure you meet the stringent requirements for maximum and minimum levels. The broadcaster you are working with will be able to tell you their required levels.

15 EXPLORING COMPOSITING TECHNIQUES

Lesson overview

In this lesson, you'll learn about the following:

- Using the alpha channel

- Using compositing techniques

- Working with opacity

- Working with a greenscreen

- Using mattes

 This lesson will take approximately 50 minutes.

Compositing comprises blending, combining, layering, keying, masking, and cropping, in any number of combinations. Anything that combines two images is compositing.

Adobe Premiere Pro CS6 has powerful tools that enable you to create professional combined layers of video in your sequences.

In this lesson, you'll learn about the key technologies that make compositing work and approaches to preparing for compositing, adjusting the opacity of clips, and keying greenscreen shots with chromakey and mattes.

Getting started

Until now, you have been mainly working with single, whole-frame images. You have created edits where you have transitioned between one image and another or edited clips onto upper video tracks to have them appear in front of clips on lower video tracks.

In this lesson, you'll learn about ways to combine those layers of video. You'll still use clips on upper and lower tracks, but now they will become foreground and background elements in one blended image.

The blend might come from cropping part of the foreground image or from *keying*—selecting specific colors to become transparent—but, whatever the method, the way you edit clips onto a sequence is the same as ever.

You'll begin by learning about an important concept that explains the way pixels are displayed and then try several techniques.

1 Open Lesson 15.prproj in the Lesson 15 folder.

   Switch to the Effects workspace.

2 Choose Window > Workspace > Effects.

3 Choose Window > Workspace > Reset Current Workspace to open the Reset Workspace dialog.

4 Click Yes.

What is an alpha channel?

Visible   Transparent   Partially transparent glow

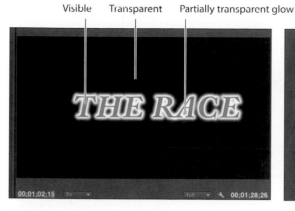

This title...

...combines with this video.

To produce this composite image, everything begins with cameras selectively recording the red, green, and blue parts of the light spectrum as separate color channels. Because each channel is monochrome (just one of the three colors), they are commonly described as *grayscale*.

Adobe Premiere Pro uses these three grayscale channels to produce the corresponding primary color channels. They are combined using primary additive color to create a complete RGB image. You see the three channels combined as full-color video.

This is not the end of the story! There is a fourth grayscale channel: alpha.

The fourth channel defines no colors at all. Instead, it defines opacity—how visible the pixel is. Several different words are used in the world of post-production to describe this fourth channel, including visibility, transparency, mixer, and opacity. The name is not particularly important. What matters is that you understand that you can adjust the opacity of each pixel independently of its color.

Just as you might use color correction to adjust the amount of red in a clip, you can use Opacity controls to adjust the amount of alpha transparency.

By default, the alpha channel, or Opacity, of a typical camera footage clip, is at 100 percent, or fully visible. On the 8-bit video scale, of 0 to 255, this means it will be at 255. Clips that are animations or text or logo graphics will often have alpha channels that control what parts of an image are opaque and transparent.

Using compositing in your projects

The use of compositing special effects and controls can take your post-production work to a whole new level. Compositing means creating new image compositions from existing ones. Once you begin working with the compositing effects available in Adobe Premiere Pro, you'll find yourself discovering new ways of filming and new ways of structuring your edit to make it easier to blend images together.

It's the combination of filming techniques and dedicated effects that produces the most impactful results when compositing. You can combine simple images of environments with complex, interesting patterns to produce extraordinary textured moods. Or, you can cut out parts of an image that don't fit and replace them with something else.

Compositing is one of the most creative parts of nonlinear editing with Adobe Premiere Pro.

Shooting videos with compositing in mind

Much of the most effective compositing work begins when you are planning your production. Right at the start, you can begin to think about how you can help Adobe Premiere Pro to identify the parts of the image you'd like to be transparent. Adobe Premiere Pro has a limited number of ways of identifying which pixels you'd like to make transparent. Consider chromakey, for example, the standard special effect used to allow weather reporters to appear in front of a map.

The weather reporter is actually standing in front of a greenscreen. Special-effects technology uses the green color to identify which pixels should be transparent. The video image of the weather reporter is used as the foreground of a composition, with some visible pixels (the reporter) and some transparent pixels (the green background).

Next, it's just a question of putting the foreground video image in front of another background image. In a weather report, it's a map, but it could just as easily be any other video or graphic image.

Planning ahead can make a big difference to the quality of your compositing. For that blue or greenscreen to work well, it needs to be a consistent color. It also needs to be a color that does not appear anywhere on your subject. Green-colored jewelry, for example, might turn transparent when the key effect is applied.

This…

…combined with this…

…becomes this.

If you're shooting greenscreen footage, the way you film can make a big difference to the finished result. Be sure to capture the background with soft light and try to avoid *spill*, where light reflected from the screen bounces onto your subject. If this happens, you'll be in danger of *keying out*, or making transparent, parts of your subject.

Essential terminology

For the purposes of this lesson, we'll be using some terms that might be new to you. Let's run through some important ones:

- **Alpha/alpha channel:** The fourth channel of information for each pixel. An alpha channel defines transparency for an image. It's a separate grayscale channel, and it can be created entirely independently of the content of the image.

- **Key/keying:** The process of selectively making pixels transparent based on their color or brightness. The Chromakey effect uses color to generate transparency (that is, to modify the alpha channel), while the LumaKey effect uses brightness.

- **Opacity:** The word used to describe the overall alpha channel value for clips in a sequence in Adobe Premiere Pro. You can adjust the opacity for a clip over time using keyframes.

- **Blending mode:** A technology originally seen in Adobe Photoshop. Rather than simply placing foreground images in front of background images, you can select one of several different blending modes that cause the foreground to interact with the background. You might, for example, choose to view only pixels that are brighter than the background or to apply only the color information from the foreground clip to the background. Experimentation is often the best way to learn about blending modes.

- **Greenscreen:** The common term that describes the overall process of filming a subject in front of a greenscreen and then using a special effect to selectively turn green pixels transparent by creating an alpha matte based on the color background. The clip is then composited over a background image in a similar fashion to a "screen" key that would use basic image luma information—which is why it's called *greenscreen*. A weather report is a good example of greenscreen.

- **Matte:** An image, shape, or video clip used to identify a region of your foreground image that should be transparent or semitransparent. Adobe Premiere Pro allows multiple types of mattes, and you will be working with them in this lesson.

Working with the Opacity effect

You can adjust the overall opacity of a clip using keyframes on the Timeline or in the Effect Controls panel.

1   Open the sequence Evening Jacket in the Sequences bin. This sequence has a foreground image of a man in a jacket, with a background image of a sunset.

2   Make sure the Video 2 track is expanded so you can see the keyframe rubber band for the Jacket foreground clip.

3   Adobe Premiere Pro allows you to use the rubber band to adjust the settings and keyframe any effect you apply to a clip. Since the fixed effects include Opacity, this option is automatically available. In fact, it is the default option, which means the rubber band already represents clip opacity. Try dragging the rubber band up and down using the Selection tool.

> **Tip:** When adjusting the rubber band, you can hold the Control (Windows) or Command (Mac OS) key for fine control.

When you use the Selection tool in this way, the rubber band is moved without additional keyframes being added.

In this example, the foreground is set to 50 percent opacity.

Keyframing opacity

Keyframing opacity on the Timeline is almost exactly the same as keyframing volume. You use the same tools and keyboard shortcuts, and the results are likely to be exactly what you expect; the higher the rubber band, the more visible a clip will be.

1 Open the sequence Race in the Sequences bin. This sequence has a title in the foreground. It's common to need to fade titles up and down at different times and with different durations. You can do so using a transition effect, just as you would add a transition to a video clip. For more control, you can use keyframes to adjust the opacity.

2 Make sure the Video 2 track is expanded so you can see the rubber band for the foreground title.

3 Hold the Control (Windows) or Command (Mac OS) key, and click the rubber band for the title graphic to add four keyframes, two near the beginning and two near the end.

▶ **Tip:** It's often easier to add the keyframe markers to the rubber band first and then drag them to adjust them.

4 Adjust the keyframes so they represent a fade-up and a fade-down in the same way that you would adjust audio keyframes to adjust volume. Play the sequence and watch the results of your keyframing.

▶ **Tip:** Once you've added a keyframe with the Control (Windows) or Command (Mac OS) key, you can release the key and start dragging with the mouse to set the keyframe position.

You can use the Effect Controls panel to add keyframes to the opacity for a clip. Like the audio volume keyframes, the Opacity setting has keyframing turned on by default in the Effect Controls panel. This means that if you would like to make a flat level adjustment to the overall opacity of a clip, it's sometimes quicker to do it on the Timeline, rather than in the Effect Controls panel.

Combine layers based on a blending mode

Blending modes are special ways for foreground pixels to combine with background pixels. Each blending mode applies a different calculation to combine the foreground *RGBA*—red, green, blue, and alpha—values with those of the background. Each pixel is calculated individually in combination with the pixel directly behind it.

The default blending mode for all clips is Normal. In this mode, the foreground image has a uniform alpha channel value across the entire image. The more opacity the foreground image has, the more strongly you will see those pixels in front of the pixels in the background.

The best way to find out how blending modes work is to try them.

1 Open the Double Identity sequence in the Sequences bin. This sequence already has a title at the end of the edited intro.

2 Select the top-level part of the title, called Title Text, and take a look at the Effect Controls panel.

3 In the Effect controls panel, expand the Opacity controls and take a look at the Blend Mode option.

4 Right now, the blending mode is set to Normal. Try a few different ones to see the results. Each blending mode calculates the relationship between the foreground layer pixels and the background pixels differently. See the Adobe Premiere Pro Help for a description of the blending modes.

In this example, the foreground has the Lighten blending mode. Only the pixels in the foreground that are lighter than the pixels in the background are visible.

Working with alpha-channel transparencies

Many types of media already will have varying alpha channel levels for pixels. A title is an obvious example: Where text exists, pixels have 100 percent opacity, and where there is no text, pixels usually have 0 percent opacity. Elements such as drop shadows behind text typically have a value somewhere in between. Keeping some transparency in a drop shadow helps it look a bit more realistic.

Adobe Premiere Pro sees pixels with higher values in the alpha channel as being more visible. This is the most common way to interpret alpha channels, but occasionally you might come across media that is configured in the opposite way.

You will immediately recognize the problem because your foreground image will become a cut-out in an otherwise black image. This is easy to address because just as Adobe Premiere Pro can interpret the audio channels on a clip, it is also possible to choose the correct interpretation of existing alpha channel information.

You can see the results very easily using the title in the Double Identity sequence.

1 Set the Timeline playhead so you can see the title in the Program Monitor.

2 Select the foreground title text and use the Effect Controls panel to set the blending mode to Normal.

3 Locate the Title Text clip in the Graphics bin. Right-click the clip and choose Modify > Interpret Footage. At the bottom of the panel, you'll find the Alpha Channel interpretation options.

4 Try each of the options, and observe the results in the Program Monitor. You will need to click OK before the display will update.

The options are as follows:

- **Ignore Alpha Channel:** Treats all pixels as having 100 percent alpha. This can be useful if you do not intend to use a background layer in your sequence.

- **Invert Alpha Channel:** Reverses the alpha channel for every pixel in the clip. This means pixels that were fully opaque will become fully transparent, and pixels that were transparent will become opaque.

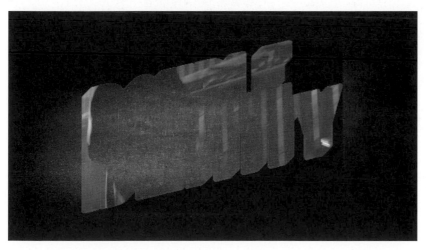

Color keying a greenscreen shot

When you change the opacity level of a clip using the rubber band or the Effect Controls panel, you adjust the alpha for every pixel in the image by the same amount. There are also ways to selectively adjust the alpha for pixels, based on their position on the screen, their brightness, or their color.

Chromakey effects adjust the opacity for a range of pixels based on their specific luminance, hue, and saturation values. The principle is quite simple: You select a color, or range of colors, and the more similar a pixel is to the color selection, the more transparent it becomes. The more closely a pixel color matches the selection, the more its alpha channel value is lowered, until it becomes fully transparent.

Open the sequence Keying Double Identity in the Sequences bin.

This is similar to the other Double Identity sequence, but the shot where the lady gets into the car has been replaced by a greenscreen version. This is a better version because it has audio, but the green parts of the image need to be removed.

The foreground video is on the Video 2 track. On the Video 1 track there's a still image background that has already been loosely keyframed to follow the camera movements of the foreground image.

All that remains is to remove the green pixels.

Preprocessing the footage

In a perfect world, every greenscreen clip you work with would have a flawless green background and nice, clean edges on your foreground elements. In reality, there are lots of reasons why you might be faced with less than perfect material.

Of course, there's always the potential problems caused by poor lighting when the video is created. However, there's a further problem caused by the way many video cameras store image information.

Because your eyes do not register color with as much acuity as they do brightness information, it is common for cameras to reduce the amount of color information stored. For DVCPro 25 video, for example, color information is only recorded for every fourth pixel.

Camera systems achieve reductions in file size using this system of reduced color capture, and the approach varies from system to system. Sometimes color information is stored for every other pixel; other times it might be recorded for every other pixel on every second line. Whatever the system, it's going to make keying more difficult because there simply isn't as much color detail as you'd like.

If you find your footage is not keying well, try the following:

- Consider applying a light blur effect before keying. This blends pixel detail, softening the edges and often giving a smoother-looking key. If the amount of blur is very light, it should not dramatically reduce the quality of your image. You can simply apply a blur effect to the clip, adjust the settings, and then apply a Chromakey effect on top. The Chromakey effect will work on the clip as it appears after being blurred.

- Consider color correcting your shot before you key it. If your shot lacks good contrast between your foreground and background, you can sometimes help the key by adjusting the picture first with an effect like the Three-Way Color Corrector or Fast Color Corrector.

Using the Ultra Key effect

Adobe Premiere Pro has a powerful, fast, and intuitive Chromakey effect called Ultra Key. The workflow is very simple: Choose a color you would like to become transparent, and then adjust settings to suit. The Ultra Key effect, like every greenscreen keyer, dynamically generates a matte, based on the color selection. The matte is adjustable using the detailed settings of the Ultra Key effect.

Let's try it.

1 Apply the Ultra Key effect to the KeyCar clip in the Keying Double Identity sequence.

2 In the Effect Controls panel, select the Key Color eyedropper. Use the eyedropper to click a green area in the KeyCar shot, visible through the windows of the car. This clip has a consistent green visible in the background, so it is not too important where you click. With other footage, you may need to experiment to find the right spot.

Tip: If you hold the Control key (Windows) or Command (Mac OS) key when you click with the eyedropper, Adobe Premiere Pro takes a 5x5 pixel sample average, rather than a single pixel selection. This often captures a better color for keying.

The Ultra Key effect identifies all pixels that have the green you selected and sets their alpha to 0%.

3   In the Effect Controls panel, change the Output menu for the Ultra Key effect to Alpha Channel. In this mode, the Ultra Key effect displays the alpha channel as a grayscale image, where dark pixels will be transparent and light pixels will be opaque.

It's clear that what appeared to be a clean key is far from it: Those windows are far too gray.

4   Change the Setting menu to Aggressive, and scrub through the shot to see whether it has nice, clean black areas and white areas. If you see gray pixels in this view where there should not be, the result will be partially transparent parts in the picture.

5   Switch the Output menu back to Composite to see the result.

The Aggressive mode works much better for this clip. The Default, Relaxed, and Aggressive modes modify the Matte Generation, Matte Cleanup, and Spill Suppression settings. You can also modify them yourself to get a better key with more challenging footage.

Each group of settings has a different purpose. Here's an overview:

- **Matte Generation:** Once you've chosen your key color, the Matte Generation controls adjust the way it is interpreted. You will often get positive results with more challenging footage by adjusting these settings.

- **Matte Cleanup:** Once your matte is defined, you can use these controls to adjust it. Choke shrinks the matte, which is helpful if your key selection misses some edges. Be careful not to choke the matte too much because you'll begin to lose edge detail in the foreground image, often supplying a "digital haircut" in the vernacular of the visual-effects industry. Soften applies a blur to the matte, which often improves the apparent "blending" of the foreground and background image for a more convincing composite. Contrast increases the contrast of the alpha channel, making that black-and-white image a stronger black and white and thereby more clearly defining the key. You will often get much cleaner keys by increasing the contrast.

- **Spill Suppression:** Spill Suppression compensates for color that bounces from the green background onto the subject. When this happens, the combination of the green background and the subject's own colors are usually different enough that it does not cause parts of the subject to be keyed transparent. However, it does not look good when the edges of your subject are green! Spill suppression automatically compensates by adding color to the foreground element edges that is positioned opposite, on a color wheel, to the key color. For example, magenta is added when greenscreen keying, or yellow is added when bluescreen keying. This neutralizes the color "spill."

For more information about each of these controls, see the Adobe Premiere Pro Help.

● **Note:** In this example, we're using footage with a green background. It is also possible you'll have footage with a blue background for keying. The workflow is exactly the same.

The Color Correction controls give you a quick and easy way to adjust the appearance of your foreground video to help it blend in with your background. Often, these three controls are enough to make a more natural match. Note that these adjustments are applied after the key, so you won't cause problems for your key by adjusting the colors with these controls.

Using mattes

The Ultra Key effect generates a matte dynamically, based on the colors in your shot. You can also create your own custom matte or use another clip as the basis for a matte.

When you create your own matte, you are defining a shape that will act as a cut-out for your video. Let's try this with a common scenario when using greenscreen clips.

1 Open the Reporter sequence in the Sequences bin.

This sequence has a reporter standing in front of a greenscreen, but the green does not reach the edge of the screen.

2 Apply the Four-Point Garbage Matte effect to the Reporter.mov clip. A *garbage matte* is a completely user-definable area that you want to define as visible or transparent.

3 Select the Four-Point Garbage Matte effect in the Effect Controls panel. You need to click the name of the effect on the list of effects to select it.

When you select the effect, Adobe Premiere Pro displays special handles in the Program Monitor.

● **Note:** The matte in the example extends beyond the edge of the image. This is fine—the main goal is to choose what you will exclude. In this case, the curtain is successfully excluded.

4 Drag the garbage matte handles so the selection excludes the black curtain.

Immediately, you can see the background layer of this sequence. The Four-Point Garbage Matte effect is already defining some pixels that should be transparent.

5 Apply the Ultra Key effect to the foreground Reporter clip in the sequence and use the techniques you used previously to key the shot.

The result is a clean key, with no curtain. You used the Four-Point Garbage Matte effect because this was a relatively simple clip to fix. There are also Eight-Point and Sixteen-Point versions of this effect for more complex shots, plus the positions of the points can all be keyframed using the standard controls in the Effect Controls panel.

Using mattes that use graphics or other clips

The Garbage Matte effects are user-defined regions that should be visible or transparent. Adobe Premiere Pro can also use another clip as the basis for a matte.

Using the Track Matte Key effect, Adobe Premiere Pro borrows the luminance information or alpha channel information from one clip to define a matte for another clip. This simple effect can produce very powerful results, with a little planning and preparation.

Using Track Matte Key

Let's use the Track Matte Key effect to create a layered background for future titles.

1   Open the Clouds sequence in the Sequences bin. This sequence has three layers:

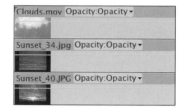

- **Video 3:** Some clouds. This clip has a Luma Curve effect applied to increase the contrast.

- **Video 2:** A sunset photo with rich colors.

- **Video 1:** A sunset photo with paler colors.

2   Apply the Track Matte Key effect to the Sunset clip on Video 2.

3   In the Effect Controls panel, set the Track Matte Key Matte menu to Video 3.

4   Set the Composite Using menu to Matte Luma.

Scrub through the sequence to see the result. The top clip is no longer visible. It is being used as a guide to define the visible and transparent regions of the clip on Video 2.

The effect is quite subtle, because the clouds move slowly. Nonetheless, the result is the appearance of pink clouds layered on the background layer.

Creating a custom matte with the Title tool

The Track Matte Key effect can use any other clip to define which pixels should be visible or transparent. It's common to use the Adobe Premiere Pro Title tool to generate simple shapes for use with the Track Matte Key effect.

Let's create a soft-edged circle we can use to highlight a region in a shot.

1 Open the sequence Mountain Race in the Sequences bin.

This sequence has a clip with two bikers racing and an adjustment layer. We want to draw attention to one of the cyclists. We'll do this by combining the adjustment layer with a graphic created using the Adobe Premiere Pro Titler.

● **Note:** When you create a new title, Adobe Premiere Pro uses your current sequence as the default dimensions. It makes life easier if you open the sequence you need the title for before you begin.

2 Go to the Title menu, and choose New Title > Default Still.

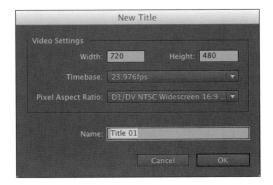

The New Title dialog appears. You could change the settings if you needed, but they should be correct based on the current sequence.

● **Note:** For more information about the Titler, see Chapter 16, "Creating Effective Titles."

3 Give the new title the name *Highlight*, and click OK.

4 There are several panels in the Titler. The panel at the top left has a series of tools for creating text and shapes. Select the Ellipse tool (●).

5 The center part of the Titler shows the current Timeline frame as a background for the title you are creating. Click into this area with the Ellipse tool and drag to create a circle. Hold the Shift key as you drag to confine the shape to a perfect circle, rather than an ellipse.

6 Switch to the Titler Selection tool. Click the circle you just created to select it. Once the circle is selected, the Title Properties panel displays options relating to the circle.

7 Change the Fill Type from Solid to Radial Gradient. This displays a color selector with two *color stops*—color pickers that blend together to create a gradient.

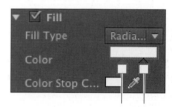

Color Stop 1   Color Stop 2

8 Click to select the second color stop; then reduce Color Stop Opacity to 0%.

● **Note:** You may need to widen the right column to see which property is Color Stop Opacity.

9 This is almost perfect, but the gradient is not strong enough. Drag the second Color Stop to the left, to increase the gradient, until the circle has soft edges.

10 Close the Titler. Your new title is automatically added to the Project panel.

Making a traveling matte

Once you have a graphic in the shape you'd like to use with the Track Matte Key effect, you can use the Motion controls in the Effect Controls panel to reposition and animate it.

Note: It's generally better to make graphics larger than you need and use the Scale control to reduce the size than to begin with the graphic too small and scale up. Scaling up might introduce hard edges because the pixels expand when you scale up.

1 Edit the soft edge circle title you just created onto Video 3. Adjust the position and duration so that it exactly matches the other clips on the Timeline. If you don't have a title to use, you can use the Highlight Example clip in the Graphics bin.

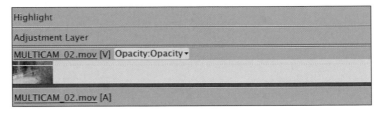

Initially, the graphic will sit rather obviously in the center of the screen.

2   Apply the Track Matte Key effect to the adjustment layer. In the Effect Controls panel, set the Track Matte Key Matte menu to Video 3.

Initially, you won't see any effect, because no changes have been made with the adjustment layer.

3   In the Effect Controls panel, turn on the Fast Color Corrector effect.

This effect was already applied and set up for the adjustment layer in order to make the image brighter.

4   Select the Highlight title on the Timeline. Use the Motion controls in the Effect Controls panel to reposition the title so that it highlights the winning rider. Use keyframes to have the circle scale and move across the screen to follow the rider.

▶ **Tip:** If you select the Motion effect heading in the Effect Controls panel, the Program Monitor becomes a direct manipulation panel, where you can click and drag the clip to a new position and size.

Using the After Effects Roto Brush Tool

Adobe Premiere Pro has up to 16-point garbage mattes to manually mask image regions in clips. This is pretty powerful but not as powerful as Adobe After Effects, which can apply precisely positioned, keyframed, Bezier-curved, multipoint mattes. The process of very precisely selecting a foreground asset with a mask is called *rotoscoping*.

Adobe After Effects has a special Roto Brush tool that dramatically reduces the amount of work required to rotoscope a foreground image.

To send a clip to After Effects and use the Roto Brush, follow these steps:

1   Right-click the clip you would like to send to After Effects, and choose Replace With After Effects Composition.

    Adobe Premiere Pro passes the clip to After Effects, where an After Effects composition will automatically be created.

2   You will need to give the new After Effects project a name and location. Consider saving the project in a subfolder with your Adobe Premiere Pro project.

3   The clip has already been added to a composition in After Effects. Double-click it inside the Timeline panel to open it, ready for editing.

4   Like Adobe Premiere Pro, After Effects has a series of tools for different tasks. In the case of After Effects, they are positioned at the top of the screen by default. Select the Roto Brush tool.

5   Using the Roto Brush tool, draw over the foreground subject. There's no need to carefully draw close to the edges. The Roto Brush tool will automatically seek and snap to the edges of your subject.

6   Click repeatedly with the Roto Brush tool to add to your selection. Hold the Alt (Windows) or Option (Mac OS) key and click to remove things from your selection.

7   Just below the time ruler in the layer panel, there is a range selection for the Roto Brush tool. Be sure to drag the end of the range to select the total duration you would like the Roto Brush tool to work on.

8   Press the spacebar. The Roto Brush tool will automatically track the edges you selected, creating a mask that sets pixels outside of the selection as transparent and the pixels inside the selection as visible.

    If the Roto Brush tool loses the edge of the selection, press the spacebar to stop the analysis, use the Roto Brush tool to adjust the selection, and press the spacebar again to continue.

9   When the Roto Brush tool has finished analyzing the clip, you can simply save the After Effects project and return to Adobe Premiere Pro. The clip will now have transparent pixels outside of the selected area, and you can use it as a foreground element in a composition.

The Roto Brush tool has effect controls, and you can access them in the Adobe After Effects Effect Controls panel that appears automatically when you begin working with the Roto Brush tool.

Be sure to save the Adobe After Effects project when you have finished, because Adobe Premiere Pro will need it to display the results of your mask.

Review questions

1 What is the difference between the RGB channels and the alpha channel?

2 How do you apply a blending mode to a clip?

3 How do you keyframe clip opacity?

4 How do you change the way a media file's alpha channel is interpreted?

5 What does it mean to "key" a clip?

6 Are there any limits to the kinds of clips you can use as a reference for the Track Matte Key effect?

Review answers

1 All of the channels use the same scale. The difference is that the RGB channels describe color information, while the alpha channel describes opacity.

2 Blending modes are under the Opacity category in the Effect Controls panel.

3 You adjust clip opacity in the same way that you would adjust clip volume. Make sure you're viewing the rubber band for the clip you want to adjust, and then click and drag with the Selection tool. You can also use the Pen tool to make subtle adjustments.

4 Right-click the file and choose Modify > Interpret Footage. The Alpha Channel options are at the bottom of the panel.

5 A *key* is usually a special effect where the color of pixels is used to define which part of the image should be transparent and which part should be visible.

6 No, you can use just about anything to create your key with the Track Matte Key effect. In fact, you can even apply special effects to the reference clip, and the results of those effects will be reflected in the matte.

16 CREATING TITLES

Lesson overview

In this lesson, you'll learn about the following:

- Using the Titler window
- Working with video typography
- Creating titles
- Stylizing text
- Working with shapes and logos
- Making text roll and crawl
- Working with templates

 This lesson will take approximately 90 minutes.

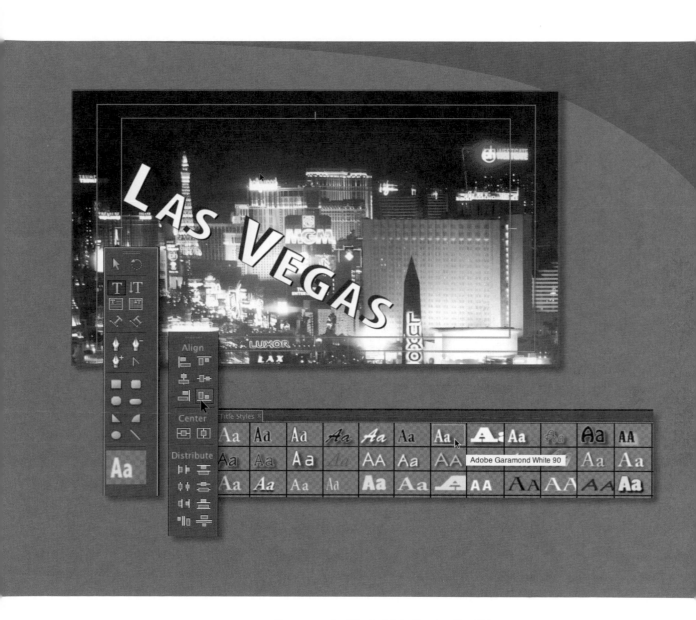

You can use the Tilter in Adobe Premiere Pro CS6 to create text and shapes. These objects can then be placed above video or used as stand-alone clips to convey information to an audience. You can create both static and dynamic titles.

Getting started

While you will rely upon audio and video sources as the primary ingredients for building a sequence, you will often need to incorporate text into your project. Text is very effective when you need to convey information quickly to your audience. For example, you can identify a speaker in your video by superimposing her name and title during the interview (often called a *lower-third* or simply an *ID*). You may also use text to identify sections of a long video (often called *bumpers*) or to acknowledge the cast and crew (with credits).

The proper use of text allows you to succinctly deliver information. It is clearer than the use of a narrator and allows for information to be presented in the middle of dialogue segments. Additionally, text can be used as a reinforcement of key information to the end viewer.

With Adobe Premiere Pro CS6, you will find a versatile Title tool. It offers you a range of text- and shape-creation tools that can be used to design effective titles. You can use the fonts loaded on your computer as well as control opacity and color. You can also insert graphic elements or logos that were created using other Adobe applications such as Adobe Photoshop or Adobe Illustrator. The Titler is an engaging and powerful tool. Its customizability makes it possible for you to create compelling titles to use in your productions.

An overview of the Titler window

In this lesson, let's start with some preformatted text and modify its parameters. This approach is a good way to get a quick overview of the powerful features of the Adobe Premiere Pro Titler. Later in this lesson, you'll build titles from scratch.

1 Start Adobe Premiere Pro, and open the project Lesson 16.prproj.

   The sequence 01 Seattle should already be open.

2 Double-click Title Start in the Project panel.

   The Titler window opens with a title already loaded over a video frame. The textbox should be selected by default; if not, click once to choose it.

Here's a quick rundown of the Titler's panels:

Title Tools panel   Title Designer panel

Title Properties panel

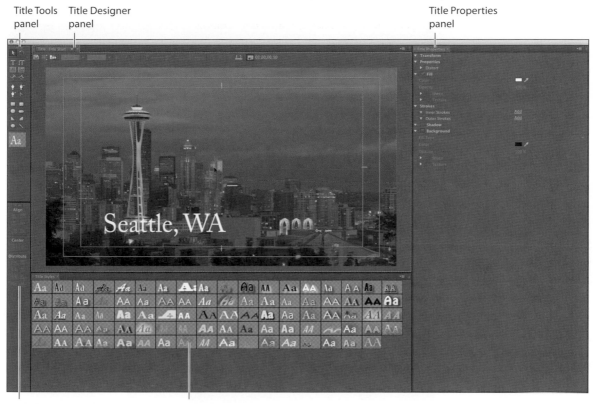

Title Actions panel   Title Styles panel

- **Title Tools panel:** These tools define text boundaries, set text paths, and select geometric shapes.

- **Title Designer panel:** This is where you build and view text and graphics.

- **Title Properties panel:** Here you'll find text and graphic options such as font characteristics and effects.

- **Title Actions panel:** You'll use these to align, center, or distribute text and groups of objects.

- **Title Styles panel:** Here you'll find preset text styles. You can choose from several libraries of styles.

● **Note:** You may have to expand the window to see all the Title Properties options.

3 Click several different thumbnails in the Title Styles panel to acquaint yourself with the styles available.

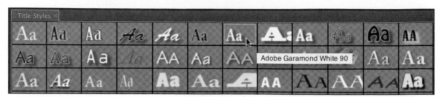

Each time you click a new style, Adobe Premiere Pro instantly changes the active or selected text to that style. When you're finished checking out some of the styles, choose the style Adobe Garamond White 90 (shown here). This style works with the mood of the scene in the video.

4 Click the Font Browser menu in the Titler. Note that the current font is Adobe Garamond Pro.

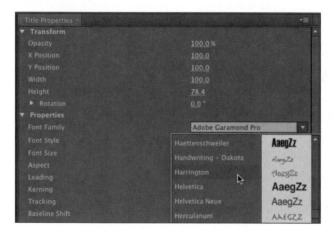

5 Scroll through the fonts, and note that as you select a new font, you see immediately how it will work with your text.

The specific fonts loaded on each system will vary. Just choose one that looks close to those used in this lesson.

● **Note:** With all the clicking and testing, you might have deselected the text. If there is no bounding box with handles around the text, select the text by clicking the Selection tool (in the upper-left corner of the Titler) and clicking anywhere in the text.

6 Click the Font Family menu in the Title Properties panel on the right of the Titler. This is another way to change fonts in the Titler. Experiment with changing the font through this panel. You can also experiment with the Font Style menu.

7 After you're done experimenting, choose Adobe Caslon Pro from the Font Family menu. Choose Bold from the Font Style menu to make the text easier to read.

8 Change the font size to 140 by typing the new value into the Font Size field or by dragging the Size number until it reaches 140. The text may become hidden; if so, resize the textbox by dragging the top handle of the bounding box with the Selection Tool.

9 In the Title Designer panel, click the Center button to center the text.

10 Change Tracking to 3.0. Tracking changes the amount of space between all of the characters in the text block.

Let's make the drop shadow more pronounced and easier to read.

11 In the Title Properties panel, change Shadow Distance to 10, Shadow Size to 15, and Shadow Spread to 45. You can enter numbers into each field or click and drag the numbers to scrub their values.

12 In the Title Actions panel, click the Horizontal Center and Vertical Center buttons to align the text to the absolute center of the screen.

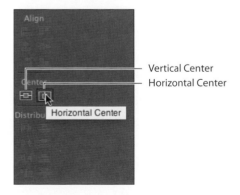

Your screen should look like the one shown here.

13 Drag the Titler floating window to the right—far enough to be able to see the Project panel.

14 In the Project panel, double-click Title Finished to load it in the Titler.

15 Toggle between the two titles by using the drop-down menu in the Titler main panel.

Your text should look similar to the Title Finished text.

16 Close the Titler by clicking the little *x* in the upper-right corner (Windows) or the Close button (Mac OS).

17 Drag Title Start from the Project panel to the Video 2 track on the Timeline, trim it so it fits above the video clip, and drag the current-time indicator through it to see how it looks over that video clip.

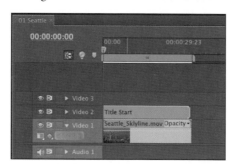

Using titles in other projects

You're likely to create common titles for location names and identification of inter-viewee names that you can use in multiple projects. However, Adobe Premiere Pro does not automatically save titles as separate files. To make a title available for use in another project, select the title in the Project panel, choose File > Export > Title, give your title a name, choose a location, and click Save. Later, you can simply import that title file the same way you would import any other asset.

Video typography essentials

When you design text for video, it is essential that you follow acceptable typography conventions. Because the text is often being composited over a moving background with multiple colors, you must attempt to achieve clarity in design. You must find a proper balance of legibility and style, all the while fitting enough information on the screen but not crowding it. Otherwise, the text will quickly become difficult to read and frustrating for the viewer.

▶ **Tip:** If you'd like to learn more about typography, consider the book *Stop Stealing Sheep & Find Out How Type Works* (Adobe Press, 2002) by Erik Spiekermann and E. M. Ginger.

Font choice

Your computer likely has hundreds (if not thousands) of fonts. This makes choosing a good font much more difficult. To simplify the selection process, try using a triage mentality and consider a few guiding questions:

- **Readability:** Is the font easy to read at the point size you are using? Are all the characters in the line of text readable? If you look at it quickly and then close your eyes, what do you remember about the text block?

- **Style:** How would you describe the font you've chosen using adjectives only? Does the font convey the right emotion for your video? Type is like a wardrobe; picking the right font is essential to the success of the design.

- **Flexibility:** Does the font mix well with others? Does it come in various weights (such as bold, italic, and semibold) that make it easier to convey significance when using that font? Can you create a hierarchy of information that conveys different kinds of information, such as a name and title for a speaker's lower-third graphic?

The answers to these guiding principles should help steer you toward better-designed titles. You may need to experiment to find the best font. Fortunately, you can easily modify an existing title or duplicate it and change the copy.

Color choice

While you have a near infinite number of possible color combinations, choosing the right colors to use in a design can be surprisingly tricky. This is because only a few colors work well for text and remain clear to the viewer. This task becomes even more difficult if your video is for broadcast or if your design must stylistically match the branding for a series or product. The text must also work once it's placed over a busy moving background (this issue is typically called *type on pattern*).

The white text in the image on the left has the most readability over the dark background. The blue text in the image on the right is more difficult to read because it is similar in color and tone to the sky.

While you may think you're being conservative, the most common color for text in video is white. Not surprisingly, the second most popular color is black. When colors are used, they tend to be very light or very dark shades. Lighter colors that work well include light yellow, blue, gray, and tan. Darker colors that can work include navy and forest green. The color you choose must provide suitable contrast from the background the text is being placed over.

● **Note:** When creating text for use in a video, you will often find yourself placing it over a background that has many colors present. This will make it difficult to achieve proper contrast (which is essential to preserving legibility). To help in this case, you may need to add a stroke, outer glow, or drop shadow to get a contrasting edge.

Kerning

As you build titles, you may decide that you want to modify the space between individual pairs of letters. This is typically done to improve the appearance of text and is a process called *kerning*. Taking the time to manually adjust text becomes more important the larger the font gets (because it just makes improper kerning that much more visible). The goal is to improve the appearance and readability of your text, while creating optical flow.

▶ **Tip:** A common place to start kerning is to adjust between an initial capital letter and the succeeding lowercase letters, particularly in the case of a letter with very little "base" like a T, which creates the illusion of excessive space along the baseline.

The original kerning is a bit loose in spots (left). After you adjust it by hand, the overall readability improves (right). Kerning is best learned by studying professionally designed materials like posters and magazines.

In Adobe Premiere Pro (and other Adobe applications), kerning is easy to adjust.

1 Click to place your cursor or move it using the arrow keys.

2 When the blinking I-bar is between the two letters you want to kern, hold down the Alt (Windows) or Option (Mac OS) key.

3 Press the left-arrow key to pull the letters closer or the right-arrow key to push them farther apart.

4 Move to the next letter pair and adjust as needed.

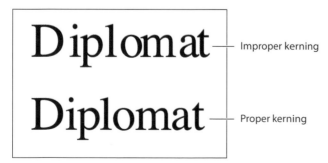

Diplomat ─┤ Improper kerning

Diplomat ─┤ Proper kerning

Tracking

Another text property (which is similar to kerning) is *tracking*. This is the overall space between all letters in a line of text. Tracking can be used to globally condense or expand a line of text so it better fits on-screen. It is often employed in the following scenarios:

- **Tighter tracking:** If a line of text is too long (such as a length title for a speaker's lower-third), you may tighten it slightly to fit. This will keep the vertical height the same but fit more text into the available space.

- **Looser tracking:** A looser track can be useful when using all uppercase letters or if you need to apply an outside stroke to the text. It is used often for large titles or when text is used as a design or motion graphics element.

Tracking is combined with the use of the Small Caps option to create a stylized title that is still easy to read.

Tracking is typically done in the Title Properties panel in Adobe Premiere Pro (or the Character panel in other Adobe applications). Tracking, like kerning, is subjective, and you can learn best how to do it by studying professional examples and looking for inspiration and guidance.

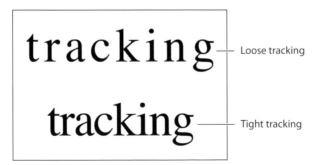

Loose tracking

Tight tracking

Leading

Just as there is a need to control the space between characters horizontally, you'll also want to control the vertical space between lines of text. This process is called *leading*, and it is pronounced *lead*-ing as in the metal, not *lead*-ing as in sheep. The name is derived from the time when strips of lead were used on a printing press to create space between lines of text.

The original leading causes the two lines of text to become difficult to read (left). Changing the leading value from 5 to 24 in the Title Properties panel increases the space between lines and improves readability (right).

In most cases, you should use the default setting of Auto for leading your text. However, you can change leading as needed to fit text into a design template or to get more information on the screen at once. To fit more text on the screen, you'll tighten the leading to produce less space between lines of text (you can also loosen it to spread text apart).

Don't set the leading too tight; otherwise, descenders from the top line (like the downward lines on *j*, *p*, *q*, and *z*) will cross ascenders from the lower line (like the upward lines on *b*, *d*, *k*, and *l*). This collision will likely have a negative impact on the readability of your text.

Alignment

While you may be used to seeing text left-justified for things like a newspaper, there are no hard-and-fast rules for aligning video text. In a general sense, the text used for a lower-third title tends to be left- or right-justified.

On the other hand, you will often center text used in a title sequence or segment bumper. In the Titler (or Paragraph panel for other Adobe applications), you'll find buttons for aligning your text. These can be used to align text left, right, or centered.

● **Note:** When setting text in an Adobe application, you often don't just want to click and type (called *point* text). Instead, you can click and drag using the Type tool to define the paragraph area first. This is called *paragraph* text and offers greater control over alignment and layout.

Safe title margin

When you're designing in the Titler, you'll see a series of two nested boxes. The first box shows you 90 percent of the viewable area, which is considered the action-safe margin. Things that fall outside of this box may get cut off when the video signal is viewed on a television set. Be sure to place all critical elements that are meant to be seen (like a logo) in this region.

The text on the left is too close to the edge (and outside the safe title margin). The image on the right shows the text properly repositioned within the title-safe margin, which improves readability for video text.

The second box, which is 80 percent of the viewable area, is called the *title-safe zone*. Just as this book you're reading has margins to keep the text from getting too close to the edge, it's a good idea to keep text inside the innermost or title-safe zone. This will make it easier for your audience to read the information.

● **Note:** You can turn off the title-safe margins or action-safe margins by opening the Titler panel menu (or choosing Title > View) and then choosing Safe Title Margin or Safe Action Margin, respectively.

Creating titles

When you create a title, you will need to make some choices as to how the text is organized on the screen. The Titler panel offers three approaches to creating text, each offering both horizontal and vertical text-direction options:

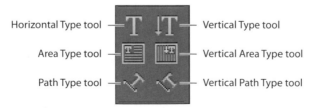

Horizontal Type tool ——— ⊤ ↓⊤ ——— Vertical Type tool

Area Type tool ——— ——— Vertical Area Type tool

Path Type tool ——— ——— Vertical Path Type tool

- **Point text:** This approach builds a text bounding box as you type. The text runs on one line until you press Enter (Windows) or Return (Mac OS) or until you choose Title > Word Wrap. Changing the shape and size of the box changes the shape and size of the text.

- **Paragraph (area) text:** You set the size and shape of the textbox before entering text. Changing the box size later displays more or less text but does not change the shape or size of the text.

- **Text on a path:** You build a path for the text to follow by clicking points in the text screen to create curves and then adjusting the shape and direction of those curves using the handles.

In the Title Tools panel, you can select a tool from the left or right side. This will determine whether the text will orient horizontally or vertically.

Adding point text

Now that you have a basic understanding of how to modify and design a title, you can build one from scratch. Let's work with a new project. You'll be creating a title that will be used to promote a conference in Las Vegas.

1 Open the sequence 02 Vegas from the Project panel.

2 To open the New Title dialog, choose File > New > Title, or press Control+T (Windows) or Command+T (Mac OS).

Note: Adobe Premiere Pro will automatically match a new title's settings to the open sequence. This means you may see different video attributes when you create a new title for frame sizes and aspect ratios. It's a good idea to have the sequence for which you want to design open and to use the default settings that Adobe Premiere Pro loads to match.

3 Type **Las Vegas** in the Name box, and click OK.

4 Drag the timecode (directly to the right of the Show Background Video button) to change the video frame displayed on the text screen.

Show Background Video

Timecode

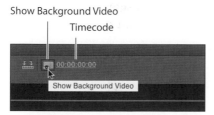

▶ **Tip:** Dragging the timecode with the text screen displayed is a useful way to position text relative to the video contents. You can also use it to evaluate how the text looks over your video and make adjustments to improve readability. The video frame displayed behind the title is not saved with the title. It is there only as a reference for positioning and styling your title.

5 Click the Show Background Video button to hide the video clip.

The background now shows a grayscale checkerboard, which signifies transparency. This means that when the title is placed above a video track in your Timeline, the transparent areas would let the video show through. If you reduce the opacity of the text, you will see some of the background show through. Remember, an opacity of 100 percent means 0 percent transparency (while an opacity of 30 percent means 70 percent transparency).

6 Click the Myriad Pro White 25 style (shown here).

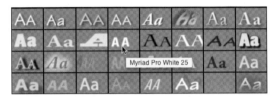

Let your cursor hover above a style for a few seconds to see its name.

7 Click the Type tool (shortcut T), and click anywhere in the Titler panel.

The Type tool creates point text.

8 Type **LAS VEGAS** to match the figure here.

● **Note:** If you were to continue typing a long title, you'd notice that point text does not wrap automatically. This will cause your text to run off the screen to the right. To make text wrap automatically when it reaches the title-safe margin, choose Title > Word Wrap. If you want to force a new line to start, press Enter (Windows) or Return (Mac OS).

9 Click the Selection tool (the arrow in the upper-left corner of the Title Tools panel). Handles appear on the text bounding box.

You won't be able to use a keyboard shortcut because you are typing into a text bounding box.

10 Drag the corners and edges of the text bounding box, and note how the text changes size and shape accordingly. Hold down the Shift key to constrain the text so it scales uniformly.

11 Hover the pointer just outside a corner of the text bounding box until a curved line pointer appears. Then drag to rotate the bounding box off its horizontal orientation.

12 After making sure the Selection tool is still active, click anywhere within the bounding box, and drag the angled text and its bounding box somewhere else on the Titler panel.

▶ **Tip:** Instead of dragging bounding box handles, you can change values in the Transform settings in the Title Properties panel. Either type new values or position your pointer on a value and drag left or right. Your changes show up immediately in the bounding box (as long as it is selected).

Try to approximately match this look. Adjust the size, rotation, and position of the text using the techniques you've learned so far.

Adding paragraph text

While point text is very flexible, you can take better control over layout with paragraph text. This option will automatically wrap the text as it reaches the edge of the paragraph textbox.

Continue working with the same title you have open from the previous exercise.

1 Click the Area Type tool in the Title Tools panel.

2 Drag a text bounding box into the Titler panel that fills the upper-right corner of the title-safe area.

The Area Type tool creates paragraph text.

3 Start typing. Start entering names of participants who will be attending the event in Las Vegas. You can use the names here or add your own.

This time, type enough characters to go beyond the end of the bounding box. Reduce the font size if needed so you can see a few lines of text at once. Unlike point text, area text remains within the confines of the bounding box you defined. It wraps at the bounding box borders.

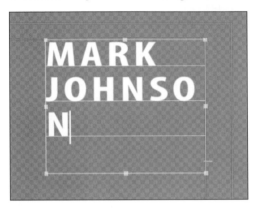

The text in this screen is too large to fit on one line, so it automatically wraps to the next. By reducing the font size in the Title Properties panel, you can fit more text on one line.

4 Press Enter (Windows) or Return (Mac OS) to go down a line.

5 Click the Selection tool, and change the size and shape of the bounding box.

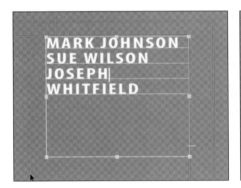 

The original text is too large to fit on one line (left). Resizing the text bounding box allows more text to fit on one line (right).

The text does not change size. Instead, it adjusts its position on the bounding box baselines. If you make the box too small to fit all your text, the extra text scrolls below the bottom edge of the bounding box. In that case, a small plus (+) sign appears near the lower-right corner outside the bounding box.

▶ **Tip:** A good way to avoid spelling mistakes is to copy and paste text from an approved script or e-mail that has been reviewed by your client or producer.

6 Close the current title you have open.

Because Adobe Premiere Pro automatically saves text to the project file, you can switch to a new or different title and not lose whatever you've created in the current title.

Stylizing text

Earlier you experimented with title styles, which quickly apply formatting to a selected text block. While title styles are fast and easy, they are only the beginning. You can use the Title Properties panel to take precise control over the appearance of your text.

Changing a title's appearance

In the Title Properties panel, you will find several options for modifying the appearance of your text. When they're used correctly (and with restraint), you can use them to improve the readability of your type and its overall appearance or style. However, it's possible to overdo it and add too many effects, which will produce amateurish results and impact readability.

▶ **Tip:** Instead of using the Color Picker to change the Color Stop Color, you can use the Eyedropper tool (located next to the color swatch) to select a color from your video. Click the Show Video button at the top of the Titler panel, move to a frame you want to use by scrubbing the timecode numbers left or right, move the Eyedropper tool into your video scene, and click a color that suits your needs.

Here are some of the most useful tools for modern typographic design. You'll find these in the Typographic Properties panel:

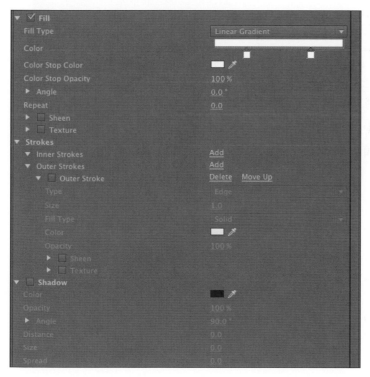

- **Fill Type:** You have several choices of fill type. The most popular ones are Solid and Linear Gradient, but you will also find additional gradient, bevel, and ghosting options.

- **Color:** Set the color for your text. You can click the swatch or enter numerical values in the Color Picker or use the Eyedropper tool to sample from your video clip.

- **Sheen:** A gentle highlight can add depth to your title. Be sure to adjust the size and opacity so the effect is subtle.

- **Stroke:** You can click to add inner and outer strokes. Strokes can be solid or gradient and add a thin edge to the outside of the text. Adjust the opacity of a gradient to create a gentle glow or soft edge. A stroke is commonly used to help keep text legible over a video or complex background.

- **Shadow:** The use of a drop shadow is a common addition to video text because it makes the text easier to read. Be sure to adjust the softness of the shadow. Also, be sure to keep the angle of shadows identical for all titles in a project for design consistency.

1   In the Project panel, double-click the Las Vegas title.

2   Modify the Las Vegas text block using the properties described in this section.

3   Continue designing until you have a look that is visually pleasing to you.

Saving custom styles

If you create a look you like, you can save time by storing it as a style. A style describes the color and font characteristics for a block of type. You can easily reuse a style to reformat the appearance of text with one click. All of the properties of the text update to match the preset.

Let's create a style from the text you've been modifying in the previous section.

1　Select a text block or object that has the properties applied that you want to save.

Use the text you formatted in the previous exercise.

2　In the Title Styles panel menu, click the submenu and choose New Style.

3　Enter a descriptive name, and click OK. The style is added to the Title Styles panel.

4　To view styles more easily, you can click the Title Styles submenu and choose to view the presets as *Text Only*, *Small Thumbnails*, or *Large Thumbnails*.

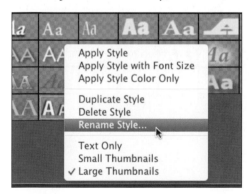

5　To manage a style, right-click its thumbnail. You can choose to duplicate a style to modify a copy, rename a style so it's easier to find, or delete a style if you want to remove it.

Creating an Adobe Photoshop graphic or title

Another choice for creating titles or graphics for Adobe Premiere Pro is Adobe Photoshop. While it is known as the premier tool for modifying photos, Adobe Photoshop also has a great deal of capabilities for creating elegant titles or logo treatments. Adobe Photoshop offers several advanced options including anti-aliasing (for smoother text), advanced formatting such as scientific notation, flexible layer styles, and even a spelling checker.

To create a new Adobe Photoshop document from within Adobe Premiere Pro, do the following:

1   In Adobe Premiere Pro, select the Project panel, and choose File > New > Photoshop File.

2   Examine the New Photoshop File window. The video settings should be correctly set for your project.

3   Click OK.

4   Choose a location to store your PSD file, name it, and click Save.

5   Adobe Photoshop or Photoshop Extended opens, allowing you to edit the title.

    The new Adobe Photoshop document you created will automatically match the current Adobe Premiere Pro Timeline in use (or the preset you chose). Now that you have a Photoshop document open, let's take a quick look at some of the functionality in Adobe Photoshop.

6   Select the Text tool by pressing T.

7   Draw a text block and, by clicking and dragging, draw from the left edge of the title-safe area to the right edge. This creates a paragraph textbox to hold the text. As in Adobe Premiere Pro, the use of a paragraph textbox in Adobe Photoshop allows you to precisely control the layout of text.

Creating an Adobe Photoshop graphic or title (continued)

8   Enter the text you'd like to use.

9   Adjust the font, color, and point size to taste using the controls in the Options bar across the top of the screen to adjust the font and text options.

10 Click the check mark in the Options bar to commit the text layer.

11 If you need transparency, be sure to disable the Background layer by clicking the visibility icon next to it in the Layers panel. You'll see a checkerboard pattern indicating transparency.

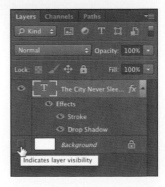

When you're finished in Adobe Photoshop, you can close and save the title. It will be automatically updated in the Adobe Premiere Pro project. If you'd like to return to Adobe Photoshop, just select a title in the Project panel or Timeline and choose Edit > Edit in Adobe Photoshop.

Working with shapes and logos

When building titles for your program, you'll likely need more than just words to build a complete graphic. Fortunately, Adobe Premiere Pro also offers the ability to generate vector shapes that can be filled and stylized to create graphic elements. You can also import completed graphics (like a logo) to enhance your Adobe Premiere Pro title.

Creating shapes

If you've created shapes in graphics-editing software such as Adobe Photoshop or Adobe Illustrator, you'll find creating geometric objects in Adobe Premiere Pro quite similar. Simply select from the various shapes in the Title Tools panel, drag and draw the outline, and release the mouse button.

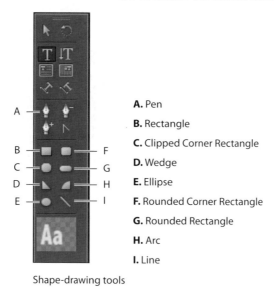

A. Pen

B. Rectangle

C. Clipped Corner Rectangle

D. Wedge

E. Ellipse

F. Rounded Corner Rectangle

G. Rounded Rectangle

H. Arc

I. Line

Shape-drawing tools

Follow these steps to draw shapes in Adobe Premiere Pro. This exercise is just for practice.

1 Press Control+T (Windows) or Command+T (Mac OS) to open a new title.

2 Type **Shapes Practice** in the Name box in the New Title dialog, and click OK.

3 Click the Show Background Video button to hide the video preview.

4 Select the Rectangle tool (R), and drag in the Titler panel to create a rectangle.

5 Click different title styles while the rectangle is still selected.

You'll notice that title styles affect shapes as well as text. Experiment with different styles or create your own.

6 Shift+drag in another location to create a square.

7 Select the Rounded Corner Rectangle tool, and Alt+drag (Windows) or Option+drag (Mac OS) to draw from the center of the shape.

The center remains in the spot where you first clicked, and the figure changes shape and size around that point as you drag.

8 Select the Clipped Corner Rectangle tool, and Shift+Alt+drag (Windows) or Shift+Option+drag (Mac OS) to constrain the aspect ratio and draw from the center.

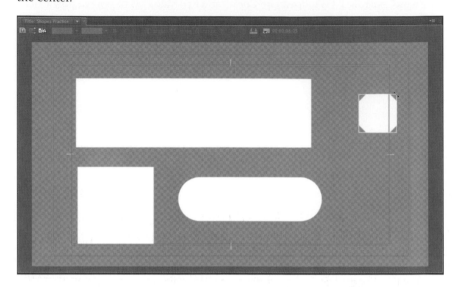

You'll also find additional tools for creating lines and free-form paths.

9 Press Control+A (Windows) or Command+A (Mac OS) and then press Delete to make another clean slate.

10 Select the Line tool (L), and drag to create a single line.

11 Select the Pen tool, and click in a blank area of the title canvas to create an anchor point (don't drag to create handles).

12 Click the Titler panel again where you want the segment to end (or Shift+click to constrain the segment's angle to a multiple of 45 degrees). This creates another anchor point.

13 Continue clicking with the Pen tool to create additional straight segments. The last anchor point you add appears as a large square, indicating it is selected.

14 Complete the path by doing one of the following:

- To close the path, move the Pen tool to the initial anchor point. When it is directly over the initial anchor point, a little circle appears underneath the Pen pointer. Click to make the connection.

- To leave the path open, Command+click (Mac OS) or Control+click (Windows) anywhere away from all objects, or select a different tool in the Title Tools panel.

Experiment with the different shape options. Try overlapping them and using different styles. The possibilities are endless.

Adding a logo

The use of a logo allows you to integrate a graphic file into your title design. You can insert common file formats including vectors (.ai, .eps) or still images (.psd, .png, .jpeg).

1 In the Project panel, double-click the file Lower-Third Start to open the title in the Titler panel.

2 Choose Title > Logo > Insert Logo.

3 Select the file logo.ai from the Lesson 16 folder, and click Open.

4 With the Selection tool, drag the logo to position it where you want it in the title.

> **Note:** If you place a vector graphic into a title, Adobe Premiere Pro converts it into a bitmap graphic. The image will appear at its original size. You can scale it smaller; if you make it larger, the image may become pixelated.

If necessary, adjust the size, opacity, rotation, or scale of the logo. Hold down the Shift key to constrain proportions when you scale to prevent unwanted distortion.

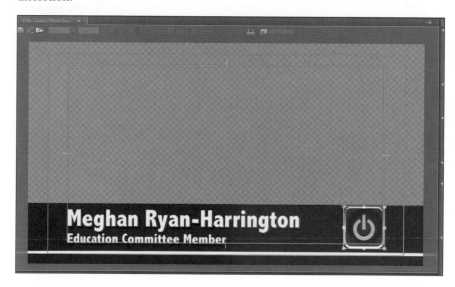

5 When finished, close the title.

If you need to restore a logo to its default size, just select it and choose Title > Logo > Restore Logo Size. If you accidentally distorted the logo, select the logo and choose Title > Logo > Restore Logo Aspect Ratio.

Aligning shapes and logos

As you design titles, you will often want to keep the design uniform and neat. The Adobe Premiere Pro Titler offers the ability to align and distribute elements with a title. Align lets an object's position match, such as the bottom edges or centers of two or more objects. You can also take three or more objects and evenly space them in relation to each other with a justify command.

1   In the Project panel, double-click the file Align Start to open the title in the Titler panel.

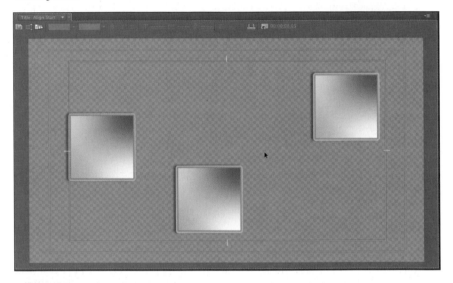

This title contains three shapes that are randomly positioned on the screen.

2   Select all three squares by Shift+clicking each one.

Notice that when more than one object is selected, the Align tools become active.

3   Click the Align Vertical Bottom button to align the bottom edges of the three objects.

The three objects are now aligned based on the bottommost object.

4 Click the Horizontal Center Distribute button to equally space the three objects from one another.

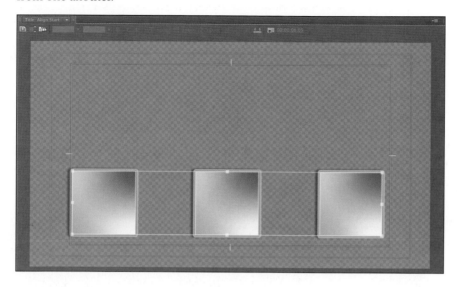

The objects are now evenly spaced and aligned with one another. Now, let's space them in relation to the canvas.

5 Click both the Horizontal Center and Vertical Center tools.

You should have three perfectly aligned squares centered in the title area.

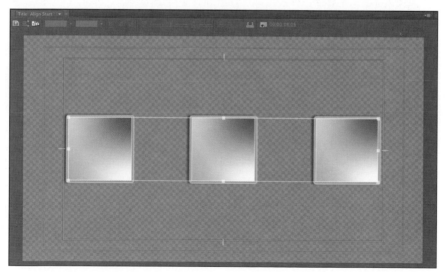

Making text roll and crawl

Using the Titler, you can make rolling text for opening and closing credits and crawling text for items such as headline bulletins.

1 From the Adobe Premiere Pro menu bar, choose Title > New Title > Default Roll.

2 Name your title *Rolling Credits*, and click OK.

3 Select the Type tool, and then type some text with the Caslon Pro 68 style.

   Create placeholder credits as shown here, pressing Enter (Windows) or Return (Mac OS) after each line. Type enough text to more than fill the screen vertically. Use the Title Properties panel to format your text as desired.

4 Click the Roll/Crawl Options button.

Roll/Crawl Options

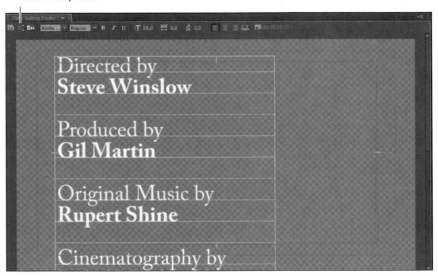

You have the following options:

- **Still:** This changes the credits to a still title.

- **Roll (scroll text vertically):** This should be selected already, because this title was created to scroll vertically, as often seen in movie credits.

- **Crawl Left, Crawl Right:** These indicate the crawl direction (rolling text always moves up the screen).

- **Start Off Screen:** This controls whether the credits start completely off the screen and roll on or whether they begin at the location as typed in the Titler.

Note: With rolling text selected, the Titler automatically adds a scrollbar along the right side that enables you to view your text as it runs off the bottom of the screen (shown here). If you select one of the crawl options, that scrollbar will appear at the bottom to enable you to view text running off the right or left edge of the screen.

- **End Off Screen:** This indicates whether the credits roll completely off the screen.

- **Preroll:** This specifies the number of frames before the first words appear on-screen.

- **Ease-In:** This specifies the number of frames at the beginning to gradually increase the speed of the roll or crawl from zero to its full speed.

- **Ease-Out:** This specifies the number of frames to slow down the roll or crawl at its end.

- **Postroll:** This specifies the number of frames that play after the roll or crawl ends.

5   Select Start Off Screen and End Off Screen, and type **5** for Ease-In and **5** for Ease-Out. Click OK.

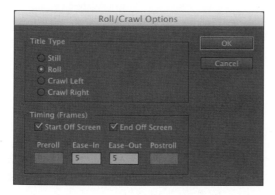

6   Close the Titler.

7   Drag your newly created Rolling Credits title to the Video 2 track of the Timeline above the video clip (if another title is there, drag this one directly on top of it to do an overlay edit).

8   With the Edit tool, grab the right edge of the Rolling Credits clip, and drag it to be the same length as the video clip in track 1.

9   With the sequence selected, press the spacebar to view your rolling credits.

▶ **Tip:** It's often easier to set your credits in a word processing application or text document. You can then copy and paste rather than type them into a title.

● **Note:** Dragging a rolling title to increase its length will cause it to roll slower. Dragging the rolling title to decrease its length will cause it to roll faster.

Animated text with Adobe After Effects

If you'd like to create animated titles for use in Adobe Premiere Pro, you'll find excellent options available in Adobe After Effects. You'll find a very deep animation engine with 17 animation properties ranging from Scale and Position to Blur and Skew.

1   To create a new Adobe After Effects composition from within Adobe Premiere Pro, choose File > Adobe Dynamic Link > New After Effects Composition.

2   The New After Effects Comp window is automatically filled in with settings that match your project settings. Click OK. A new Adobe After Effects composition is added to both your Timeline and Project panels.

3   You are automatically switched to Adobe After Effects. Name the project, and click Save.

    Store the project with your Adobe Premiere Pro project file so that your media path structure is easy to preserve. Any additional clips sent to Adobe After Effects from your current Adobe Premiere Pro project will automatically join this linked Adobe After Effects project.

4   Select the Text tool, and click in the After Effects Composition panel to enter text.

    You can click the buttons beneath the composition window to turn on a title-safe overlay. If you are unsure of what a button does, just hover your cursor over it to see a tool tip.

5   Adjust the text properties with the Character panel to improve its style and legibility.

6   An easy way to animate the layer is with presets. Select the text layer in the Timeline panel. Position the current-time indicator (playhead) at the start of the timeline.

Animated text with Adobe After Effects (continued)

7 Select the Effects & Presets panel (if it's not visible, you can choose it in the Window menu). Click the submenu in the upper-right corner of the Effects & Presets panel and choose Browse Presets. Adobe Bridge launches with the default presets shown.

8 Select the folder named Text, and double-click to open it. Double-click other subfolders to examine other animation presets. You can click an .ffx file to see a preview movie in the Preview pane. Use the navigation path at the top of the window to switch to a different folder.

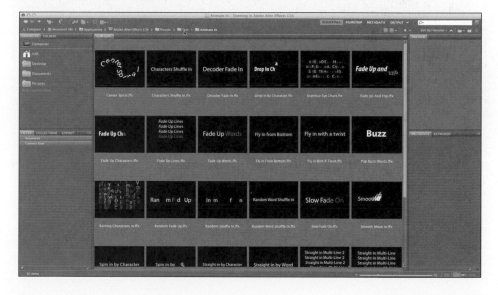

(continues on next page)

Animated text with Adobe After Effects (continued)

9 Select a preset effect and double-click to apply it to your selected text layer. For this exercise, choose Animate In > Raining Characters In.ffx. Adobe Bridge is minimized, and Adobe After Effects becomes the active application.

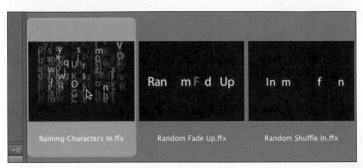

10 In the Preview panel, click the RAM Preview button to preview the text animation. In this animation, the timing might be different than you'd like, but you can easily modify it.

11 With the layer in Adobe After Effects selected, press U to see all your user-added keyframes. You can drag the keyframes to new positions in the Timeline to adjust the start and end time of the animation.

12 You can adjust the individual parameters of the text effects. Click the disclosure triangle next to the Range Selector to close it; then click it again to open it and show all the animation properties. Click the triangle next to Advanced to see all those properties as well.

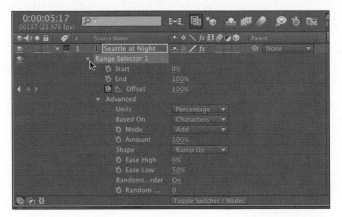

Animated text with Adobe After Effects (continued)

13 Experiment with the different Advanced properties to see the results. In particular, experiment with the following properties, and click RAM Preview occasionally to view the changes:

- Randomize Order: Randomizes the order in which the property is applied to the characters affected by the Range Selector.

- Random Seed: Affects the method used to calculate randomness. Try inputting a different value to produce a varied animation.

- Shape: Affects the shape used to select characters between the start and end of the range. Choosing different options will result in subtle but significant changes. You can choose Square, Ramp Up, Ramp Down, Triangle, Round, or Smooth.

14 If you're happy with the animation as is, save your Adobe After Effects project and return to Adobe Premiere Pro. You can now edit the new Adobe After Effects composition into your Timeline just as you would any other title.

Review questions

1 What are the differences between point text and paragraph (or area) text?

2 Why display the title-safe zone?

3 Why might the Align tools be dimmed?

4 How do you use the Rectangle tool to make a perfect square?

5 How do you apply a stroke or drop shadow?

Review answers

1 You create point text with the Type tool. Its bounding box expands as you type. Changing the box shape changes the text size and shape accordingly. When you use the Area Type tool, you define a bounding box, and the characters remain within its confines. Changing the box's shape displays more or fewer characters.

2 Some TV sets cut off the edges of the TV signal. The amount lost varies from set to set. Keeping your text within the title-safe margin ensures that viewers will see all your title. This is less of a problem with newer digital TVs, but it is still a good idea to use the title-safe zone to frame your titles.

3 The Align tools become active if more than one object is selected in the Titler. The Distribute tools also become active when more than two objects are selected.

4 To create a perfect square, hold down the Shift key as you draw using the Rectangle tool.

5 To apply a stroke or drop shadow, select the text or object to edit, and click its Stroke (Outer or Inner) or Shadow box to add a stroke or a drop shadow. Then start adjusting parameters, and they will show up on the object.

17 MANAGING YOUR PROJECTS

Lesson overview

In this lesson, you'll learn about the following:

- Working in the Project Manager
- Importing projects
- Managing collaboration
- Managing your hard drives

 This lesson will take approximately 25 minutes.

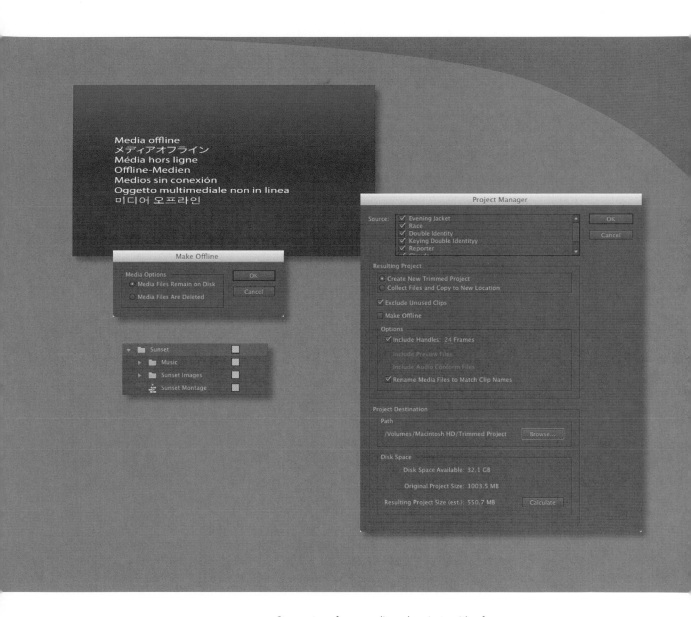

Media offline
メディアオフライン
Média hors ligne
Offline-Medien
Medios sin conexión
Oggetto multimediale non in linea
미디어 오프라인

Make Offline

Media Options
● Media Files Remain on Disk
○ Media Files Are Deleted

OK
Cancel

▼ 📁 Sunset
  ▶ 📁 Music
  ▶ 📁 Sunset Images
  ✦ Sunset Montage

Project Manager

Source:
☑ Evening Jacket
☑ Race
☑ Double Identity
☑ Keying Double Identityy
☑ Reporter

OK
Cancel

Resulting Project

● Create New Trimmed Project
○ Collect Files and Copy to New Location

☑ Exclude Unused Clips
☐ Make Offline

Options
☑ Include Handles: 24 Frames
☐ Include Preview Files
☐ Include Audio Conform Files
☑ Rename Media Files to Match Clip Names

Project Destination
Path
/Volumes/Macintosh HD/Trimmed Project   Browse...

Disk Space
        Disk Space Available: 32.1 GB
        Original Project Size: 1003.5 MB
Resulting Project Size (est.): 550.7 MB   Calculate

Stay on top of your media and projects with a few
simple steps.

In this lesson, you'll learn how to stay organized when working with multiple Adobe Premiere Pro CS6 projects. The best kind of organizational system is one you already have when you need it—not when you're caught up in the creative process. This lesson will help you to be more creative with a little bit of planning.

Getting started

When you start creating projects with Adobe Premiere Pro, you may not feel the need to invest time in staying organized. Perhaps you're just working on your first project now, and if that's the case, it's going to be nice and easy to find it on your hard drive.

Once you start working on multiple projects, staying organized gets a little more complicated. You'll be using multiple media assets taken from multiple places. You'll have multiple sequences, each with its own particular layout, and you'll be generating multiple titles. You may also have multiple effect presets and title templates. All in all, you'll need quite a filing system to keep all these project elements organized.

The solution is to create an organizational system for your projects and to have a plan in place for archiving those projects you might want to work on again.

The thing about systems for organization is that they're usually easier to use if they exist before you need them. Look at this idea from the other direction: If you don't have an organizational system in the moment you need it—when you have a new video clip to put somewhere, for example—you might be too busy to think about things like names and file locations. Consequently, it's common for projects to end up with the same name, stored in the same place, with a mix of files that don't go together.

The solution is simple: Make your organizational system in advance. Map it out with pen and paper if it helps, and work out the journey you'll take, starting from getting your source media files, moving through your edit, and finishing with output, archiving, and beyond.

In this lesson, you'll begin by learning about features that help you stay in control, without losing focus on what matters most—your creative work.

Then you'll learn about some positive approaches to collaboration.

1 To begin, open Lesson 17.prproj in the Lesson 17 folder.

2 Choose Window > Workspace > Editing to switch to the Editing workspace.

3 Choose Window > Workspace > Reset Current Workspace.

   The Reset Workspace dialog opens.

4 Click Yes in the Reset Workspace dialog.

The Project menu

Though most of your creative work can be performed using buttons in the interface or keyboard shortcuts, some important options are available only in the menus. The Project menu gives you access to the Project Manager, a tool that automates the process of streamlining your project. It also includes options to make clips *offline*, disconnecting the media file from the clip.

Project menu commands

The options available under Project Settings are the ones you used to create your project. Note that the only thing you can't change here is the location of the project file, though you could easily do that by exiting the project and moving the file using Windows Explorer (Windows) or Finder (Mac OS).

You'll find some duplication of functionality in the Project menu. Link Media and Make Offline are also in the Project panel, when you right-click a clip.

So is Automate to Sequence, a feature you learned about in Lesson 5, "Essentials of Video Editing."

Batch lists are for capturing; see Lesson 3, "Importing Media."

The Project Manager automates the process of backing up your project and discarding unused media files. We'll look at the Project Manager in a moment.

The Remove Unused command automatically removes clips from your project that are not used in any sequences. This is useful if you're looking to tidy up your project.

Making a clip offline

The words *offline* and *online* have different meanings in different post-production workflows, depending on the context. In the language of Adobe Premiere Pro, they refer to the relationship between clips and the media files they link to:

- **Online:** The clip is linked to a media file.
- **Offline:** The clip is not linked to a media file.

When a clip is offline, you can still edit it into a sequence, and even apply effects to it, but you won't be able to see any video. Instead, you'll see the Media Offline warning.

In almost all operations, Adobe Premiere Pro is completely nondestructive. This means no matter what you do with your clips in your project, nothing will happen to the original media files. Making a clip offline is a rare exception to this rule.

If you right-click a clip in the Project panel or go to the Project menu and choose Make Offline, you'll have two options:

- **Media Files Remain on Disk:** This simply unlinks the clip from the media file and leaves the media file in place and unchanged.

- **Media Files Are Deleted:** This deletes the media file. The effect of deleting the media file is that the clip goes offline, because there is no media file to link to anymore.

The benefit of making clips offline is that they can be reconnected with new media. If you've been working with low-resolution media, this means you can recapture tape-based media, or reimport file-based media, at a higher quality.

▶ **Tip:** You can make multiple clips offline in a single step. Just select any clips you would like to make offline before you choose the menu option.

Working with low-resolution media is sometimes desirable if you have limited disk storage or a large number of clips. When your editing work is complete and you're ready for fine-finishing, you can replace your low-resolution, small file-size media with selected high-resolution, large file-size media.

Do be careful with the Make Offline option, though! Once your media file is deleted, it's gone. Use the option to delete the actual media file very cautiously.

Using the Project Manager

Let's take a look at the Project Manager. To open it, go to the Project menu and choose it.

The Project Manager provides several options that automate the process of *streamlining* your project, or gathering together any media files you've used in your project.

It is very useful if you intend to archive your project or if you want to share your project. By using the Project Manager to gather all of your media files, you can be confident nothing will be missing— or offline—when you hand the project over to your creative colleagues.

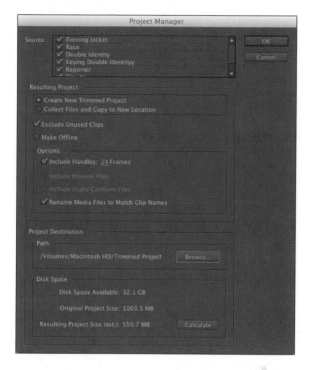

The result of using the Project Manager is a new, separate project file. Because the new file is independent of your current project, it's safe to try using the Project Manager and double-check that everything is fine before you delete anything.

Here's an overview of the options:

- **Source:** Select one or all of the sequences in your project. The Project Manager will choose clips and media files based on the sequences you select.

- **Resulting Project:** Create a new project with new media files based only on the trimmed parts of clips you have included in your sequence(s), or create a new project that has full copies of the clips you have included in your sequence(s).

- **Exclude Unused Clips:** With this option selected, the new project will not include clips you have not used in your selected sequence(s).

- **Make Offline:** When you choose this option, Adobe Premiere Pro will automatically unlink clips captured from tape, so they are ready to be recaptured using Batch Capture. This is useful if you originally captured your media at low resolution and now want to recapture only the parts you used at high quality. This option has no effect on media imported from files.

● **Note:** Some video formats, such as XDCAM, cannot be trimmed. When you create a trimmed project that includes these formats, full copies of media files are included.

- **Include Handles:** This adds the number of frames you specify to the new trimmed versions of the clips in your sequence(s). The extra content gives you the flexibility to trim and adjust the timing of your edits.

- **Include Preview Files:** If you have already rendered your effects, you can include the preview files with your new project so you won't need to render the effects again.

- **Include Audio Conform Files:** This includes the audio conform files with your project, so Adobe Premiere Pro won't need to conduct analysis of your audio again.

- **Rename Media Files to Match Clip Names:** As the name implies, this option renames your media files to match the clip names in your project. Consider carefully if you would like to use this option, because it can make it difficult to identify the original source media for your clips.

- **Project Destination:** Choose a location for your new project.

Working with a trimmed project

To create a new trimmed project file that includes only the parts of the clips you have used in your selected sequence(s), do the following:

1 Go to the Project menu and choose Project Manager.

2 Select the sequence(s) you want to be included in your new project.

3 Select Create New Trimmed Project.

4 Choose Exclude Unused Clips, unless you want to be able to recapture or reimport files that will now be offline.

5 Select Make Offline if you intend to recapture all tape-based clips. In most cases, you will not want to choose this option.

6 Add some handles. The default is one second on each end of the clips used in your sequences. Consider adding more if you'd like to have more flexibility to trim and adjust your edits in the new project.

7 Decide whether you want to rename your media files. Generally, it's better to leave your media files with the original names. However, if you are producing a trimmed project to share it with another editor, it might be helpful for them to identify the media files if they are renamed.

8 Click Browse and choose a location for your new project file.

9 Click Calculate to have Adobe Premiere Pro estimate the total new size of your project, based on your selections. Then click OK.

The benefit of creating a trimmed project is that you no longer have unwanted media files cluttering up your hard drive. It's a convenient way of transferring your

Note: Choosing to add 5 or 10 seconds of media at each end of the clip will do no harm; it will just mean your media files are a little larger.

project to a new location using the absolute minimum amount of storage space, and it's great for archiving.

The danger with this option is that once your unused media files are deleted, they're gone! Be sure that you have a backup of your unused media or that you definitely do not want to use the media before you create a trimmed project.

When you create your trimmed project, Adobe Premiere Pro will not delete your original files. Just in case you selected the wrong items, you can always go back and check before manually deleting the files on your hard drive.

Collecting files and copying them to a new location

To collect all of the files used in your selected sequences to a new single location, follow these steps:

1   Go to the Project menu and choose Project Manager.

2   Select the sequences you want to be included in your new project.

3   Select Collect Files and Copy to New Location.

4   Choose Exclude Unused Clips. If you want to include every clip in your bins, regardless of whether they are used in a sequence, deselect this option. Deselect this option if you are creating a new project to organize your media files a little better—perhaps because you have imported them from lots of different locations. When the new project is created, every media file linked to the project will be copied to the new project location.

5   Decide whether you would like to include existing preview files to save you from having to rerender your effects in the new project.

6   Decide whether you would like to include Audio Conform Files to save Adobe Premiere Pro from having to analyze the audio files again.

7   Decide whether you want to rename your media files. Generally, it's better to leave your media files with the original names. However, if you're producing a project to share it with another editor, it might be helpful for them to identify the media files if they are renamed.

8   Click Browse and choose a location for your new project file.

9   Click Calculate to have Adobe Premiere Pro estimate the total new size of your project, based on your selections. Then click OK.

Collecting all of your media files this way is very helpful if your media files are located in lots of different places and it's hard to find them. Adobe Premiere Pro will make copies of the original files in a single location.

If you intend to create an archive of your entire original project, this is the way to do it.

Final project management steps

If your goal is to give yourself maximum flexibility to reedit your sequences based on the new project, consider using the Remove Unused option, available under the Project menu, before you use the Project Manager.

Remove Unused will leave you with only those clips currently used in sequences. However, unlike the option to create a trimmed project file, when you use the Project Manager to collect your files to a new location, the entire original media file will be copied. This is perhaps the best of both worlds, balancing hard drive space with creative flexibility when working on the newly created project.

Importing projects or sequences

As well as importing many kinds of media files, Adobe Premiere Pro can import sequences from existing projects, along with all of the clips used to create them.

You can try it now:

1   Use any method you prefer to import a new media file. If you double-click a black area in the Project panel, the Import dialog will appear.

2   Select the file Sunset.prproj in the Lesson 17 folder, and click Import.

The Import Project dialog appears, with just two options:

- **Import Entire Project:** This imports every sequence in the project you are importing and every clip already imported into a bin.

- **Import Selected Sequences:** This allows you to select the specific sequence you would like to import. Only clips used in that sequence will be imported.

3   The project you're importing has only one sequence, so leave Import Entire Project selected, and click OK.

Adobe Premiere Pro adds a new bin to the project, containing the sequence that has been imported, and further bins containing the clips used in the sequence.

This is a nice way to work because Adobe Premiere Pro has automatically organized the new clips for you, based on the project you imported.

Managing collaboration

Being able to import other projects unlocks novel workflows and opportunities for collaboration. You could, for example, share work on different parts of a program between different editors, all using the same media assets. Then, one editor could import all of the other projects to combine them into a completed sequence.

Project files are small—usually small enough to email. This allows editors to email each other updated project files, open them and compare, or import them to do a side-by-side comparison in the project, provided that each editor has a copy of the same media files.

Remember, you can also add markers with comments to a Timeline, so when updating a sequence, consider adding a marker to highlight changes for your collaborators.

Be warned: Adobe Premiere Pro does not lock project files when they are in use. This means two people can access the same project file at the same time. This could be creatively dangerous! As one person saves the file, it updates. As the next person saves the file, it updates again. Whoever saves the project file last defines the file. If you intend to collaborate, it would be better to work on separate project files and import.

There are several dedicated media servers made by third parties that help you to collaborate using shared media files. These allow you to store and manage your media in a way that is accessible by multiple editors at the same time.

Keep these key questions in mind:

* Who has the latest version of the edited sequence?
* Where are the media files stored?

As long as you have simple answers to these questions, you should be able to collaborate and share creative work using Adobe Premiere Pro.

Managing your hard drives

Once you've used the Project Manager to create a new copy of your project or you have completed your project and finished with its media, you'll want to clean up your drives. Video files are *big*. Even with very large storage drives, you'll quickly need to think about which media files you want to keep and which you want to discard.

To make it easier to remove unwanted media when you have finished a project, consider importing all media files via your project folder or via a specific location on your media drive for your project. This means putting copies of your media into a single location before importing because, when you import media, Adobe Premiere Pro creates a link to it wherever it is on your computer.

By organizing media files before you import them, you'll find it much easier to remove unwanted content at the end of the creative workflow, because everything is conveniently located in one place.

Remember that deleting clips in a project, or even deleting the project file itself, will not delete any media files.

Additional files

The media cache uses storage space as you import new media files to your projects. Also, each time you render effects, Adobe Premiere Pro creates preview files.

To remove these files and reclaim extra space on your hard drive, do the following:

- Choose Edit > Preferences > Media (Windows) or Premiere Pro > Preferences > Media (Mac OS), and click Clean in the Media Cache Database section.

- Delete render files associated with your current project by choosing Sequence > Delete Render Files. Alternatively, locate your Preview Files folder by checking under Project > Project Settings > Scratch Disks. Then delete the folder and its contents using Windows Explorer (Windows) or Finder (Mac OS).

Consider carefully when choosing the location of the media cache and your project preview files. The total size of these files can be significant.

Media management with Dynamic Link

Dynamic Link allows Adobe Premiere Pro to use After Effects compositions as imported media while they are still editable in After Effects. To do this, Adobe Premiere Pro must have access to the After Effects project file that contains the composition, and After Effects must have access to the media files used in the composition.

While working on a single computer with both applications installed and your media assets located on internal storage, this is achieved automatically.

If you use the Project Manager to collect files for a new Adobe Premiere Pro project, it will not bring copies of Dynamic Link files. Instead, you will need to make copies of the files yourself, in Windows or Mac OS. If you have created your Dynamic Link projects in a single unified location, this is very easy to do; just copy the folder and include it with the assets collected already.

Review questions

1 Why would you choose to make a clip offline?

2 Why would you choose to include handles when creating a trimmed project with the Project Manager?

3 Why would you choose the Project Manager option called Collect Files and Copy to a New Location?

4 What does the Remove Unused option in the Project menu achieve?

5 How can you import a sequence from another Adobe Premiere Pro project?

6 Will the Project Manager collect Dynamic Link assets, such as After Effects compositions, when creating a new project?

Review answers

1 If you're working with low-resolution copies of your media files, you'll want to make your clips offline so you can recapture them or reimport them.

2 Trimmed projects include only the parts of your clips used in sequences. To give yourself some flexibility, you'd add handles; 24 frame handles would actually add 48 frames to the total duration of each clip, because one handle is added at the beginning and end of each clip.

3 If you have imported media files from lots of different locations on your computer, it can be difficult to find everything and stay organized. By using the Project Manager to collect all of the media files into one location, you'll make it easier to manage your project media files.

4 When you choose Remove Unused, Adobe Premiere Pro removes any clips from your project that are not used in a sequence. Remember, no media files are deleted.

5 To import a sequence from another Adobe Premiere Pro project, import the project file as you would import any media file. Adobe Premiere Pro will invite you to import the entire project or selected sequences.

6 The Project Manager does not collect Dynamic Link assets when creating a new project. For this reason, it's a good idea to create any new Dynamic Link projects in the same location as your project folder or in a dedicated folder for your project. This way, it is easier to locate and copy the assets for the new project.

18 EXPORTING FRAMES, CLIPS, AND SEQUENCES

Lesson overview

- Choosing the right export options
- Exporting single frames
- Creating movie, image sequence, and audio files
- Using Adobe Media Encoder
- Exporting to Final Cut Pro
- Exporting to Avid Media Composer
- Working with edit decision lists
- Recording to tape

 This lesson will take approximately 45 minutes.

Exporting your project is the final step in the video production process. Adobe Media Encoder offers multiple high-level output formats: Adobe Flash, QuickTime, and MPEG formats. Within those formats you have dozens of options and can also export in batches.

Getting started

One of the best things about editing video is the feeling you have when you can finally share it with your audience. Adobe Premiere Pro CS6 offers a wide range of export options—methods of recording your projects to tape or converting them to additional digital files.

Increasingly, the primary form of distribution is the use of digital files. To create these files, you can use Adobe Media Encoder. Adobe Media Encoder is a stand-alone application that handles exports in batches, so you can export in several formats simultaneously and process in the background while you work in other applications, including Adobe Premiere Pro and Adobe After Effects.

● **Note:** Adobe Premiere Pro can export clips selected in the Project panel, as well as sequences or Work Areas within sequences. The content that's selected when you choose File > Export is what Adobe Premiere Pro will export. Be sure to exercise care and make sure that the item you want to export is selected so you do not waste precious time rendering content from the Project panel rather than your sequence.

Overview of export options

Whether you've completed a project (or just want to share an in-progress review), you have a number of export options:

- You can select a whole sequence as a single file to post to the Web or burn to a disc.
- You can export a single frame or a series of frames to post to the Web or attach to an e-mail.
- You can choose audio-only, video-only, or full audio/video output.
- You can export directly to videotape.

Beyond the actual export formats, you can set several other parameters as well:

- You can choose to create files at the same visual quality and data rate as your original media, or you can compress them.
- You may need to specify the frame size, frame rate, data rate, or audio and video compression techniques if a particular preset doesn't fit your needs precisely.

You can use exported files for further editing, in presentations, as streaming media for Internet and other networks, or as sequences of images to create animations.

Exporting single frames

While an edit is in progress, you may want to quickly export a still frame to send to a team member or client to review. Additionally, you could choose to export a specific thumbnail image to use as the thumbnail of your video file when you post it to the Web. Adobe Premiere Pro offers a simplified workflow for still-image export.

Let's look at the Export Frame function. To select a frame, simply place the playhead over the frame you want to use. You can use the Export Frame function in two ways:

- You can load a clip from the Project panel into the Source Monitor. When using the Export Frame function from the Source panel, Adobe Premiere Pro will create a still image that matches the resolution of the source video file.

- You can move the playhead in the Timeline or Program Monitor to choose a frame. When using the Export Frame function from the Timeline, Adobe Premiere Pro will create a still image that matches the resolution of the selected video sequence.

Let's give it a try.

1 Start Adobe Premiere Pro, and open Lesson 18_01.prproj.

2 Click somewhere in the Review Copy Timeline to select the sequence.

3 In the Program Monitor, click the Export Frame button on the lower right.

If you don't see the button, it may be because you've customized the panel's buttons. You can press Shift+E to manually invoke the command.

4 In the Export Frame dialog, enter the desired filename.

5 Using the pop-up menu, choose the correct still-image format for your needs.

- JPEG, PNG, BMP, and GIF work well for compressed graphic workflows (like web delivery).

- TIFF and Targa are suitable for print and animation workflows.

- DPX is often used for digital cinema or color-grading workflows.

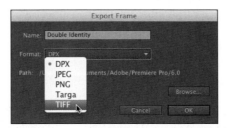

6 Click the Browse button to open the Browse for Folder dialog. Create a new folder on the desktop and select it.

7 Click OK to export the frame.

● **Note:** In Windows, you can export to the BMP, DPX, GIF, JPEG, PNG, TGA, and TIFF formats. On the Mac, you can export to the DPX, JPEG, PNG, TGA, and TIFF formats.

Exporting a master copy

Creating a master copy allows you to make a pristine digital copy of your edited project that can be archived for future use. A master copy is a self-contained digital file that contains all of the content of your sequence at its highest resolution and best quality. Once created, you can then use that file to produce other compressed output formats.

Matching sequence settings

Ideally, your master file will closely match the settings (frame size, frame rate, and codec) as the primary material in your sequence. Adobe Premiere Pro makes this fairly easy, because you can choose to match sequence settings, which makes it simple to create a file that matches your edit. There is no guesswork, provided you chose the right sequence preset (or let your sequence autoconform). Let's give it a try.

● **Note:** In some cases, the Match Settings option cannot write an exact match of the original camera media. For example, XDCAM EX will write to a generic MPEG2 file. In most cases, the file written will have an identical format and closely match the data rate of the original sources.

1 Continue working with Review Copy in Lesson 18_01.prproj.

2 With the sequence selected (in either the Project or Timeline panel), choose File > Export > Media.

   The Export Settings dialog opens. We'll explore this interface in-depth later in this lesson.

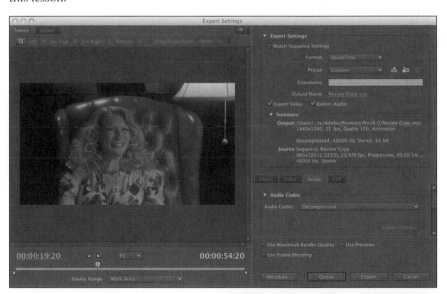

3 In the Export Settings dialog, select Match Sequence Settings.

4 Click the gold hypertext for the Output Name option to choose a target.

5 Choose a target (such as the Lesson 18 folder), and name the sequence *Review Copy 01.mxf.*

6 Click Save.

7 Examine the text in the Summary area to confirm that the output format matches the sequence settings. In this case, you should be using DVCPRO HD media (as MXF files) at 23.976fps.

8 Click the Export button to write a single file, which is a digital clone of the sequence.

▶ **Tip:** If your sequence to export has a lot of items that are scaled (such as photos or mixed-resolution video), you can use the Maximum Render Quality option. This is much slower but produces excellent results.

Choosing another codec

When you export a project as a self-contained movie, you can change the codec that is used. Some camera formats (such as DSLR and HDV) are heavily compressed. Using a higher-quality mastering codec can improve the quality of the master file you created.

Many popular third-party codecs such as ProRes, Avid DNXHD, and Cineform can be installed and used. These codecs may require a purchase, can come bundled with third-party hardware, or in some cases can be downloaded for free.

1 Use the same project as the previous exercise.

2 Choose File > Export > Media or press Control+M (Windows) or Command+M (Mac OS).

3 In the Export Settings dialog, click the Format pop-up menu and choose QuickTime as the format.

4 Click the output name (the gold text), and give the file a new name, *Review Copy 02.mov.* Save it to the same destination as the previous exercise.

5 Click the Video tab near the bottom of the window.

6 Choose a mastering codec that you have installed.

One option that should be installed on your system is the Animation codec. This file produces a very high-quality (but large) file. Check the frame size and frame rate to match your source settings. You may need to scroll the window or resize the panel to make it easier to see. Use the settings you see here.

● **Note:** The JPEG 2000 option is another good cross-platform choice to create high-quality files for archiving. On a Windows machine, you can also explore some of the high-quality AVI presets.

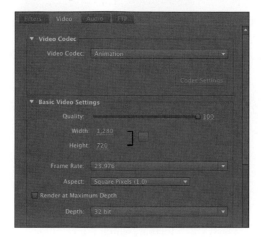

7 Click the Audio tab and choose Uncompressed for the audio codec. In the Basic Audio Settings section, choose 48000 Hz as the sample rate, Stereo for Channels, and 16 bit for Sample Size.

● **Note:** The Animation codec is very high-quality but cannot be viewed in real time without an extremely fast disk array.

8 Click the Export button at the bottom of the dialog to export the sequence and transcode it to the specified file format.

Working with Adobe Media Encoder

Adobe Media Encoder is a stand-alone application that can run independently or can be launched from Adobe Premiere Pro. One advantage to using Adobe Media Encoder is that you can submit a job directly from Adobe Premiere Pro and then continue working as the encoding is processed.

Choosing a file format for export

Adobe Premiere Pro and Adobe Media Encoder can export in a number of formats; let's run through them quickly to identify when you should use them.

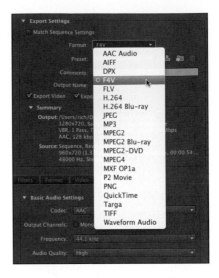

- **AAC Audio:** The Advanced Audio Coding format is the audio-only format that is often used with most H.264 encoding.

- **Audio Interchange File Format:** This is an audio-only file format popular on the Mac.

- **DPX:** DPX stands for Digital Picture Exchange and is a high-end image sequence format for digital intermediate and special-effects work.

- **F4V:** This is a newer version of the Flash video format, which is a popular way to distribute video online. F4V files use the H.264 video codec/AAC audio codec.

- **FLV:** This is the more compatible Flash video format for use with older computers. FLV files use the VP6 video codec/MP3 audio codec.

- **H.264:** This is the most flexible and widely used format today, with options for devices such as the iPod and Apple TV, TiVo Series3 SD and HD, and services such as YouTube and Vimeo. H.264 files produced via this option can also be transmitted to smartphones, such as Android, Blackberry, and iPhone devices, or used as high-quality, high-bit-rate intermediate files for working in other video editors.

- **H.264 Blu-ray:** This option produces H.264 files specifically for Blu-ray Discs.

- **JPEG:** This setting will create a sequential series of images at the target destination.

- **MP3:** This compressed audio format is very popular on the Internet.

- **MPEG2:** This older file format is primarily used for DVD and Blu-ray Discs. Presets in this group allow you to produce files that can be distributed for playback on your own or other computers. Some broadcasters also use MPEG2 as a format for digital delivery.

- **MPEG2 Blu-ray:** This will create a Blu-ray-compliant MPEG2 video and audio file from your HD material.

- **MPEG2-DVD:** Use this preset to create standard-definition DVDs.

- **MPEG4:** Selecting this codec produces lower-quality H.263 3GP files for distribution to older cell phones.

- **MXF OP1a:** These presets let you create files compatible with Sony's IMX and XDCAM (other than EX) systems.

- **P2 Movie:** This output option is used for rendering sequences back to P2 cards.

- **PNG:** This is a lossless but efficient still-image format for Internet use or for image sequences that contain transparency.

- **QuickTime:** This container format can store files using multiple codecs. All QuickTime files use the .mov extension, and it is the preferred format for use on Macintosh computers.

- **Targa:** This is a rarely used uncompressed still-image file format.

- **TIFF:** This popular high-quality still-image format offers both lossy and lossless compression options.

- **Waveform Audio:** This uncompressed audio file format is popular on Windows computers using the .wav formats.

The following formats are available only on Windows:

- **Microsoft AVI:** This "container format," available only in the Windows version of Adobe Premiere Pro, can store files using multiple compression technologies, or *codecs*. While not officially supported by Microsoft for a number of years, it is still in widespread use in Windows systems primarily for large intermediate files within an editing project, such as renders transferred between applications in a Window-only environment. It is rarely, if ever, used for distribution of video files to the public.

- **Windows Bitmap:** This is an uncompressed, rarely used still-image format with a .bmp extension. It's available only on the Windows version of Adobe Premiere Pro.

- **Animated GIF and GIF:** These compressed still-image and animated formats are used primarily on the Web. They're available only on the Windows version of Adobe Premiere Pro.

- **Uncompressed Microsoft AVI:** This is a very high-bit-rate intermediate format that is not widely used and is available only on the Windows version of Adobe Premiere Pro.

- **Windows Media:** This option produces WMV files for playback using the Windows Media Player and is used in some playout server applications and is ideal for Microsoft Silverlight applications (Windows only).

That's only a brief overview of the formats, but it should provide some useful direction when it's time to produce your videos.

Using the formats

Adobe Media Encoder supports many formats. Knowing which setting to use can seem a little overwhelming. Let's take a look at some common scenarios and review which formats are typically used. While there are few absolutes, these should get you close to the correct output. Be sure to always test your output with a short file first before going live with it.

- **Uploading to a website for Flash deployment:** When you choose the FLV|F4V format, choose an FLV preset for producing the file with the older On2 VP6 codec, and choose F4V for the newer, higher-quality H.264 format. If you don't know which format to use, go with F4V. In terms of resolution, the 720p Source, Half Size presets in both F4V and FLV formats encode your video at 740 x 360 (for HD source), which is a conservative resolution that should look quite good. Check with your web administrator for the format, resolution, data rate, and other details.

- **Encoding for DVD/Blu-ray:** Generally, you'll use MPEG2 for both—namely, MPEG2-DVD for DVD and MPEG2 Blu-ray for Blu-ray Discs. MPEG2 looks indistinguishable from H.264 in these high-bit-rate applications and will encode much, much faster. However, the H.264 format can let you fit more content in a smaller space. Better yet, input your sequence without rendering in Encore (choose File > Adobe Dynamic Link > Import Adobe Premiere Pro Sequence).

- **Encoding for devices:** Use the H.264 format for current devices (Apple iPod/iPhone, Apple TV, and TiVo), as well as some generic 3GPP presets; use MPEG4 for older MPEG4-based devices. Be sure to check the manufacturer's specifications on their website, and make sure the files that you produce don't exceed these specs.

- **Encoding for uploading to user-generated video sites:** H.264 has presets for YouTube and Vimeo in widescreen, SD, and HD. Use these presets as a starting point for your service, being careful to observe resolution, file size, and duration limits.

- **Windows Media or Silverlight deployment:** The Windows Media format is your safest option, though more recent versions of Silverlight can play H.264 files. If producing H.264 for Silverlight, follow the Flash rules provided earlier, since Silverlight should play any file produced for Flash.

In general, the Adobe Premiere Pro presets are proven and will work for your intended purpose. Don't adjust parameters when encoding for devices or optical discs, because changes that seem subtle can render the files unplayable. Even with other presets, resist the urge to tinker unless you know what you're doing from an encoding perspective. Most Adobe Premiere Pro presets are conservative and will deliver very good quality using the default values, so you probably won't improve the output by tinkering, and you could even degrade it considerably.

Configuring the Export

To export from Adobe Premiere Pro with Adobe Media Encoder, you'll need to queue the project. The first step of this involves using the Export Settings dialog to make initial choices about the file you're going to export.

1   If necessary, open Lesson 18_01.prproj.

2   Choose File > Export > Media.

It's best to work through the Export Settings dialog from the top down, first choosing your format and presets, then picking the output, and finally deciding whether you'd like to export audio, video, or both.

3   Choose the H.264 format from the Format preset. This format is a popular choice for creating files for uploading to video-sharing websites. Choose the YouTube HD 720p 23.976 preset.

This correctly loads the settings that match the frame size and frame rate of the source footage. It also adjusts the codec and data rate to match the requirements of the YouTube website.

4   Click the output name (the gold text), and give the file a new name, *Review Copy 03.mov*. Save it to the same destination as the previous exercise.

5   Examine the Summary below the preset lists to see the effects of choices so far. Note that the tabs presented on the bottom right of the Export Settings dialog will vary by format. Most of the critical options are contained on the Format, Video, and Audio tabs, and the options here will vary by format as well. Here's an overview of the various tabs:

•   **Filters:** The filter available for encoded output is Gaussian Blur. Enabling this filter reduces the video noise introduced by slightly blurring the video. Export the project without this filter to see whether noise is a problem. If it is, increase noise reduction in small amounts. Increasing noise reduction too much will make the video blurry. Judicious use of Gaussian Blur is often a very good way to reduce a file's bit rate (particularly with very detailed high-resolution material that is scaled down considerably for distribution). It can remove some of the excessive fine detail that can result in "ringing" or "shimmering."

- **Video:** The Video tab allows you to adjust the frame size, frame rate, field order, and profile. The default values are based on the preset you chose.

- **Audio:** The Audio tab allows you to adjust the bit rate of the audio and, for some formats, the codec. The default values are based on the preset you chose.

- **Multiplexer:** These controls let you determine whether the encoding method is optimized for compatibility with a specific device (like an iPod or PlayStation Portable).

- **FTP:** This tab primarily allows you to specify an FTP server for uploading the exported video when it is finished encoding. Fill in the appropriate FTP values supplied by your FTP host if you want to enable this feature.

Source and Output panels

Moving to the left side of the Export Settings dialog, look over the Source Range drop-down list, where you can choose to export the Work Area bar selected in the sequence, a range you selected by placing an In point and an Out point on your sequence, a region selected using the handles directly above the drop-down list, or the entire sequence. This is useful when you want to export selected regions on the Timeline rather than the entire sequence.

Also on the left, note the Source/Output tabs, the latter of which shows a preview of the video to be encoded. It's useful to view the video on the Output tab to catch errors such as unwanted letterboxing or distortion caused by the irregularly shaped pixels used in some video formats.

Queuing the export

When you're ready to export your sequence or selected range, you'll need to look over a few last items that will determine important details about your exported file.

Be sure to closely analyze the impact of each of these settings on your export.

- **Use Maximum Render Quality:** Consider enabling this setting whenever scaling from larger to smaller formats during rendering, but note that this option requires more RAM than normal rendering and can slow rendering by a factor of four or five. This option is not often needed except in situations that involve scaling and where the highest-quality output is needed.

- **Use Previews:** This option uses previews created while producing your project as the starting point for the final rendered file, rather than rendering all video and effects from scratch. This can shorten encoding time but can also degrade quality when rendering to a format different from your sequence preset. Use this option when you need only draft-quality output and you're in a big rush.

- **Use Frame Blending:** Enable this option to smooth motion whenever you change the speed of a source clip in your project or render to a different frame rate than your sequence setting.

- **Metadata:** Click this button to open the Metadata Export panel. You can specify a wide range of settings including information about copyright, creator, and rights management. You can even embed useful information such as markers, script, and speech transcription for advanced delivery options like Flash authoring.

● **Note:** On the Video tab you'll also find a Render at Maximum Depth check box. This can improve the visual quality of your output by using a wider gamut to generate colors when rendering. However, choosing this option can add significantly to the render time.

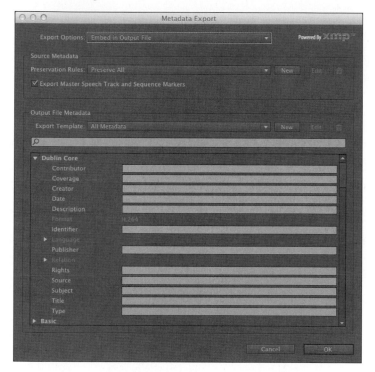

- **Queue:** Click the Queue button to send the file to Adobe Media Encoder, which should open automatically.

- **Export:** Select this option to export directly from the Export Settings dialog rather than rendering via Adobe Media Encoder. This is a simpler workflow, but you won't be able to edit in Adobe Premiere Pro until the rendering is complete.

Click the Queue button to launch Adobe Media Encoder and submit the file.

Additional options in Adobe Media Encoder

Working with Adobe Media Encoder has several additional benefits. While it involves a few extra steps over just clicking the Export button in the Export Settings panel of Adobe Premiere Pro, the extra options are worth it.

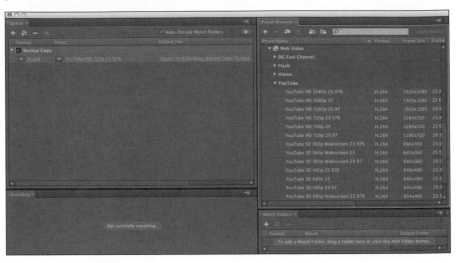

● **Note:** Adobe Media Encoder does not have to be used from Adobe Premiere Pro. You can start Adobe Media Encoder from your list of Adobe programs and add files to it that already exist on your file system.

Here are some of the most useful features you'll find in Adobe Media Encoder:

• **Add additional stand-alone files:** You can add stand-alone files to Adobe Media Encoder by choosing File > Add Source.

• **Import Adobe Premiere Pro projects directly:** You can choose File > Add Premiere Pro Sequence to select an Adobe Premiere Pro project file and choose sequences (without ever launching Adobe Premiere Pro).

• **Render After Effects Projects:** You can import and encode compositions from Adobe After Effects by choosing File > Add After Effects Composition. This method is similar to the previous in that you don't need to open Adobe After Effects.

• **Use a Watch Folder:** If you'd like to automate some encoding tasks, you can create watch folders by choosing File > Add Watch Folder and then assigning a preset to that watch folder. Source files dragged into the folder later will be automatically encoded to the format specified in the preset.

• **Modify an item:** You can add, duplicate, or remove any tasks by using the like-named buttons and drag any tasks that haven't yet started encoding to any place in the queue. If you haven't set the queue to start automatically, click the Start Queue button to start encoding. Adobe Media Encoder encodes files serially, rather than in parallel, and if you add any files to the queue after starting encoding, they'll be encoded as well.

- **Modify presets:** You can choose a format/preset separately with each approach. Once the encoding tasks are loaded into Adobe Media Encoder, administration is straightforward. To change any encoding setting, click the target task and then the Settings button on the right.

Exchanging with other editing applications

The need for collaboration is often essential in video post-production. Fortunately, Adobe Premiere Pro can both read and write project files that are compatible with many of the top editing and color-grading tools on the market.

Exporting a Final Cut Pro XML file

The use of Final Cut Pro XML allows you to exchange an Adobe Premiere Pro project with many applications. You can bring your project directly into Final Cut Pro 7 and 6 or convert it to Final Cut Pro X using 7toX for Final Cut Pro from Assisted Editing. You can also export your project to other applications such as Davinci Resolve and Grass Valley Edius. At a high level, exporting from Adobe Premiere Pro to Final Cut Pro—and importing the XML file into Final Cut Pro—is simple.

1 To begin, in Adobe Premiere Pro, choose File > Export > Final Cut Pro XML. Click Yes to save your project.

2 In the Final Cut Pro XML - Save Converted Project As dialog, name the file, choose a location, and click Save. Adobe Premiere Pro will let you know whether there were any issues exporting the XML.

This file can now be imported into another application. You will likely need to import or capture the media into the other application and relink it.

Exporting to OMF

The Open Media Framework (OMF) has become a standard way of exchanging audio information between systems (typically for audio mixing). When you export an OMF file, the typical method is to create a single file with all your audio tracks inside. When the OMF file is open by a compatible application, it will show all of the tracks.

Here's how to create an OMF file:

1 With a sequence selected, choose File > Export > OMF.

2 Enter a name for the file in the OMF Title field.

3 Check that the Sample Rate and Bits per Sample settings match your footage; 48000 Hz and 16 bits are the most common settings.

4 From the Files menu, choose one of the following:

- **Encapsulate:** This option exports an OMF file that contains the project metadata and all the audio for the selected sequence. Encapsulated OMF files typically are large.

- **Separate Audio:** This option exports individual mono AIFF files into an omfiMediaFiles folder.

5 If using the Separate Audio option, choose between the AIFF and Eave formats. Both are high-quality, but check with the system you need to exchange with. AIFF files tend to be the most compatible.

6 Using the Render menu, choose either to use Copy Complete Audio Files or to use the Trim Audio Files to reduce the file size. You can specify to add handles (extra frames) to give you some flexibility when modifying the clips.

7 Click OK to generate the OMF file.

8 Choose a destination, and click Save. You can target your lesson folder for now.

Exporting to AAF

Another way to exchange files is the Advanced Authoring Format (AAF). This method is typically used to exchange both project information and source media with Avid Media Composer.

1 Choose File > Export > AAF.

2 In the AAF - Save Converted Project As dialog box, choose a location and click Save.

3 In the AAF Export Settings dialog box, you have two additional choices.

- **Save as legacy AAF:** This makes a file more compatible but doesn't support as many features.

- **Embed audio:** This option attempts to embed audio into the file to reduce the need for relinking.

4 Click OK in order to save the sequence to an AAF file at the specified location. The AAF Export Log dialog box opens to report any issues.

Working with edit decision lists

An *edit decision list* (EDL) harkens back to the days
when small hard drives limited the size of your video
files and slower processors meant you could not play
full-resolution video. To remedy this, editors used
low-resolution files in a nonlinear editor like Adobe
Premiere Pro, edited their project, exported that to
an EDL, and then took that text file and their original
tapes down to a production studio. There they would
use expensive switching hardware to create the finished, full-resolution product.

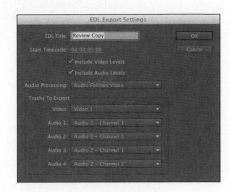

These days, there isn't much call for that kind of offline
work, but filmmakers still use EDLs because of the size
of the files and other complexities associated with going from film to video and back to film.

If you plan to use an EDL, you need to keep your project within some narrow guidelines:

- EDLs work best with projects that contain no more than one video track, two stereo (or four mono) audio tracks, and no nested sequences.
- Most standard transitions, freeze frames, and clip-speed changes work well in EDLs.
- Adobe Premiere Pro supports a key track for titles or other content. That track has to be immediately above the video track selected for export.
- You must capture and log all the source material with accurate timecode information.
- The capture card must have a device control that uses a timecode.
- Videotapes must each have a unique reel number and be formatted with the timecode before you shoot the video to ensure there are no breaks in the timecode.

To view the EDL options of Adobe Premiere Pro, choose File > Export > EDL, which opens the EDL
Export Settings dialog.

Your options are as follows:

- EDL Title: This specifies a title to appear in the first line of the EDL file. The title can be different from the filename. After clicking OK in the EDL Export Settings dialog, you will have the opportunity to enter a filename.
- Start Timecode: Here you set the starting timecode value for the first edit in the sequence.
- Include Video Levels: This includes video opacity-level comments in the EDL.
- Include Audio Levels: This includes audio-level comments in the EDL.
- Audio Processing: Here you specify when audio processing should occur. Options are Audio Follows Video, Audio Separately, and Audio At End.
- Tracks To Export: This specifies which tracks to export. The video track directly above the video track selected for export is designated as the key track.

Send to Adobe SpeedGrade

Adobe offers its own robust color-grading utility called SpeedGrade that is included with the Creative Suite Production Premium software families. It offers a comprehensive tool set for manipulating and improving color. You should send files to Adobe SpeedGrade only when you're near the very end of a project and you have "picture lock" and merely want to improve your program. You should not use SpeedGrade when you still intend to make edits to the content or duration of your project.

1 Choose File > Save to capture any changes in your sequence.

2 Choose File > Send to Adobe SpeedGrade.

3 In the new dialog box, choose a destination to save the new file.

4 Click Save when ready.

> A new project file is generated, and an image sequence (using the DPX file format) is created for each clip in your project.

Recording to tape

While tape is becoming less and less common, there still are industries and parts of the world where it is the preferred output method. For example, many broadcasters require master tapes on formats like HDCAM SR or DVCPRO HD. If you shot on a format like DV or HDV, going back out to tape is a popular choice to back up the project.

If you own a tape deck or camera, you can use the project Lesson 18_02.prproj. This contains both a DV and HDV sequence that can be output.

Preparing a project for tape output

To play a project out to tape, you need to be able to play back the sequence perfectly. This means no dropped frames or untendered effects. You'll need to ensure that you have fast enough hard drives and a well-tuned machine. Here are a few other details to check:

- **Device Control settings:** Make sure Adobe Premiere Pro can see your recording deck. Open Adobe Premiere Pro Preferences and choose Device Control. In the Devices menu, choose the appropriate type of device control for your deck. Click the Options button and attempt to match your device as close as possible. If you're using a professional deck or capture card, you may need to install additional drivers.

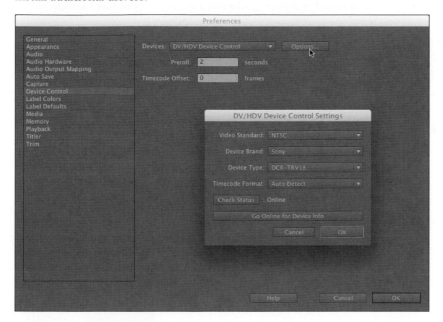

- **Audio channel assignments:** You should check that your audio channels in the sequence are assigned to the correct output. Some decks like DV allow for only two channels of audio, while other formats can support 4, 8, or even 16 channels. Using the Audio Mixer, you can assign each audio track in your sequence to a specific output.

Preparing a tape for output

To record to tape, you need to prepare the tape first. Typically, this is called *striping* or *blacking* a tape. This process sets the timecode on the tape and ensures that it is ready to record to.

This process varies greatly from deck to deck, so be sure to see the owner's manual of your hardware. It is common to start a tape at 00:58:00:00 to accommodate bars, tone, slate information, and a countdown. The primary video will typically start at exactly 1:00:00:00.

Recording to a DV or HDV deck

Out of the box, Adobe Premiere Pro has the ability to connect to a DV or HDV deck. If you captured your original video from DV or HDV tape, you may want to write the finished project back to tape for safekeeping. If so, follow the steps listed here:

1 Connect your DV or HDV camcorder to your computer, just as you did when you captured the video.

2 Turn it on, and set it to VCR or VTR (not to Camera, as you might expect).

3 Cue the tape to where you want to start recording.

4 Select the sequence you want to record.

5 Choose File > Export > Tape.

If you're working with a DV camcorder, you'll see the Export to Tape dialog shown here.

Here's a rundown of the options:

- **Activate Recording Device:** When you select this option, Adobe Premiere Pro will control your DV device. Deselect it if you want to record to a device that you'll control manually.

- **Assemble at timecode:** Select this option to pick an In point on the tape where you want recording to begin. When this option is not selected, recording will begin at the current tape location.

- **Delay movie start by _x_ frames:** This is for the few DV recording devices that need a brief period of time between receiving the video signal and recording it. Check your device's manual to see what the manufacturer recommends.

- **Preroll _x_ frames:** Most decks need little or no time to get to the proper tape-recording speed. To be on the safe side, select 150 frames (5 seconds), or add black video to the start of your project.

The remaining options are self-explanatory.

6 Click Record (or Cancel if you don't want to make a recording).

If you haven't rendered your project (by pressing Enter [Windows] or Return [Mac OS] for playback instead of the spacebar), Adobe Premiere Pro does that now. When rendering is complete, Adobe Premiere Pro starts your camcorder and records your project to it.

Using third-party hardware

Video Input/Output devices are available from several companies such as AJA, Blackmagic Design, Bluefish444, and Matrox. These cards let you connect professional-quality video decks to your computer.

The following features are useful when working with professional decks:

- **SD/HD-SDI:** Serial Digital Interface (SDI) carries standard-definition or high-definition video and up to 16 channels of digital audio. Over a single cable, you can output your video to a deck, as well as all of the audio that you might need.

- **Component video:** Some decks still rely on other connection types. You can use component video for both analog (Y'PrPb) and digital (Y'CbCr) connections. Component connections can carry only a video signal, not audio.

- **AES and XLR audio:** If you're not relying on an embedded SDI audio signal, then many decks also offer dedicated audio connections. The two most common are AES (either XLR OR BNC types) or analog XLR audio.

- **RS-422 deck control:** Professional decks employ a type of device control known as RS-422. This serial connection is used for frame-accurate control of the deck.

▶ **Tip:** To learn more about supported hardware cards, visit *www.adobe.com/ products/premiere/ extend.html.*

Review questions

1 What are the main formats for exporting digital video if you want to be able to edit the files in the future?

2 What Internet-ready media options are available in Adobe Media Encoder?

3 What encoding format should you use when exporting to most mobile devices?

4 Must you wait for Adobe Media Encoder to finish processing its queue before working on a new project?

5 When you click Record in the Export to Tape dialog, your camcorder remains paused. What's going on?

Review answers

1 The primary options for SD are Microsoft DV AVI and QuickTime MOV in DV format. For HD files, try producing a file using the Match Sequence Settings option, or use a third-party codec.

2 This varies by platform. Both operating systems include Flash (FLV|F4V), H.264, and QuickTime, with the Windows version including Windows Media as well.

3 H.264 is the encoding format used when exporting to most mobile devices.

4 No. Adobe Media Encoder is a stand-alone application. You can work in other applications or even start a new Adobe Premiere Pro project while it's processing its render queue.

5 Before Adobe Premiere Pro can start recording a project to tape, it has to render it. You can do that in advance by opening a sequence and pressing Return or Enter. Otherwise, when you click the Record button, you'll have to wait a while for Adobe Premiere Pro to process any unrendered portions of your sequence.

INDEX

SYMBOLS

` (grave) keys, 78, 89, 103
+ button, 138

NUMBERS

32-bit color effects, 301
5.1 audio mixes, 248, 266
64-bit applications, 31
7.5 IRE controls, 333

A

A/B mode, 153, 161–165
AAC (Advanced Audio Coding) format, 436
AAF (Advanced Authoring Format) files, 44, 443–444
AATCs (Adobe Authorized Training Centers), 6
Absorption controls, 275
ACA (Adobe Certified Associate), 6
acceleration
    CUDA, 30–31
    GPUs for, 29–31
    introduction to, 3, 12
    of video effects, 301
action-safe margins, 392
action scenes, 232
Activate Recording Device, 448
active frames, 103
Add Edit to all tracks shortcuts, 143
Add Edit to selected tracks shortcuts, 143
add In and Out points (Shift + /), 114, 146
Add Marker, 105
add shapes (Shift+drag), 403
adjustment layers, 304–307

Adobe After Effects CS6
    animated text with, 410–413
    Dynamic Link and, 65, 426
    high-bit-depth effects in, 301
    introduction to, 14–15
    markers for, 128
    media cache databases in, 64–65
    rendering projects in, 442
    Roto Brush Tool in, 378
    sending clips to, 308–310
    for titles, 410–413
Adobe Audition CS6
    5.1 mixes in, 266
    audio effects and, 269
    introduction to, 14–15
    media cache databases in, 64
    post-production audio in, 259
    removing background noise in, 290–292
Adobe Authorized Training Centers (AATCs), 6
Adobe Bridge CS6, 14
Adobe Certified Associate (ACA), 6
Adobe Community Help, 3, 5
Adobe Design Center, 5
Adobe Dynamic Link
    file formats in, 438
    importing media with, 65
    introduction to, 14–15, 65
    for project management, 426
    sending clips to After Effects with, 308
    sending titles to After Effects with, 410
Adobe Encore CS6
    authoring DVDs with, generally, DVD:2–DVD:4
    Autoplay DVD creation, DVD 9–12
    Blu-ray disc creation, DVD:18

S

Production Notes

The *Adobe Premiere Pro CS6 Classroom in a Book* was created electronically using Adobe InDesign. Art was produced using Adobe Photoshop. The Myriad Pro and Warnock Pro OpenType families of typefaces were used throughout this book.

Team Credits

Writers: Richard Harrington and Maxim Jago
Adobe Press Editor: Victor Gavenda
Senior Editor: Karyn Johnson
Production Editor: Katerina Malone
Development Editor: Stephen Nathans-Kelly
Technical Editor: Tim Kolb
Copyeditor: Kim Wimpsett
Compositor: David Van Ness
Proofreader: Amy Jean Petersen
Indexer: Jack Lewis
Media Producer: Eric Geoffroy
Cover Design: Eddie Yuen
Interior Design: Mimi Heft

Contributors

 Richard Harrington is a director, producer, and editor with national PSAs and Ciné award-winning productions. He owns the visual communications company RHED Pixel (www.rhedpixel.com) in Washington, D.C. Rich is also a Master Trainer for Adobe Premiere Pro. He has extensive experience with other editing tools and has held instructor certifications with both Apple and Avid. He has written and co-written a number of books including *Motion Graphics with Adobe Creative Suite 5 Studio Techniques* (Adobe Press, 2010), and *An Editor's Guide to Adobe Premiere Pro* (Peachpit Press, 2013). Rich consistently shares his knowledge as a regular contributor to Creative COW, Photofocus, and his personal blog at www.RichardHarringtonBlog.com.

 Maxim Jago is a media trainer, stage presenter, filmmaker and the author of several media technology courses. He is an Adobe Master Trainer, Grass Valley Master Trainer, and Avid Certified Instructor. Maxim has developed his own approach to making complex technologies accessible and meaningful for creative minds, called the ESP Teaching System. He presents internationally at media events, has trained editors all around the world, has been published in magazines and quoted in books, and teaches everyone from schoolchildren to professors, from ABC in Australia to the BBC in the UK. His Web sites are www.123training.co.uk (as a trainer) and www.maximjago.com (as a film maker).

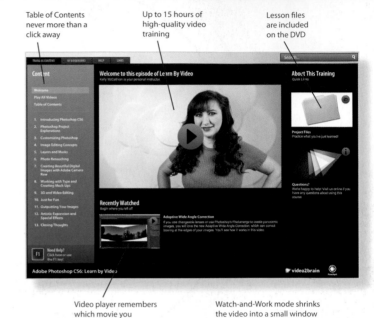

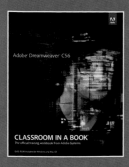

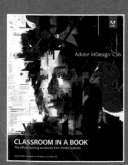

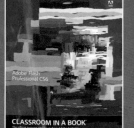

The fastest, easiest, most comprehensive way to learn

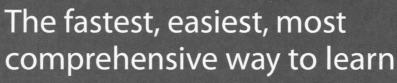

Classroom in a Book®, the best-selling series of hands-on software training books, helps you learn the features of Adobe software quickly and easily.

The **Classroom In a Book** series offers what no other book or training program does—an official training series from Adobe Systems, developed with the support of Adobe product experts.

To see a complete list of our Adobe® Creative Suite® 6 titles go to
www.peachpit.com/adobecs6

Adobe Photoshop CS6 Classroom in a Book
ISBN: 9780321827333

Adobe Illustrator CS6 Classroom in a Book
ISBN: 9780321822482

Adobe InDesign CS6 Classroom in a Book
ISBN: 9780321822499

Adobe Flash Professional CS6 Classroom in a Book
ISBN: 9780321822512

Adobe Dreamweaver CS6 Classroom in a Book
ISBN: 9780321822451

Adobe Muse Classroom in a Book
ISBN: 9780321821362

Adobe Fireworks CS6 Classroom in a Book
ISBN: 9780321822444

Adobe Premiere Pro CS6 Classroom in a Book
ISBN: 9780321822475

Adobe After Effects CS6 Classroom in a Book
ISBN: 9780321822437

Adobe Audition CS6 Classroom in a Book
ISBN: 9780321832832

Adobe Creative Suite 6 Design & Web Premium Classroom in a Book
ISBN: 9780321822604

Adobe Creative Suite 6 Production Premium Classroom in a Book
ISBN: 9780321832689

AdobePress